FIVE
OF THE FEW

Winston Churchill, House of Commons, 13 May 1940:
We have before us an ordeal of the most grievous kind.
We have before us many, many long months of
struggle and of suffering. You ask, what is our policy?
I will say: It is to wage war, by sea, land and air, with all our
might and with all the strength that God can give us;
to wage war against a monstrous tyranny...

FIVE
OF THE FEW

SURVIVORS OF THE
BATTLE OF BRITAIN
AND THE BLITZ TELL
THEIR STORY

Steve Darlow

First published in 2006 by Grub Street Publishing,
4 Rainham Close, London, SW11 6SS

This edition published in 2011 by Bounty Books,
a division of Octopus Publishing Group,
Endeavour House, 189 Shaftesbury Avenue, London WC2H 8JY
www.octopusbooks.co.uk

An Hachette UK Company
www.hachette.co.uk

Text and © 2006 Steve Darlow

978-0-753720-67-7

Line drawings by Tim Callaway

Printed and bound in China by Imago

Contents

Dedication

On 11 March 2006 the life of a fine young basketball player, Frank Empson, was tragically cut short. Frank was an extraordinary young man and one who I had come to know quite well. In him I saw similarities with the character of the Second World War RAF airmen I wrote about. This group of men were extraordinary in their own right. At such a young age they had to face up to extremes of experience time and time again. I often wonder what kind of a young man could do this – what was it in their make up that enabled them to accept and deal with these challenges. Quite honestly when I used to watch Frank, in particular, and some of his other team mates at Ware, Hertfordshire, playing basketball, I would see that same sense of pride, determination, camaraderie, responsibility and sheer youthfulness that could also be said to be attributable to the RAF pilots who fought against and defeated their opponents. The clear similarities between groups of men such as these, separated by sixty plus years of history, gives great hope for the future – the continuity of what is right, proper and good.

This book is dedicated to the memory of Frank Empson, who had the same qualities as the 'Few'.

Acknowledgements

Of course my sincerest thanks go to the five veterans, Ken Lee, Terry Clark, Tony Pickering, Peter Olver and John Ellacombe, who were willing to share their stories and put up with my questioning.

My thanks to John Davies at Grub Street whose support is invaluable. Thanks also extend to Luke Norsworthy at Grub Street, for his toleration. Colin Smith at Vector Fine Art, whose original idea this was, also deserves mention providing contacts and helping promote the book. Thanks to Rob Thornley for his thoughts as the project developed, to my unofficial librarian Steve Fraser, and to Mike Lindley. Jim Sheffield and Robin Brooks gave good advice as the idea formed. Thanks to Bud and my appreciation also extends to Andrew Mckerlie, at Brook Lapping Productions, Cathy Pugh and the Second World War Experience Centre in Leeds, David Ross, Ian Brentnall, Tim Callaway for his drawings and Robert White at the Imperial War Museum Sound Archive.

The BBC have been kind enough to allow me the use of extracts from their WW2 People's War website – an online archive of wartime memories contributed by members of the public and gathered by the BBC. The archive can be found at bbc.co.uk/ww2peopleswar.

Special Acknowledgement
Terry Clark's story is dedicated to the memory of his wife Margaret, 'who was the first to give me pad and pencil and say – you must write your story.' The account of Terry's career in this book draws heavily on the story Terry put together. Because of this he would like to give due acknowledgement of those who helped him:

My sincere thanks to a very good friend Stephen Teasdale,

who had the courage to read the sheets of paper that came out of my typewriter, and gave excellent advice and encouragement. More very helpful advice was received from Dr. Jon Tan, who taped our conversations about my RAF service. Finally I must thank my son Roger, who was always there to give his advice.

Introduction

Churchill's 'Few' will forever be remembered by history as the men who thwarted the seemingly invincible German war machine, when all seemed lost. They countered the full force of the Luftwaffe in the daylight battles during the summer of 1940, and in the night skies of the winter and spring of 1940/41. They were at the time, and still are, perceived as knights of the air. To the British people, who gazed up at the contrails, witnessed dogfights, aircraft crashing and exploding, and men falling to earth under silk canopies, they were heroes. Those on the ground who suffered under the Luftwaffe onslaught will never forget their experiences. They will also remember that the men of the RAF had given them hope for survival – and delivered as well.

Five of the Few is a personal wartime human history of five of Churchill's Few, who fought Fighter Command's air battle in the summer of 1940, and earned the right to wear their Battle of Britain clasp with pride. It tells of their experiences and the effect on their lives. It is a story of immaturity and idealism, courage and bravado, fear and heroism, memory and reflection.

The officially recognised timeframe of the Battle of Britain is given as 10 July 1940 to 31 October 1940. There is also opinion, particularly with German historians, that the Battle of Britain actually extended beyond those summer and early autumn months to include the night blitz that went on until May 1941. In *Five of the Few* the experiences of the five airmen cover both periods.

Ken Lee opens the book. The Battle of France sets the scene for the air siege of Britain and Ken was certainly in the thick of the air fighting as the Germans blitzkrieged their way to early victory. Ken's story then turns to the early stages of the Battle of Britain through to the middle of August 1940. John Ellacombe's account then takes up the Battle of Britain story as the intensity of the air battle escalates in the second half of August 1940. Into September 1940 and Tony Pickering's tale is set within the context of the change in Luftwaffe strategy, the switch to mass attacks on London. The final element of the day battle provides the background to Peter Olver's entry into the Battle of Britain. Then the Luftwaffe night offensive in the winter of 1940/41 and spring of 1941 provides the context for Terry Clark's account.

Thus the entire Battle of Britain and early night Blitz story is covered. There is of course some slight overlapping and an effort has been made to avoid repetition, although occasionally it is necessary to ensure the flow of each airman's experiences.

However this book is not just about the Battle of Britain and the Blitz. It is about the airmen's full wartime careers. Each of their stories continue beyond 1940, and they combine to give quite a full picture of the fighter pilot experience in the European theatre of operations. Ken, John, Tony, Peter and Terry build on the experience and combat knowledge they gained defending England, and utilise this as the Allies move over to the offensive in North Africa and the Mediterranean, and during the Normandy invasion of 1944 and beyond. Each man made his own personal contribution towards the final defeat of Nazism in Europe. Promotions and decorations would come their way, along with command responsibilities. There were further air battles and combats, but experience was no guarantee of survival as will be demonstrated.

When John Davies of Grub Street first approached me, asking me if I would consider writing this book, he felt it necessary to use a few persuasive words. As I told him, they were not required. I was being given the opportunity to record and write up the recollections of five Battle of Britain veterans for goodness sake. Persuasion was absolutely not necessary. It was going to be a privilege.

The book has been challenging. It has required Ken, John, Peter, Terry and Tony to drag up recollections of events that are now sixty-six years old. As it was they managed with a great clarity of thought. I have always tried to match up their recollections with official records. Any errors that have arisen are of course my responsibility.

I would like also just to add a brief note about combat claims. It has not always been the case that a veteran's recollections and his logbooks agree with officially credited claims. As this story has not been written as a scoreboard, but as a telling of experience, I have gone with the veteran's accounts and logbooks. That's what they wrote down at the time and remember now. So it is only right that I have kept faith with it too.

The BBC recently sent out a request for reminiscences of the Battle of Britain and the Blitz. Many of those that came in were from people who were children at the time. At the start of each veteran's story I have opened with an excerpt from one of these accounts, from a civilian who witnessed the air conflict. Their accounts give a small flavour of what their generation witnessed. What they say gives just a small indication of why the Few were held in such high esteem then, and why that regard continues to the present day. They witnessed the RAF airmen's fight, 'undaunted by odds, unwearied in their constant challenge and mortal danger.' They appreciated then and now that so much was owed, 'by so many to so few' and still is.

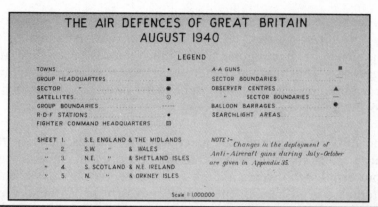

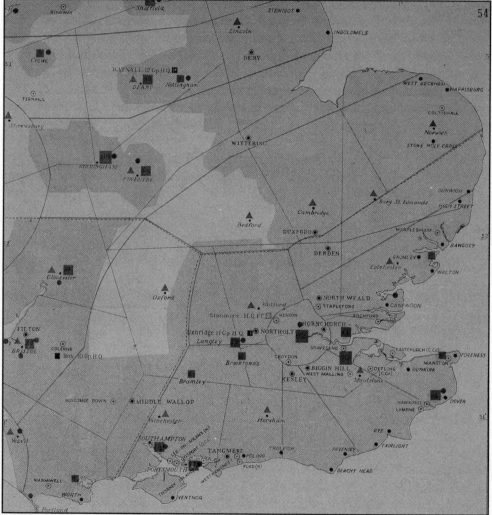

12

Chapter 1

The Frying Pan and the Fire

Doug Bukin was ten years old when war was declared. He would never forget what he witnessed in the summer of 1940.

> *Through the eyes of a ten-year-old the Battle of Britain was quite exciting. The aircraft seemed about the size of a swallow on a summer's day, high up in the sky. They were wheeling around and sometimes you'd see something coming down on a smoke trail. Another time a big white*

mushroom, obviously a pilot baling out. I expect the majority of people didn't know the drama that was going on but for me it was just exciting to watch it. You realised in a way what was happening, but you didn't significantly think that there's a British pilot and a German pilot possibly facing death. Surprisingly enough, although all this was going on, there was no noise. They were so far up you wouldn't hear the machine-gun fire or the explosions but you could see something. The poor old pilots, unfortunately many of whom didn't come back.[1]

Back in May 1940, two months before the Battle of Britain began in earnest, Ken Lee was in France, itching to take his weapon of war into the air, to try and prevent enemy airmen using theirs. For Ken and the other pilots of his squadron (501) pre-war training – in Ken's case lasting nigh on a year and a half – was now to be put to the ultimate test and there was almost a professional curiosity as to what the outcome would be.

On 11 May 1940 notification had come through of a big enemy raid, so Hawker Hurricanes of the Royal Air Force's 501 Squadron duly took off from their aerodrome in France, to seek out and engage the opposing force. Ken, who had arrived in France that very same day, was one of the pilots seeking to intercept the raid. His chance had come at last.

Ken Lee was born in Birmingham on 23 June 1915. An only son whose father had served in the Royal Navy and experienced at first hand torpedo attacks, Ken grew up in Edgbaston, Birmingham, attending King Edward VI high school before going to work in a paint factory. When twenty-one, in January 1937, Ken joined the Royal Air Force Volunteer Reserve. The RAFVR had been created in 1936 as a 'Citizen Air Force', to be part of the second line of defence behind the RAF 'Regulars'.

I read about the formation of the Volunteer Reserve and I said to my boss that I would like to join. He, being a military man, agreed, so they gave me two months leave to go to the initial course in Perth, Scotland.

I had always been very keen on the first world war and the aces and the flying and when the opportunity came to have a go myself I wanted to join immediately. Really just to learn to fly. I never thought I would get into a fighter squadron.

The VR was only for part-time flying at weekends. When I had built up a lot of experience in the VR, over 400 hours, the air force noticed that I had too many flying hours as a peace-time pilot. In January 1939 they asked me to sign up for six months regular service.

Once with the regular RAF, Ken joined 111 Squadron, flying Hurricanes.

The first morning they took me out and said, 'Here's a Hurricane go and fly it.' It was very different from anything I had flown but I got round and back.

Ken was soon to receive a commission.

One day the station warrant officer called me over and said, 'Lee. What are your initials, my boy?' 'K N T sir'. He said, 'Congratulations you're an officer, now bugger off and have your lunch in the officer's mess.' I arrived a sergeant pilot and then this day, to my astonishment, I became an officer.

Ken transferred to 43 Squadron at Tangmere in March, still on Hurricanes, practising attacks, dog fighting and air-to-air firing through the spring of 1939. Training not only taught him the skills of flying, it also schooled him in the ways of the RAF, the command structure, the history and responsibility for that history, the importance of the group, the flight, the squadron, the command. As the threat of war with Germany turned to reality Ken was posted to 501 'County of Gloucester' Squadron of the Auxiliary Air Force. The Auxiliaries, described as 'educated men of independent means', and 'the weekend playboys' also made up the RAF's second line of defence with the pilots of the RAFVR.

501 Squadron was short of pilots, they only had about seven, and they needed to make up their numbers. So they got some VRs, like myself, who had been in regular squadrons. We were more experienced than the Auxiliaries, they only had about five hours flying on the Hurricanes. We arrived with about one hundred hours day and night.

When the war was actually officially declared we were still not engaging the enemy, they weren't coming over England. We were still practising and we were well prepared and anxious to go. After a year of doing the same thing you wanted to try it out on a real target. We were often at readiness and we often scrambled but we never made contact.

Historians record the state of the French Air Force prior to the opening of the ultimately victorious great German offensive in May 1940 as suffering from 'serious ills', the Dutch Air Force as 'miniscule', and the Belgian Air Force as 'puny'. Consequently, on 10 May 1940 the Luftwaffe took command of the skies over and beyond the battle front, asserting a numerical and technical superiority. As the air battle unfolded the defending air forces were found wanting. The RAF's light bomber force was exposed as totally inadequate. But there was a ray of light. The Hurricane appeared up for the task and 501 Squadron played its part.

We were supposed to be a mobile squadron, going wherever we were needed. We had been kitted up to move to Norway but that was cancelled. This meant that we were just sitting there waiting for an order. When the fighting started in France we were told to get to Bétheniville. I was excited.

Royal Air Force Squadron Operation Record Books (ORBs) usually, but most certainly not always, provide a good primary source for the daily details of squadron activities. The personality of the author has an effect and so of course does the circumstances the squadron finds itself in. One can hardly criticise the diarist for brevity if the squadron is in the midst of an intense air campaign. The needs of the historian at a future date will be far from his thoughts. As it was the RAF left a lot of its detailed records in France following its evacuation in June. Nevertheless a daily summary does survive for 501 Squadron giving a fairly good picture of the squadron's highs and lows during the campaigns of May and June 1940 and it is this that forms the background to Ken Lee's time there.

Sixteen pilots of 501 Squadron arrived at Bétheniville, near Reims, late on the afternoon of 10 May 1940. The airfield comprised merely flat grass fields, a couple of Nissen huts, tented accommodation for the ground crews and a small café for the officers. The squadron was straight into operations that evening with success, Flying Officer Pickup downing a Dornier 17.

The next day ground personnel and the remainder of the pilots crossed the sea to the battle area, on Ensign and Bombay transport aircraft. Ken was in charge of the rear party.

> I loaded the transports and into one of them as a last thought we put the squadron motorcycle. I ordered everybody on board and I got into the other aircraft, just by chance. When we landed at Bétheniville, we were just getting out and somebody said, 'Good Lord, look there chaps!' At the other end of the landing strip a Bombay was turning over and diving into the deck.

A tragic opening to the squadron's time in France, three lives were lost, the aircraft crew and six others were taken to hospital. As David Watkins would write in *Fear Nothing* – a history of the squadron, 'The holiday mood with which the squadron had departed to France had now gone, replaced with the grim realities of war and a determination to prove themselves as a fighter squadron.' Operationally however the squadron's pilots would soon meet with success, no doubt restoring some, if there indeed was any, loss of morale.

> *Ken Lee:* We carried out patrols maintaining radio silence all the time because we didn't want to betray the fact that we'd actually come to France. And this is where we first saw any numbers, sixes and twelves of Me110s, and Dorniers and Heinkels, unescorted just flying around northern France looking for targets of opportunity. When we managed to find them they were just sitting targets.

That day two Do17s, two Me110s and two He111s were claimed as falling to the guns of 501 Squadron's Hurricanes. Ken Lee was one of those who would engage the enemy that day, something he appeared eager to do:

> We climbed up through a little break in the cloud and I saw some Heinkels. I spotted them first, came round in front of the squadron and led them through this hole in the cloud. When we came through there were Heinkels as far as the eye could see. I was very excited at seeing them at long last after practising all these attacks for years. But I couldn't get up close enough quick enough. We'd been waiting and waiting and waiting and practising and at long last they were there. I pulled up in front of the squadron and waggled my wings. There seemed a terrible lot, probably about fifty or so.

There's a certain setting on the throttle with a wire to prevent you going any further. Except in real cases of emergency, if you do go through it without permission you would come back and a flight sergeant engineer would tell you you had ruined his engine. I was pushing it as far as I could without actually breaking the wire and worrying because I didn't seem to be catching up quick enough. I actually reported that they'd been throwing coils of wire out of the back of these aircraft because there were little circles of grey stuff coming towards me. These I believe now were tracer bullets from the Heinkels, their airscrews causing the trails of smoke. Then I did notice there were little slots appearing in my wings from time to time. We had fabric wings which they just tore into.

You've got to remember the wing span of a Heinkel and set it on your sight. And make sure that you switch the firing button on. It's no use arriving there and pressing the button to find that nothing happens. You have to lower your seat, to give you as much protection as you can, switch on the guns, then switch on the Aldis sight, which you use for the actual air firing, fitting in the calibration of the aircraft you're attacking. When it's exactly into the slot it's exactly three hundred yards away. We were instructed time and time again about this circle of fire three feet wide, at three hundred yards. All eight guns were going through this circle, so if you were shooting accurately you were hitting. It was in fact a bitter mistake. We were sticking with the drill when we should have been closing in.

When you fire you don't really hear anything, the aircraft shudders and you can actually notice a check in engine speed. If you're lucky enough to knock bits off the enemy, then of course you know how well you're doing. Otherwise you want to see glycol or petrol coming out. You're after something to show that you've caused damage. And of course it's always very satisfactory when the rear gunner stops firing because you've protected yourself to some extent. If they're flying in vic [aircraft abreast in the shape of a V] and if we're flying in vic then three aircraft attack three aircraft and the three enemy air gunners are going to spread their fire between the three of us instead of having all three shoot at you at the same time.

The one that I really concentrated on started smoking from its left engine and pulling over, down to the left, but I'd fired bursts that were far too long. I had no more ammunition left. The only thing to do was to go back and refuel. No use hanging around.

We'd found the buggers at last. Everybody's saying did you see mine, did you see this and did you see that. Everyone was trying to get confirmations from the others of anything that he'd done.

I can't stress enough that we had been playing at war up to that point. I had been since January 1939 and it was now May 1940. I had done nothing but prepare for this for over a year. At long last we got them and we got away virtually unscathed. We were elated.

The sun was barely up the next morning when hostile bombers were seen and a brief ORB entry recorded the day's events as including some intense activity. Intense it most certainly was, twelve enemy aircraft claimed, a mixture of Do17s, He111s and Me110s. The success came at a price, Flying Officer Rayner and Flying Officer Smith killed. Ken Lee claimed a success. A Dornier 17 over the Belgian border.

We were doing three or four patrols a day. It was fairly regular, from dawn to dusk. We met some enemy nearly every time. But they never really attacked us. One time we were jumped, I was on patrol with Griffiths and Smith and Malfroy and we were flying at about 8,000 feet near Vusier. I was the weaver behind. [The weaver was positioned thus to protect the formation from attack from the rear. A tactic that would become somewhat exposed later that year.] I glanced over the side and saw bomb bursts on the ground. I followed the direction in which they were going and then I saw four Dorniers flying along happily about 2,000 feet below. So again according to everything we practised and maintaining radio silence, which we were compelled to do at that time, I flew in front, wiggled, pointed down and dived. The idea, which we had practised many many times, was that they should join on to me and all of us should come in behind these four Dorniers and spread the fire. I dived down, put my seat down, switched on the guns, put on the wing span of a Dornier and got ready for the attack.

I looked round to see if my comrades were alongside me but there was not a soul to be seen. They had interpreted my signal as indicating I was going back to base with engine trouble. They stayed up there on the patrol line and, I believe, got jumped by some 109s. That's when Flying Officer Smith got killed. Anyway these four Dorniers had tightened up into a box and shot the hell out of me. I had 37 strikes on the aircraft. I went round behind one, put a lot of rounds into him and he signalled, waved his wings in surrender and put his flaps down and went down to land.

Ken Lee, in discussing his feelings towards the Luftwaffe airmen he was fighting against, echoes what appears to be a general consensus amongst fighter pilots, which was that they were intent on shooting down an enemy machine, not the pilot, thus providing a protective barrier against the feeling of killing another human being:

I didn't hate the Germans at all. They were only scores. You had been trained for a year to shoot aircraft down and when the chance came that's what you did. No personal feelings whatsoever. It was a game with certain risks. No hate. They were targets and it was our job to shoot them down.

There was no great moral issue in it. My generation had only just recovered from the 14 to 18 war. The Germans came again so we fought them again, no question. No misgivings but at the same time no hate. Here they come again silly buggers, was what you felt.

When setting his sights, the fighter pilot is doing so with regard to the dimensions of a machine, an aircraft. The infantry man is setting his sights on the image and dimensions of a man. Not only does the fighter pilot have to find a way of protecting himself against the realities of his task, it is also best that he forms some kind of barricade of indifference against losses of squadron friends and colleagues. And this is what most of them did.

When you find out someone is missing I suppose my initial reaction was that I was jolly glad it wasn't me. If it was a really close friend it would affect you. But if it was just somebody in the other flight who you didn't know particularly well you'd just sort of think hard bloody luck.

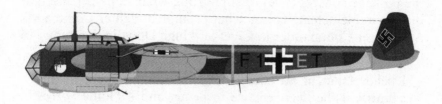

Dornier 17

13 May had 501 adding to its claims, six aircraft including a Me110 for Ken.

> We were on patrol and I was doing rear cover, as usual. I spotted these 110s coming up through a cloud below us. So I flew up in front and signalled and we all went down. I took a deflection shot of the leader and he immediately spouted smoke and flames. I went past him and turned back but he had gone vertically down and the others had dispersed. It was one pass, one shot.

On 14 May a Do 17 and four He111s were claimed. 15 May another four enemy aircraft. On 16 May the squadron moved from Bétheniville to Anglure, away from the Germans who had forced a crossing of the river Meuse and were rapidly advancing west.

Anyone who uses the story of 501 Squadron as the start of their enquiries into the air campaign during the Battle of France, would get the initial impression that the RAF had the upper hand. Further reading into the history of other units would soon set matters straight. In particular the Fairey Battle squadrons were suffering terribly. The Battles of 103 Squadron shared Bétheniville with Ken's 501 Squadron.

> We knew what was happening with the Battles, because they asked us to escort them but we were refused permission. We knew they were having terrible losses. We

were only too willing to escort them.

Losses were indeed mounting, leading to considerable debate at high levels about the likely outcome of the battle in France and the possible consequences of supporting what some perceived as the inevitable defeat. This is what prompted Fighter Command's Air Officer Commander-in-Chief Sir Hugh Dowding's famous 16 May 1940 memorandum, which made his position clear.

> I believe that, if an adequate fighter force is kept in this country, if the fleet remains in being, and if Home Forces are suitably organized to resist invasion, we should be able to carry on the war single-handed for some time, if not indefinitely. But, if the Home Defence Force is drained away in desperate attempts to remedy the situation in France, defeat in France will involve the final, complete and irremediable defeat of this country.

Dowding foresaw the consequences of wasting his resources in France. To him it was of paramount importance to maintain a force that could defend Britain's airspace. But whilst the military leaders and politicians debated the conduct of the Battle of France, the soldiers on the ground and the pilots in the air maintained a presence on and above the battle front.

For 501 Squadron, 17 and 18 May, in terms of contact with the enemy, were uneventful. On 19 May during patrols the enemy was seen but not engaged, notable because on one patrol the pilots were ordered to engage only fighters. There was little incident of note next day. The ORB on 21 May recorded that from the four patrols that day, 'none yielded anything of note to report.' Two new pilots arrived one of whom was Johnny Gibson.

Ken Lee: The first real friend I made on the squadron was Johnny Gibson, when he came to join us as a first replacement for the people we had lost in the first week. He seemed to be a little man but was absolutely irrepressible. And liked to have a jar. When he arrived on the airfield he hadn't ever seen a Hurricane. He'd only flown bi-planes. The CO told him to go and have a little ride in a Hurricane on his own, remember this was not on a proper airfield, this was on a piece of 'ploughed land'. He took it off perfectly, came back and landed perfectly. Never having seen one before!

On 23 May anti-aircraft fire disrupted a patrol, one pilot reporting his aircraft, 'completely turned over by concussion.' And on 24 May anti-aircraft fire again was the main opposition on operations. The next day the ground fire would finally claim a 501 Squadron pilot, Pilot Officer Sylvester missing from a patrol supporting an aerial attack on enemy troop movements. He had lost his way following an engagement with a Dornier, landing at another airfield and eventually returning to the squadron. Ken remembers him:

> Sylvester was one of the auxiliaries, the best auxiliary of all. He was the one who really had determination to get going at the enemy. He was always being shot down in France, but he got so well organised that he had a special escape kit including a clean shirt, underneath his seat. He always seemed to force land in the grounds of some chateau and he would come back two or three days later having been wined and dined. He was a tall man, very distinguished and he always seemed to come out on the right side. But he was shot down and lost forever one day [when the squadron had returned to England]. A girlfriend gave me a Jiminy Cricket mascot, which I had put in the new aircraft I had just got. Sylvester borrowed the aircraft and never came back. Jiminy Cricket didn't do him any good.

Ken's reference to a mascot highlights the importance that many fighter pilots put on a talisman of whatever kind – be it an item or ritual, however simple – a necklace, a piece of a girlfriend's clothing, or even a toy grasshopper.

The next day patrols, without notable incident, continued and a further move, the squadron operating from Boos. It had been a lean time for the 501 Squadron pilots following the initial intensity of combat. That was to change on 27 May. Thirteen Hurricanes took off at 1345 hours to patrol the Blangy – Abancourt area. Ten minutes later an estimated twenty-four He111s and twenty Me110s were found, 'eleven He111s were for certain brought down', and one Me110, 'almost for certain', with three more He111s possible. An extraordinary tally achieved without loss. Ken Lee was credited with a Heinkel 111. The remainder of May went without incident, poor weather hindering operations.

I was doing the rear cover for the squadron. It was rather

like herding sheep. You're weaving behind the squadron to
try and spot any enemy coming down. This is the origin of
the Hawkeye business [his nickname] – I saw the buggers
before they saw me. We'd had these two or three victories
to begin with. I'd spotted the aircraft and led the squadron
onto the target. Unintentionally I was eavesdropping outside the mess window and I heard them say, 'you know that
bugger is not too bad after all. Let's not call him boss eye
anymore (I had a dropped eyelid) let's call him Hawkeye.'
And I've been known as Hawkeye ever since. I was delighted
to know that I wouldn't be called boss eye anymore.

I was happy with the job I was doing. And everyday I
wanted to do it. When I heard the others say, 'We hope
Hawkeye's doing the rear cover today', I felt proud of
myself.

When you're flying in formation you have to concen-
trate on the lead aircraft in order to stay in position. The
wing tips are only three or four feet apart. So you can't be
keeping an eye out for the enemy. One man at the rear of
the formation would fly along slowly behind, or weaving
from side to side. He didn't have to watch the other aircraft
too closely, he was able to look around and survey the sky
in every direction. To give warning of any attack this was
the safeguard we created after a few months.

Into June 1940 and the fact that the ORB entries are short and
to the point (and perhaps written a few weeks after the events)
are no doubt indicative of the general disarray as a total
evacuation of the British presence in France became necessary.
The ORB's entry for 1 June could only comment on operations
thus, 'numerous contacts were made with the enemy resulting in
several victories.'

2 June brought a squadron withdrawal to Le Mans, whilst
501's Hurricanes operated from Boos covering the evacuation of
Allied troops from the Dunkirk beaches. Pilot Officer Claydon
was killed in action on 5 June and on 8 June Dickie Hulse and
Sergeant Lewis were also lost. Ken added another enemy aircraft
to his score, a Dornier 17 on 6 June. Two further aircraft would
fall to the guns of John Gibson on 8 and 10 June, bringing what
would be 501's claimed final score in France to seventy-one
enemy aircraft destroyed, at a cost of eighteen Hurricanes and
eight pilots. On 16 June there was a further withdrawal to

Dinard, to protect the ports of St Malo and Cherbourg and on 18 June orders came through for the evacuation of France. The rapidity of the withdrawal would sometimes prove problematic.

At one point we were staying in the Hotel de la Poste in Rouen and we'd been flying from Bouserre nearby. Suddenly, we were told to get out and evacuate immediately. We all got in the truck and went out to the aerodrome to get an aircraft. But we forgot about Johnny Gibson and left him behind in the hotel. He only got out of a back door of the hotel when the Germans came in the front. He got across the Seine and joined us again. He said, 'you rotten buggers you left me behind.' He just got overlooked. He'd only been with us a few days.

Of course during all these moves the pilots still had operational duties. On 10 June Ken fell to enemy guns.

I never saw the man that shot me down in France. I had been attacking a bunch of Heinkels that dived into a cloud. I followed them in and then something hit me. I never really knew what it was. The control column was entirely loose. I couldn't do anything with it. You're too busy to be scared. It was instinct. If you can't do anything about the situation, can't control it where you are, then you have to get out and start again. I came out of this cloud, diving pretty swiftly. I tried to fly straight and level but it wasn't possible. I decided to jump out. We had never had any instruction in those early days about the use of a parachute except to jump out and pull the rip cord. I was going so fast that when I tried to get out the wind blew me back in again. The aircraft turned on its side, I fell out and hit the tailplane with my leg. I was over Bernaise, just south of the Seine, with this huge forest below me. We'd had no instruction on how to control the direction of fall. You'd get out and wait a few moments to get clear of the aircraft and then pull to open the parachute and down you came. I got down to about four or five thousand feet and I heard bullets going past me. Some French were shooting at me and I could hear them going 'parachutist, parachutist'. I called 'Je suis Anglais'. I crashed down into the top of a tree and bounced into the lower branches and onto the ground. I had a bullet in my hand and my leg had got quite badly hit on the tailplane. That's why I wasn't able to fly back with the squadron when they returned to England.

The Frenchmen picked me up and tried to help as soon as they realised who I was. I knew a little French at the time and was able to show them my identity card. Good job I didn't drop it as I came down.

We were given a series of retirements from up near the French/Belgian border all the way back to Le Mans and then down into Normandy. We'd been trained to do as we were told and when they said go back, we went back. And when they said go forward we went forward.

When the French surrendered locally we were in the mess with a French squadron. When it became clear that they were going to surrender to the Germans they wanted us to capitulate as well. In fact they tried forcibly almost to keep us in the mess. We never dreamt of it. We just went back and again we were told either go to Jersey or get on boats back to England if possible. Because I'd been wounded I had to go back by sea. I couldn't fly, my right hand was bandaged up. I got on a little boat called the *Hull Trader* and, from St Malo, went all night long to Torquay.

I think my finest hour was in France, It's where I came into my own and I got the confidence. I think it was there that I conquered any possibility of fear because I was confident and felt sure that I could do what I was trying to do and get away with it every time.

For the rest of the squadron a day was spent operating from St Helier, Jersey covering the BEF's departure from Cherbourg. On 20 June the squadron was back in England, the air party landing at Tangmere, the following day reforming at Croydon.

France capitulated on 22 June 1940. It appeared Hitler had Europe at his mercy. The focus of defiance in western Europe rested in Britain, whose Prime Minister Winston Churchill would now rally his nation's morale, making clear in whose hands the future lay.

Winston Churchill, House of Commons, 4 June 1940: ...the cause of civilisation itself will be defended by the skill and devotion of a few thousand airmen. There never has been, I suppose, in all the world, in all the history of war, such an opportunity for youth.

Winston Churchill, House of Commons, 18 June 1940: I look forward confidently to the exploits of our fighter pilots – these splendid men, this brilliant youth – who will have the glory of saving their native land, their island home, and all they love, from the most deadly of all attacks.

One pool of brilliant youth was the pilots of 501 Squadron. On their return from France the airmen were given four days' special leave. Apart from the arrival of Squadron Leader Harry Hogan as squadron CO, little of note occurred during the remainder of June. Hogan already had a distinguished flying career to his name. Pre-war he had taken part in a record-breaking long distance flight, piloting a Vickers Wellesley from Ismailia to Darwin. He would go on to earn the respect of the pilots at 501 Squadron, including Ken.

When Harry Hogan took over the squadron, the atmosphere changed altogether and we began to ignore seniority of rank. When we started the war, if you were senior you led, whether you knew what you were doing or not. Now we were making the experienced pilots section leaders, even sergeant pilots, as long as they knew what they were doing.

We were British to the core. We were all comrades and that's all there was to it. Throughout it all nobody ever let me down, and I don't think I let anybody down either. We were from the generation which thought the teacher was always right and all policemen were good. You belonged to the squadron and therefore you did your duty.

Amazingly from the resources available it was possible to bring the squadron up to strength with new Hurricanes immediately. We were never short of aircraft. We could be short of pilots, sometimes down to fourteen, which for a squadron that's got to put twelve in the air, only two in reserve, was a little bit scarce.

Ken recalled his thoughts of England on his and the squadron's return from France.

The first impression was that nothing had changed. I was wounded and had my arm in a sling. So I went back to my home. I was walking around in uniform without a cap, I'd lost it in France. I was in the main street in Birmingham, which didn't look any different. I just wondered what they all thought about the war. I could see no reaction to me in my state.

July had started quietly for 501 Squadron, by now based at Middle Wallop, but from 10 July, which is now recognised as the first official day of the Battle of Britain, the attrition of war would once again take its toll. The Luftwaffe and the RAF would now seriously start to engage over the English Channel and the coast of south-east England. Shipping convoys and harbours were targeted. On 11 July Sergeant Frederick Dixon was lost to an Me109 when, despite baling out and despite a considerable sea search, he was presumed to have drowned. On 12 July Pilot Officer Duncan Hewitt was lost off Portland, whilst engaging a Dornier, plummeting into the sea, his body never recovered. Ken Lee had remained non-operational during this period recovering from his injuries, but he was back to operations on 13 July, when numerous patrols were carried out by the squadron. Between 14 and 20 July operations continued amidst training flights and Ken completed at least seven sorties. But there was little contact with the enemy until the last day of this period, during which Pilot Officer Sylvester's luck finally ran out, he too being swallowed by the sea. The opening days of the Battle of Britain had not gone well for 501 Squadron. Possibly their tactics were being exposed through contact with the enemy fighter aircraft.

Ken Lee: We were still sticking with the numbered attacks [formation manoeuvres aimed at bringing the greatest firepower against unescorted bombers]. There was no noticeable change in tactics. We were still flying in vic formations, when we wanted to go from one place to another as a squadron. These kind of attacks certainly restricted manoeuvrability, the pilot acting as somewhat of an automaton. Although it has to be said that such attacks did lead to familiarity in combat, and therefore acted as a means of countering any apprehension, particularly for the inexperienced. The Germans were all flying loose pairs, which was far more effective. I'm sorry to say I do think our training and our theory were poor. We'd have done much better if we'd taken notice of the tactics the Germans had used in Spain.

We were beginning to realise that we were firing from too far away. The theory we had been spoon fed was wrong.

When all had seemed lost at Dunkirk, Winston Churchill had asked his military thinkers to advise him on the potential outcome if Britain stood alone against the Nazis. His Chiefs of Staff responded, 'Our conclusion is that *prima facie* Germany has most of the cards; but the real test is whether the morale of our fighting personnel and civil population will counter-balance the numerical and material advantages which Germany enjoys. We believe it will.' Chester Wilmot in *The Struggle for Europe* summed up the scene.

> To the rest of Europe, and indeed to most of the world it seemed that the odds were weighted overwhelmingly in favour of the Luftwaffe, but... Britain was not altogether unready for the onslaught that was about to break upon her from the skies. That she was prepared at all was the result of the foresight and persistence of a small band of enlightened and progressive men who through the years of public complacency and political neglect had worked to give the country a scientific system of air defence. Their preparations had begun immediately after the Nazis walked out of the Disarmament Conference, and out of the League of Nations, in October 1933.[2]

Key scientific thinkers and developers would be allied with those of leadership and foresight to build this defence system. For leadership and foresight read Air Marshal Sir Hugh Dowding, the Commander-in-Chief of Fighter Command from July 1936. For a key scientific developer and thinker read Robert Watson-Watt, the man behind radar.

What this small band of men had strived for and achieved was the expansion of the Home Defence Air Force during the mid to late 1930s, the design and production of the aerial weaponry, the Hurricane and the Spitfire, and a highly technical, scientific and organised system of defence with which to marshal, deploy and command the aircrews of the RAF who would man the aerial front line. The efficiency of the ground defence system would be tested to the utmost in the summer and autumn of 1940 but this would prove irrelevant if the RAF did not have the trained pilots who could fly sufficient numbers of modern aircraft with which to oppose enemy incursions into British airspace.

Since Dunkirk and the Fall of France, Dowding's command had concentrated on building up squadron strength, resting pilots, training new pilots, producing more fighters. German armed forces were merely the breadth of the English Channel away and the RAF had to be prepared not only to assist in the repulsion of a seaborne assault but also to bloody the Luftwaffe without attrition seriously diminishing strength and effectiveness. While the country braced itself for the Nazi onslaught, Fighter Command prepared for the ultimate test of Dowding's foresight, the defensive system he had overseen since his command appointment.

Fighter Command was made up of four separate fighter groups covering Britain. No 10 Group covered the south-west, No 11 Group the south-east, No 12 Group the centre and No 13 Group the north. It would be 11 Group in the breach of the battle during the summer months, although reinforcements could come in from other groups when necessary. Each group was further divided into geographical sectors, which had main sector stations. Also there were satellite airfields within each sector, controlled by the respective sector station. At Command, Group and Sector level there were operations rooms where the developments of the day's activities could be monitored, therefore informing command decisions. Information from the Chain Home radar stations, looking out from the coast, the Observer Corps tracking raids inland and radio direction finding stations, was filtered to provide a picture of the air situation. It was all there in theory. Adolf Hitler now decided to put it to the test.

On 16 July 1940, with Britain unrespondent to suggestions of peace, Hitler issued War Directive No 16.

> As England in spite of her hopeless military position has so far shown herself unwilling to come to any compromise, I have decided to begin preparations for and, if necessary, to carry out the invasion of England.
>
> This operation is dictated by the necessity of eliminating Great Britain as a base from which the war against Germany can be fought. If necessary, the island will be occupied...

I therefore issue the following orders:

1) The landing operation must be a surprise crossing on a broad front extending approximately from Ramsgate to a point west of the Isle of Wight... The preparations... must be concluded by the middle of August.

2) The following preparations must be undertaken to make a landing in England possible:

a) The English Air Force must be eliminated to such an extent that it will be incapable of putting up any substantial opposition to the invading troops.

b) The sea route must be cleared of mines.

c) Both flanks, the Straits of Dover and the Western approaches to the Channel... must be heavily mined as to be completely inaccessible.

d) Heavy coastal guns must dominate and protect the entire coastal front area...

3) The invasion will be referred to by the codename *Seelöwe* [Sealion].

So the stakes were now clearly set. The survival of England, of Britain and all the Kingdom stood for now depended on repulsing Operation Sealion.

From 21 to 31 July the squadron diary has Ken Lee carrying out seventeen operations. Steadily the battle for control of the sky was heating up. The 25 and 26 July saw another move for 501 Squadron personnel to Gravesend, as Ken recalled, 'right under where the big raids were coming in.'

Usually we were in a dispersal tent and we'd get a telephone call, vector such a direction. We'd take off and go straight off in that direction to the height indicated. No hesitation, no thought about what we would find when we got there. You're hearing, Blue Leader, Blue Leader, vector 10, vector 120, angels 15. If you see them 'Tally Ho' was the cry, or 'there go the bastards'.

We weren't practising any longer. We reckoned we knew it all and we were waiting for them. Just waiting and virtually every day we were off, sometimes, three, four or five times. You could climb up to five or eight thousand feet and be in an engagement and be back on the ground in twenty-five minutes, refuelled and rearmed and off again within the hour.

For the Hurricanes there wasn't a terrible lot of air combat dog fighting. It was mainly finding the enemy and coming in behind them, trying to shoot them down. The Spits' job was to stay up and keep the Me109s off our backs. It's now been agreed that the Hurricane squadrons did quite a lot more than people have given them credit for without the glamour of the Spits.

We slept at Gravesend, just an ordinary little airfield with the aircraft dispersed around the edge. No protection, just an open field. At dawn we would take off for Hawkinge, land there, again no protection, just dispersed widely all the way round the perimeter. That is the edge of the field, we were still on grass, no runways. There were four dispersal points each with a tent where we sat while waiting for something to happen. We were connected up and could get scrambles from there. Probably four times during the day. The last thing in the evening we would be on standby and if we had half an hour we used to fly back to Gravesend. If not we'd just stay at Hawkinge for the night, kipping down with blankets in this big tent.

On 27 July, operating from Hawkinge (acting as a forward base), the pilots of 501 Squadron countered the enemy over Dover Harbour. Flight Lieutenant 'Pan' Cox was lost, the ORB recording that it was believed that he had been shot down by the Dover anti-aircraft fire. As Ken recalled:

We had to dive down through the barrage coming up from Dover in order to get at this huge mass of Stukas. We all went through the middle of it and one of our better known pilots was hit by a rocket. As soon as we got out to sea we were in the middle of them. In fact while I was shooting at one I happened to glance over my shoulder and see the Stuka behind me standing on its tail shooting at me.

Ken Lee, flying as Blue 1 would submit a combat report with regard the action on 27 July. Time attack was delivered – 1725 hours, place – over Dover, height of enemy – 3,000 feet, claim – 1 Me109 damaged. His combat report reads as follows:

The squadron was patrolling one and a half miles north-east of Dover. I sighted enemy aircraft diving onto Dover docks and immediately led the squadron towards them, when the Dover Defence Barrage opened up. I engaged 1 Me109 pulling up from machine gunning or bombing the docks, at first with a full deflection and then followed it round to take a further shot from full astern. My tracer ammunition passed through the enemy aircraft, which dived steeply towards the sea, followed by Blue 3, who himself could not get within effective range and quickly lost sight of it. There were our Spitfires and other Me109s engaged in the vicinity.

On 29 July 501's diarist would be able to record later in the day, 'a major engagement'. It is interesting to note that the 11 Group Intelligence bulletin for 29 July opens with, 'the main feature of the day was a large-scale attack on Dover Harbour at about 0735-0745 hours by a force estimated at approximately forty Ju87s with an escort of approximately the same number of Me109s'. Of course with respect to the size of attacks prior to this date it was 'large-scale'. With respect to the attacks that would be developing in the following few months it was not. Over Dover that morning, German airmen, flying Ju87s and Me109s, were to fight for their lives with the pilots of 501 Squadron. The 501 Squadron ORB would later record six enemy aircraft claimed destroyed, confirmed or probable, and six more claimed damaged (although the 11 Group bulletin would later record, with respect to 501 Squadron, two Ju87s destroyed confirmed, two Ju87s destroyed unconfirmed, one Me109 destroyed unconfirmed and four Ju87s damaged). Ken Lee was one of those who made a claim as his combat report for that day testifies.

501 Sqn Hurricane

Number of enemy aircraft – 40 + Ju87s and Me109 escort
Time attack was delivered – 0745 hours
Place attack was delivered – 10 miles south-east of Dover
Height of enemy – 2,000 feet
Range at which fire was opened – 300 yards
Estimated length of bursts – 10 secs
Total number of rounds fired – 1,350

The squadron left Hawkinge at 0725 hours to patrol over Dover at 5,000 feet, which was later changed to 8,000 feet. After flying north-east over Sandwich I led the squadron round south-west towards Hawkinge. At this moment approximately at 0745 hours I saw about 40 dive-bomber Ju87s coming out of the sun. As we had been warned not to cross over the Dover AA Barrage, I led the formation round on the west of it and then turned to intercept the Ju87s, which by this time had finished their bombing and had climbed to about 2,000 feet. The squadron dived to the attack and a general dogfight developed. I chose a Ju87 and got on to its tail firing at it for 10 secs at about 300 yards, seeing my tracer entering it. It dived down pouring out white smoke and owing to the general confusion I lost sight of it. As the enemy aircraft took evasive action in the form of steep dives and climbs there is nothing to suggest that it was more than damaged. I returned to Hawkinge at about 0801 hours.

In total the 11 Group intelligence bulletin for the day summarised events as six destroyed confirmed, ten destroyed unconfirmed, two destroyed probable and nine damaged. In addition anti-aircraft claimed a further two Ju87s shot down on the raid. Here we have a clear example of the overclaiming that would become a feature of both sides' battle summaries throughout the Battle of Britain. Accurate figures could of course never be achieved at this stage, the reports of the returning pilots had to be relied on in the first instance. These pilots had just been in an aerial melee, with the combatants fighting at high speed and in three dimensions. A definitive account of the engagement would be an impossibility. Yet assessments of the fighting were needed so that commanders could gauge the success of their tactics, to inform future strategy. What is now known though is that it was the Germans who would be put at the most disadvantage by the overclaiming, believing, as the battle developed, that Fighter Command was nearing defeat. When this defeat continually failed to materialise morale and rational thinking about future strategy suffered.

On 30 July 501 Squadron would lose two more airmen. Pilot Officer Ralph Don was seriously injured in a parachute fall, while Pilot Officer Gordon Parkin's injuries proved serious from an accident undershooting the airfield at Gravesend. At the end of July the squadron strength was down to sixteen pilots. But had morale deteriorated? It did not seem so to Ken Lee.

> The fact that we couldn't beat them never occurred to us, any of us. We were just doing our best and muddling along. We were going to be alright in the end. There certainly was never any despondency that I ever encountered.

Ken was also developing a mature attitude towards losses, responding to the situation with the sense of fatalism, which historian Richard Holmes sums up, as a 'view characteristic of soldiers of well developed combat experience, men who have already seen just how nasty and random battle really is.'[3] Ken's view was, 'If it's going to happen, it's going to happen.'

July had certainly cost the Royal Air Force, but the attrition rate was acceptable. Indeed Park and Dowding were not going to let it be anything else. They knew that the RAF's primary task was to be the defence of more important targets than those currently under attack and their air forces were marshalled accordingly. However the course of the battle was now to change and more important targets were to be sought out by the enemy bombers. On 1 August 1940 Adolf Hitler issued Directive No 17, 'In order to establish the necessary conditions for the final conquest of England I intend to intensify air and sea warfare against the English homeland.' The Directive's first requirement demanded:

> 1. The German Air Force is to overpower the English Air Force with all the forces at its command, in the shortest time possible. The attacks are to be directed primarily against flying units, their ground installations, and their supply organizations, but also against the aircraft industry, including that manufacturing anti-aircraft equipment.

The directive went on to require continued attacks 'against ports', 'stores of food', 'provisions in the interior of the country'.

Goering in response directed his airmen to 'wipe the British Air Force from the sky.'

The first week of August was fairly quiet for 501 Squadron, however. Ken carried out eight active patrols and recalled the lull, 'There was nothing outstanding and we weren't at that time suffering very much ourselves.' New pilots came in, Flight Lieutenant Putt, and Polish airmen Flying Officer Lukaszewicz, Pilot Officers Zenker and Kozlowski, and Flying Officer Witorzenc.

> We got these Poles, people we'd never heard of, who could hardly speak English. But from the moment they came they were seen to be superb pilots. And superb fighting men. We got on with them very well indeed.

It remained quiet for the squadron until 10 August when a Do17 was engaged but it escaped into cloud. Indeed Ken carried out no active operations. Battles of life and death were happening elsewhere. On 11 August Ken completed two patrols, again with no contact, but the next day there was plenty of intense fighting.

Hitler's 1 August directive had included the date of 5 August as the start of the intensification of the air war, but this was subject to the combat readiness of the Luftwaffe and the weather conditions. On 2 August preparations for *Adler Tag* – Eagle Day – were set in motion and 10 August was chosen for the launch. Poor weather would bring about a postponement that day, similarly the next day and so 13 August was set as *Adler Tag*. But the day prior to this there was a noticeable escalation in the air fighting as the German air force attacked radar stations along with shipping in the Channel and Thames estuary. 501 Squadron's ORB records the bare facts of the day, with respect to its experiences.

> A.M. Weather was fine and clear. The Squadron left for Hawkinge at 0824 hours and patrolled from 0939 to 1015 hours. No interceptions were made. Squadron were ordered to patrol at East of N. Foreland and over the Estuary off Westgate and took off at 1100 hours and landed again at 1155 hours. Squadron Leader Holland forced landed in a field near Dover. Between Deal and Ramsgate the Squadron encountered a force of 30 to 40 Ju87s flying between 3,000 and 4,000 feet over the Thames

Estuary. The Squadron attacked and broke formation as the enemy were at various heights. Several aircraft were destroyed confirmed and unconfirmed. Pilot Officer Lukaszewicz was reported missing believed killed after this engagement [His Hurricane hit the sea west of Ramsgate].

P.M. The Squadron encountered another force of enemy aircraft off West of Ramsgate. The Squadron broke formation and attacked individually. One Me110 was destroyed and two 110's damaged. The Squadron (12 aircraft) took off from Hawkinge at 1725 hours and landed at Gravesend at 1840 hours. Pilot Officer Gibson landed at Hawkinge after shooting down a Me109. The Squadron was unable to operate from Hawkinge owing to the damage caused by bombing by enemy aircraft.

At Hawkinge, one hangar was smashed, another partially wrecked. Machine-gun bullets had peppered the aerodrome and buildings. Fire had spread in the main stores and there was not much left of the clothing store. Workshops were wrecked. Twenty-eight craters were left in the landing ground. Two civilians and three airmen were killed, six airmen severely injured. Two Spitfires were severely damaged. Just one example of the type of damage that would befall numerous airfields over the coming weeks.

In the air airmen from both sides had fought for their lives, but of course the authors of the ORBs are not required to dramatise the events. Ken Lee recalls what it was like taking part in the August battles, in contrast to July.

The numbers of aircraft coming in multiplied by three or four. And formations of a hundred aircraft came at one time, so that definitely you could see the increase of activity. But the more there were, the more there were to shoot down. Normally we'd be flying south-east. You would see black in the distance and you'd be climbing and climbing and climbing all the time, pressing on. You're always looking for height and as a raid, say twenty or thirty plus would be coming towards you you'd try to judge the curve, climbing to come round behind them.

Unless we got above them we couldn't attack from head on. We were struggling for height all the time. Eventually when you get up there you're in these vic formations, doing these supposed mass attacks to spread the counter fire. Go in squirt off and hope bits fall off. When you've used the ammunition pull off go back and get some more.

In contrast to France there were more of them. They weren't so vulnerable, they had some protection and were flying much bigger formations with much more fire power. We didn't know it was the Battle of Britain. Nobody told us. We were still going by the fact that we were getting these odd victories here and there. We were losing a few people, most of them coming back having jumped out. Some were slightly wounded but they came back to the squadron within a few weeks and so we were still a going concern. And we were never short of aircraft.

You haven't got much firing time with eight guns. You've got to give measured short bursts, two or three seconds each. It's no use just pushing your button and squirting out at God knows what. You've got to get a good sight. You can do that as you are diving and as you are closing in you can put in little bursts to begin with to liven them up or distract the rear gunners. And then you get to your 300 yards, which was supposed to be the optimum range but it is quite a long way away. It didn't seem close. Your sights had the wing span of this aircraft on it so that you knew exactly where you were. If it fitted the gap you were exactly 300 yards. I have even throttled back when I have been in a good position so I didn't get too close. I should have carried on and got as close as I could.

When you spot them they are always above you. You're still climbing towards them. 'Tally Ho' is when you actually see them. You don't need the ground control any longer. You've got them in the eyeball. You look for your wing men, make sure you're flying in an appropriate formation and then it's really a case of coming round behind them and hoping that your rear cover and your weavers are going to keep anybody off your tail. If you're doing the weaving, which I normally was, then if any aircraft dived down towards you, you would turn to face them and try to get a shot at them. The moment they saw some aggression they didn't come down so close.

It was a long, long climb always pushing trying to get there. It's only four or five miles difference in the speed, especially when you're climbing and they're going straight and level. You're not closing fast, so that's the waiting period, the time to get close enough to do the damage. The luxury of being able to dive in from above them was unheard of except for those early days in France when we did find them in all kinds of compromising situations. I don't remember any misgivings, or drawing back from anything. When you saw them you went at them.

The fighter controllers were very casual in their instructions, very matter of fact and cheerful about the whole thing. 'Alright boys now there's...' or 'I've got a nice lot for you today.' We felt very happy with them, especially when they'd given you a couple of good directions. Any chat came from the controller. Occasionally in the excitement of the battle you'd hear somebody had left his transmitter on. You were supposed to be listening, and only putting in the transmitter when you have something to say. You don't have much to say unless in the excitement of the moment you say got the bugger or something like that.

Success came Ken's way on the second morning patrol of 12 August. His combat report as detailed to the squadron Intelligence Officer outlined the engagement:

Number of enemy aircraft – 30
Type of enemy aircraft – Ju87
Time attack was delivered – 1130
Place attack was delivered – 10 miles east of North Foreland
Height of enemy – 100 feet
Range at which fire was opened – 250 to 75 yards
Estimated length of bursts – 1 burst, 12 secs
Total number of rounds fired – 220
I attacked dive bombers returning from attacking shipping in Thames Estuary, two stragglers, one was attacked by another Hurricane and crashed on fire into the sea. Pilot jumped out. Self attacked other enemy aircraft and closed to 75 yards pulling away to avoid enemy aircraft. Saw explosion and flash in enemy aircraft and on turning to engage again, enemy aircraft had disappeared. There being no cloud at that height enemy aircraft considered definitely destroyed.

In authenticating the action of the pilot, intelligence officers had great power; and in recording and collating the experiences as told to them, they had a position of great authority, as Ken recognised:

> Everybody wanted to get their victories confirmed. You could have probables and halves, but to get your own fully confirmed aircraft at a certain time and a certain date that's what you wanted. It's rather like playing cricket, you wanted to score more runs than everybody else.

On 13 August 501 Squadron, owing to the damage at Hawkinge, operated exclusively from its 'parent station' Gravesend, but made no interceptions. On 14 August the squadron was able to use Hawkinge again as a forward base. Patrols were flown, Ken Lee completing four, but any enemy presence remained elusive. The squadron was called to readiness the next morning at 0410 hours and later that morning flew to Hawkinge. Ken Lee flew three active operations before midday. On a late morning sortie the pilots of 501 Squadron reported twenty Ju87s to line up in their sights and in the ensuing melee fourteen enemy aircraft were claimed destroyed or damaged, against a cost of two Hurricanes lost, the pilots surviving, and one damaged.

The day was far from over for 501 Squadron though. Twice more the enemy were engaged, eight enemy aircraft claimed destroyed or damaged. Ken completed one more patrol late that evening. This day, 15 August, is now seen as one of the most important days of the Battle of Britain. On it the RAF claimed 182 German aircraft, which history has now reduced to seventy-five. The RAF lost thirty-four aircraft, seventeen pilots dying, sixteen injured. Attrition rates were high for both sides, the battle was reaching its most crucial phase. Pilots, of course, were aware of the losses and strains on their own particular squadron, but what of the general situation?

> We were inclined to see our own particular phase and if we were doing well and we were getting away with some results and not too many casualties we were entirely happy. Certainly no time clock hung over us. We never thought like that.

On 16 August during one engagement an enemy aircraft was damaged, and Ken flew one patrol without incident. On 17

August 501 Squadron flying was curtailed. This no doubt provided a welcome respite from the high intensity levels of recent days, thus affording the squadron personnel a chance to relax. Drink of course has long been a means to alleviate the stresses of military battle. Quite possibly it helped the airmen get some sleep. It also provided the opportunity to engage in some group bonding, bringing together the men who would be fighting alongside each other.

Except for our half day a week in London, we didn't get out very much. We were on the aerodrome from dawn til dusk and then a half hour in the pub before the ten o'clock closing. In the streets of London, and the clubs and the restaurants we would go to, there was no noticeable change in the way we were treated.

We came up the steps in Piccadilly Circus and there was the Regent Palace, the Canadian Riding School (that's where the Canadians took their girlfriends, and a lot of good rides took place in the Riding School) on one corner and up the side street at the end there was a street called Denham Street where there were one or two nice little café restaurants and bars. One of them, Chez Moi, was frequented by the pilots from a lot of the fighter squadrons. There was a cartoonist who worked there and the walls were covered with drawings of the pilots. That was our main meeting place. The first time I went there, there was a girl sitting at the bar, she turned round, looked up the stairs as I came down and said, 'Good God, there's Kenny Lee, raped me in a tent when I was twelve.' When I was about twelve I had probably had a look at her knickers or something like that. I had a bit of trouble living that down I must say.

There was a downstairs bar in the Regent Palace. Always full of single women, sitting in there on their own. You could chat most of them up. They weren't just easy, you still had to work at it a little bit, wine and dine probably. These casual engagements weren't what you call romantic. They were just fun and taking advantage of the situation. I had money, twelve and six a day, and when I was released I was free to do what I wished as long as I turned up at the squadron in the morning at the right time. You were footloose and fancy free.

The black out was very, very intense. But the moment the door opened of whatever place you were going to a wave of sound and excitement would overwhelm you.

Many many young men would give their eye teeth to be a member of a fighter squadron, have some authority and be respected, a section leader, have your own aircraft and your own ground crew. You were the centre of your own little world and with all the other fellows together you formed a unit.

On the morning of 18 August 501 Squadron was at fifteen minutes availability from dawn to 0830 hours, at which point the aircraft became airborne setting course for Hawkinge. Patrols were carried out, Ken completing two. At 1230 hours he was airborne again when disaster struck.

It was the first time we had flown in an action when I wasn't doing the weaving for the squadron. We were supposed to be on our way back to base and I had taken the lead position. I was acting flight leader, but regardless of that I had always been doing the weaving until that day. I would definitely have seen these 109s coming down, but there were two new boys doing the weaving. According to the German account they saw nothing and were both shot down, giving us no warning whatsoever.

We had been told to go back to Gravesend to be released for the afternoon. We took with me leading. There were six aircraft in front of me and I was in the box. I had two aircraft following either side of me and one in the box behind me. The eleventh and twelfth aircraft were doing the weaving, practising. We set off for Gravesend. Half way there the controller came on saying we had got a very big raid coming in and giving us height and direction. We climbed up and up and up, to about 17,000 feet. The first thing I knew was a bang and my leg shot up in the air.

The Hurricanes had been 'bounced' by Me109s of the German unit JG26. The commander Gerhardt Schoepfel took out the two weavers first, Pilot Officer Kozlowski, seriously injured, and Pilot Officer Bland killed. Schoepfel then sent Sergeant McKay's Hurricane to earth, the pilot baling out slightly burned. The German pilot then turned his guns on to Ken's Hurricane.

A bullet had hit me in the back of the leg. Immediately there was smoke and flames coming out from underneath the main tank. I was right in the middle of the formation so this seemed inexplicable. I was without full control, there was smoke and flames. I rolled it on its back and pushed myself out. Then I did something incredible, which I don't quite believe myself. I set my stopwatch and did a minute drop. There had been rumours that the Germans were shooting down people in parachutes and I didn't intend to be hung up there waiting to be shot. I dropped down to about 5,000 feet, I was going round and round, head over heels, and I pulled the chute. It came up between my legs and I could well have got wrapped up in it like a parcel. It was pull the chute and hope for the best. I came wafting down into a cornfield. An old chap, with a military cap on, jumped up from the corn. He had a gun, which he apparently had captured in Gallipoli himself, from the Turks. I wasn't in uniform, it was such a beautiful day and we were only going back to base. I had taken my jacket off and put it in the tail. I was just in shirtsleeves with no means of identifying myself. Consequently I was held at gunpoint until the London Irish arrived, who took me off to the local golf club for a refresher. My boot was sogging with the blood, like a Wellington you have got wet in a stream. It wasn't gushing out but it was very wet. My back was peppered with little bits of explosive bullet so my shirt was stained. They took me to the golf club, we went in and I was given a brandy. There were all these people, 'you know old chap, I was on the fourth tee and this aircraft came so low it made me miss my stroke!'

I blame myself entirely. I had no idea we were going to be engaged. As far as I was concerned we were just going back to base. If I thought we were to be engaged I would have done the weaving myself and I don't think we would have lost four aircraft. I would have warned them in time, to break up.

I was taken to Leeds Castle and they had to take the bullet out of my leg. I didn't get back to the squadron for four weeks.

Ken had little choice now but to spend some time away from the battle, which continued at full intensity. Colleagues added to their scores. Colleagues fell to German guns. Whilst recovering from his injuries, Ken remained fully aware of the course of the battle.

> I was in Maidstone, Kent and could see the raids going on. I was annoyed I was not there. We saw them going past us to London. We'd see them being shot down occasionally and we'd see the vapour trails of aircraft up above. You just regretted you weren't up there getting a couple more on your score sheet.

On 10 September 501 Squadron had moved to Kenley and Ken Lee would return to his squadron colleagues later that month. As he recalled:

> We had a lot more pilots. Earlier in the battle we only had about sixteen pilots. So twelve in the air and little in reserve. At Kenley we had twenty or more pilots. We were comfortable. We weren't living in tents any longer. We were back in the mess at Kenley and it was a very organised life. It was just the same as it had been in peacetime except that there were real targets when you got out there.
>
> The battle did die down, and it was mainly patrols. When we were at Hawkinge we were right in amongst them but when we were back at Kenley they had to penetrate a long way before we intercepted them, and we just didn't find many.

Ken would complete some operational patrols in October 1940. But he would not be experiencing anything like the intensity of previous air battles. During this period his operational career to date would be recognised. He received the Distinguished Flying Cross on 22 October 1940, the *London Gazette* entry reading, 'This officer has led his section and flight with marked success. He has displayed great dash and determination and has destroyed at least six enemy aircraft.' However Ken's time with 501 Squadron was about to run out and he left in November 1940.

Chapter 2

Sand and Wire

After the Battle of Britain Ken Lee was posted as a flight commander to an operational training unit for Hurricanes.

> They thought I had completed my ration and they needed instructors so I went to 53 OTU, Crosby-on-Eden, Carlisle. I commanded C Flight there and we got our quota of pilots through without any casualties. Most had trained on Harvards so they knew monoplanes and were easy to convert. I had a good time there. After a couple of courses, about six months, they decided they wanted more senior experienced fighter pilots in the Middle East so I was sent there. I had no choice.
>
> I went to Liverpool and collected fifty odd young newly trained fighter pilots. I was to be their officer in charge on a boat going in convoy to Madagascar, via the mid Atlantic. They were to drop us off at Takoradi.

The Takoradi route, from the Gold Coast, West Africa, had been established to provide a safe routing for aircraft and pilots to the hostile skies over the Middle East. When Ken Lee arrived there it, 'had been well established as an assembly post for aircraft and after we were put ashore we went off in dribs and drabs, in convoys, across Africa to the Sudan and to bases in Egypt.'

> The idea was for one Beaufighter or Blenheim to escort six aircraft, doing the navigation right across the centre of Africa; from Takoradi to Lagos then up to Kano, across to Maiduguri, across Chad to El Fasher, and to arrive at the Nile and Khartoum. They would let you go up on your own then follow the Nile, until you reached Cairo. It should have taken about three days, it took me two weeks.

On our first stage we were so ahead of schedule that the pilot in charge of the convoy decided to put us down in a place in the bush in the middle of southern Nigeria. We landed on the strip and they said, 'What the bloody hell are you doing here mates.' We said, 'We've come to refuel and fly out.' They responded, 'Bloomin hard luck, we ain't got no fuel.' We had to wait a week before they brought the barrels up the river Niger to refuel us. When we eventually refuelled we joined other convoys that were going by, and went on to Kano.

Coming in to El Fasher I got into the slipstream of a Polish ferry pilot who was coming in at ground level. I never saw him. I slipped and turned down onto the runway and I put my wingtip in. So I had to stay there for a while. But when I was there they asked if I could do them a favour by going and getting an aircraft that had crash landed in the desert. So off I went with the airscrew from my aircraft on the back of the truck. We eventually found this place where the aircraft had crashed. All the bush was being cleared away by local natives, who were being bribed. They dug a hole under the aircraft, then let the wheels down and pulled it slowly back up a ramp. It was pretty tattered and torn with the crash landing. The wings were fabric so they got some natives with bone needles and sinews to stitch up the slits on the Hurricane. They put my airscrew on, we revved it up, they stood back and off we went and flew it back to base. The airscrew was then put back on my aircraft and I joined the next convoy until I reached Khartoum and the Nile. Then I flew along the Nile, a very easy and pleasant trip.

When Ken arrived in the Middle East he went straight to the top to sort out his posting.

I went to see the AOC, Air Vice-Marshal Arthur Coningham. He said, 'Well you haven't flown in the desert so we won't give you a flight right away.' I was a flight lieutenant at the time. 'We'll send you up to Billy Drake, with 112 Squadron.' I responded that that was a good thing, I knew Billy from before the war. When I got there to my surprise they were not flying Hurricanes, they were flying Kittyhawks with Allison engines, a bloody awful aircraft. The Allison engine wasn't reliable. When we were dive bombing the airscrew would run away with you and it was difficult to pull out of the dive.

The situation in North Africa at this stage was not good for the Allies. The advantage lay with the Axis forces, which, under the leadership of General Erwin Rommel, were steadily pushing the Allied forces east beyond the Egyptian border, where the front eventually congealed at Alamein.

In this period Ken Lee would suffer a bout of dengue fever and in mid-September he was posted to 260 Squadron. Ken commented on the retreat, his time with 112 Squadron and with 260 Squadron flying Kittyhawks over Alamein.

When we had to retreat all the pilots who had been there before me got in an aircraft and flew off, leaving me to follow behind, all the way back through the desert, in a pick-up truck. We weren't panicking!

We didn't see much of the Luftwaffe, it was so different from France and England. We saw the Italians once or twice, but in the air we really had air superiority. Although we were being pushed back all the time, we were always raiding their front lines with the Bostons. We escorted them but very, very seldom did we get jumped.

We couldn't understand why we were going back except we were told 'Rommel's coming'. When we had stopped retreating and settled down the squadron base was on the road from Cairo to Alexandria. Then every day more and more heavy vehicles and tanks came past us to reinforce the front. All of a sudden supplies became really quite plentiful, including Budweiser beer, which we had never seen before.

What Ken was witnessing was the build-up to one of the most decisive battles of the war. He recalled the activity prior to the battle of El Alamein:

I remember the night of 23 October 1942. They gave us an hour's notice of the start of the barrage, then all of a sudden the whole horizon lit up and it went on for about three days. When the Army began to move we followed them slowly. The nature of ops was to escort a bomber to the target, carrying a bomb, and when the bombers dropped their bombs, we dropped ours. No question of aiming them. And then they turned for home and we dived down to the deck and strafed our way home, as long as there was no air opposition, which there seldom was.

Diving down on a target with a Breda gun firing straight up at you was far more dangerous than my experiences in the Battle of Britain. He's on the ground aiming at an aircraft which is coming directly towards him. He's only got to have a good shot and he's going to hit you. You got hit occasionally. We were very, very lucky on the dive bombing and strafing.

The battle of El Alamein was fought ferociously on the ground and in the air, but eventually the Allied strength broke the Axis line. Rommel's forces now began the long retreat west that would ultimately take them to Tunisia, and then ejection from North Africa. They would be continually harassed by the RAF. Ken Lee played his part and he would claim his seventh and final enemy aircraft destroyed for the war (an Mc202) on 10 November 1942.

We had been on a raid and we were coming back strafing low level and this fellow came down behind me. Fortunately I caught a glimpse of him in my mirror. I did a really sharp, sharp, sharp turn. He went straight on and I nipped in behind and that's all there was to it. We were quite low. I don't know what he was doing, he didn't hit me although I had been hit by ground fire. When I turned he made no evasive action whatsoever. It was the only one I ever saw.

The Allied land forces pushed on across North Africa through the rest of 1942 and into 1943, and in March 1943, as Ken recalled:

When we got so far forward, they retired some of the squadrons from the front line. I was then sent off to Tehran to take command of a flight of Hurricanes which was supposed to be defending the Caucasus from Hitler. We were used as a protective screen to defend Iran from the Germans. But the Führer heard I had come up there so he went back, didn't come any further. Six Hurricanes there and six down at Abadan, down on the Gulf. Their job and my job then, when we moved back down there, was to fly around the Red Sea and if you saw any Japanese submarines you were supposed to shoot the periscope off. It was a real backwater of the war.

I was then given command of 123 Squadron in Iran and I was instructed to bring it back to the Western Desert in May 1943. I brought it back up to near El Adem at which point preparations for the landing in Sicily were underway.

Ken's time at El Adem was spent, 'doing absolutely nothing except practice formations and evasive action.' But the opportunity to see some action soon came.

One day Max Aitken, who was the Group commander, had the idea that we should stir up the Germans in Crete. He assembled all the Hurricane squadrons that were left in the desert at El Adem. We were to go off and beat up Crete. All the squadrons flew in and we'd had a big marquee erected. We all sat down and Max said, 'Right chaps, tomorrow morning two Beaufighters are going to come over and navigate for you. You are going to fly all the way to Crete at sea level and knock hell out of the place.' I had known Max before, he had been in 1 Squadron in peacetime when I was there. So I said, 'Well Max, who's leading this thing.' He said, 'You are!' That was the first I knew about it. No maps. No photographs. And no targets. Just go and give them hell.

Off we went [23 July 1943] at ground level, and we arrived right on schedule. We had long-range tanks which we dropped as we approached the coast. We went up a valley, but all we could see was beautiful scenery, full of olive trees. Not a soul was in sight. We were looking backwards and forwards, searching for something to shoot at. We got to the end of the valley, turned round and made the fatal mistake of coming down the same valley, by which time they were waiting for us. I was first in so I was supposedly in the safest position of them all.

As I came back out of the valley and then back over the beach I had a little check round the aircraft as we were going to be flying over the Mediterranean. To my horror my trousers were covered in oil, the oil line was spurting like mad. I glanced around, the oil temperature was way up as was the engine temperature. There was no way I was going to fly back across the Mediterranean like that. We had already decided on a plan as to where to go and crash land, and be picked up by the Resistance. So I turned back and as I came back over the coast the engine cut out. I suppose it overheated. I had to get down. I had been flying a Hurricane and other fighter aircraft every day for six years. I really could put an aircraft down on a postage stamp. I saw this little slot between the olive trees and went in there. When I was later interrogated the Germans didn't believe it, they thought it wasn't possible. They kept asking me how I had managed it and whether I had some kind of secret weapon.

The drill was to try and set your aircraft on fire after you landed. I got out the little thermite bomb and set it off, put it on the wing and then headed for the bushes. I ran across an open space and after about fifty yards I felt a terrific blow in the guts. Someone on the ground had taken a shot at me and the bullet had gone through my webbing belt, through the buckle and out through the ammunition pouch on the other side. I was really lucky, a few millimetres over and it would have ripped my stomach open. Anyway it knocked me flat and when I sat up someone was standing over me with the gun. [Ken was now a captive and made to hand over his hand gun.] He frightened me in a way. When we marched up this hill he was shooting my pistol off and I thought he was going to shoot me.

I was marched up to the local village where the German army officers were all having their breakfast, and they stood up and saluted, 'Guten Morgen, Herr Myorr [Major]. Have you been *wownded (sic)*? Have you had your *brek fast (sic)*?' I had an omelette and a brandy with them. One of these fellows came to me and said, 'Tell me sir, would you be kind enough, when you are interrogated would you say that it was my machine guns on that hill that shot you down and not those buggers over there?'

A staff car came to collect me. As a squadron commander I was a comparatively rare object to catch and they wanted to know whether we were really going to invade. I was taken immediately back to the headquarters at Heraklion, and put in a prison cell until the evening. I went to sleep, and when I woke up I couldn't believe it. I couldn't believe that I had been captured. It got dark and then they came in and tied my hands behind my back. I wondered what the hell was going on. They marched me out to a Junkers 52 transport plane and took me to Athens. They put me in a hut there with half a dozen other people who had been shot down on the same raid. The next night they flew me to Vienna. I had two Luftwaffe officers as an escort. They took me to the Ringstrasse gaol and said, 'Well we are off on the town now, see you in the morning.' I said, 'if I give you my parole can I come with you?' They said, 'Good idea', and they asked the Commandant, but he wouldn't let me go.

The morning after that I went on the train to the interrogation centre Dulagluft, Frankfurt-am-Main, Germany. They got me there as quickly as possible. They thought they would get some information as to whether we were going to land in Crete as well as Sicily. I didn't have any information. I didn't even know if we were going to land in Crete. It was Max Aitken's idea to stir them up. They had been having it so easy there.

The Germans were very clever. The moment I arrived they came along, all saluting, 'Hello Squadron Leader. How are the boys in 501 Squadron', the squadron I had been in during the Battle of Britain. That was three years previous, they were a bit out of date. 'Congratulations on your decoration...' and so on. They thought they knew everything. Then they tried a little bit of bullying although they never laid a finger on me, it was just threatening behaviour. After I had been in solitary confinement for a week they had one last try and said, 'Let's go for a little walk in the woods. There is a lovely inn there. We can have a drink and meet some girls.' Well that didn't work either and they just put me back into the flow, to Stalag Luft III at Sagan.

Ken was moved to Stalag Luft III in a cattle wagon, locked in, bucket in the corner. He recalls the sight when he arrived.

There was a row of faces at the wire watching me. I was isolated for a day while they found out who I was from someone who knew me, to make sure I wasn't a German plant. I was reconciled with what had happened to me and I immediately set about finding something to do. I studied

Economics and French and did the cooking for the group I was with.

Ken is unable to recall exactly which part of the camp he was put in on first arrival but he was later moved into North Compound, where he would play his part in one of the most famous escape attempts of the war, immortalised as 'The Great Escape'.

I did my bit with regard distributing the sand from the tunnel and watching for guards to make sure they didn't interrupt anything. I had seen the tunnel and been down the shaft. The sand was packed in socks, which you had slung round your neck and down your trouser leg. There were nails in the bottom of the sock, with a string attached to the nail. As you walked around the compound you would pull the string. The nail came out of the sock and the sand ran down over your boots to the ground and you scuffed it in to disguise it.

Sometimes I was on guard duty. I'd sit at a corner with a particular target, an entrance, where the guards came in or went out. I'd read a book and if the guards came I'd close the book and people watching you from the hut would tap on the floor or say close down.

Everyone who worked on the tunnel was in line for a place when the escape attempt came, but I was something like number 300 on the second day. The idea was that they were going to close the tunnel down after 150 people had got out and then open it again the next night.

On the night of 24/25 March 1944 the break out began. For a while everything went well, seventy-six men managing to pass through the tunnel, surface the other side of the wire and 'disappear' into the night. Then the tunnel was discovered.

On the actual night we all knew it was going on. We all had our heads down. We were waiting for something to happen. We heard the shooting. 'Oh God, they've found it.' We were very depressed but there was nothing we could do. We had no reason then to be dejected about the loss of life because we didn't know there had been any.

As most people now know the German reaction to the escape was extreme. The majority of the escapers were caught, only three managed to reach the UK, and fifty would be shot.

The Camp commandant told us, 'We're sorry to tell you that fifty of your escapers were shot trying to re-escape.' We knew something queer had gone on. It's possible one or two could be shot trying to re-escape, but not fifty. It was a huge shock.

Escape attempts were strictly controlled by an escape committee because they didn't want one escape interfering with another. We didn't have any major escape attempts after this.

The course of the war could be followed by the POWs, as Ken recalled, 'the BBC news was announced in the huts at night.' By January 1945 the Germans were withdrawing on both fronts, east and west. The Russian advances to the east soon led to the evacuation of the Stalag Luft III compounds. North Compound was evacuated at 4 am on 28 January.

We could hear the battle, so they decided they would move us out, in two feet of snow! We had been preparing, greasing our boots and building our sledges. And they let us take all the red cross parcels we could carry. But after a day in the snow they were being thrown away, people just couldn't carry them anymore.

The extreme wintry conditions on the forced march west caused great discomfort over the next few days. Not just for the prisoners either, the guards were also suffering.

It wasn't a question of supervision, it was a question of survival. We were helping the guards. One of our guards had been a POW in England in the first world war. We finished up putting him onto a sled. It was terrible. Overnight I recall staying in a chicken hut and a beer cellar.

The cold and exhausted POWs from North Compound arrived at Spremberg on the afternoon of 2 February. Here they were entrained, leaving late that night and arriving at Tarmstedt station, a few kilometres to the north-east of Bremen, late on the afternoon of 4 February. Then followed a rain-soaked walk of a few kilometres to Marlag und Milag Nord, which had hosted Royal Navy and Merchant Navy prisoners. The RAF men from North Compound settled into the 'appalling conditions' of Marlag. Eventually the time came for this camp to be evacuated also, as the Germans retreated from the advancing British forces.

So on 10 April another march began in the direction of Lübeck. But on arrival in the area the allocated camp was deemed completely unsuitable and the Senior British Officer Group Captain L. E. Wray RCAF persuaded the Germans to take the POWs back to more suitable accommodation.

> We came across a large farm with huge cattle sheds. Very comfortable. Se we stopped there and said we were not going any further. The Germans resigned themselves to that. They said, 'Alright, we'll look after you now, but when your chaps come over the hill, we'll give you the rifles and you look after us.'

On 2 May 1945 British forces finally arrived.

> A scout car arrived and a fellow opened the hood, stood up and said, 'Who are you?' We said, 'We're Stalag Luft III.' He said, 'We've been looking for you all over Germany!' The guards were all taken away. There were one or two who had been brutal and we pointed them out and they were dealt with. We wandered out into the town. I went down the road and came to an artillery unit. They asked who I was and I told them. They invited me for a meal and served white bread. During the eighteen months in Germany I had had nothing but black bread and I thought this would be marvellous. But after the black bread the white bread tasted like straw. I was very disappointed.
>
> There was an incredible sense of relief. We were taken to an airfield and the Lancasters came in. We were loaded, eight or nine of us, and flown back to England. I went to an interrogation centre in Manchester, was quickly passed through and then sent home for some leave. I knocked at the door of our house. My father opened it and said, 'Welcome home lad!'

After some rest Ken now had to make a decision about his future, whether or not to stay in the RAF.

> I had lost all seniority and I wasn't going to get a squadron. I didn't want to go back to being under the command of people I had trained. And I couldn't really see a future in flying after being warned that the air force would probably be reduced in size and you would find yourself without a

job after ten years.

So I took my father's advice, that I should get a decent job while they were going. I went to the United Africa Company and took a position as a branch manager in Tanganyika, trading in native produce such as beeswax, ivory, cotton. I had really enjoyed the flight during the war from Takoradi to Khartoum, across the centre of Africa. I thought I would like to go back, and ended up spending ten years out there.

Whilst Ken was in Africa, recognition of the importance of the Battle of Britain grew. Not that Ken was aware initially:

It was only several years after the war that it began to be recognised. It happened whilst I was in Africa and it was only when I came back, to Ireland, that my father wrote to me saying, 'What's all this thing about the Battle of Britain? Why aren't you a member of the society?' So I did something about it.

Ken took up residence in Dublin, running a wholesale plumbing business for the next thirty years. He retired to Spain but has since returned to England, living in Sheffield. In the sixty or so years since the Battle of Britain, the drama of those fateful days in the summer of 1940 has grown in the public mind. The heroic, even mythic, story of the battle in the skies, and the men who fought it, is still alive and strong. How does one of the Few reflect upon this portrayal?

We do find now that a lot of youngsters are interested, which is gratifying. I have no misgivings and no second thoughts about what happened. I hate the people who keep raking over these things, trying to find fault with what was done and what wasn't done. I would rather thought went into the effort that was put in at the time and that that is left unsullied. It will be like other military stories eventually. When the survivors die away, it will be like how the Battle of Waterloo is remembered, as a historical fact.

Does Ken have a sense of pride about his involvement in the Battle of Britain?

No. Satisfaction that I was there.

Air Commodore John Ellacombe, CB, DFC and Bar

Chapter 3

A Very Fine Adventure

Douglas Cooper lived in Kent during the summer of 1940 and witnessed the air battles that went on daily in the skies above.

The battle raged on in the sky, there were aircraft everywhere, and big puffs of smoke where the anti-aircraft shells were bursting. Some aircraft were on fire, black smoke pouring out behind them, and by this time the bombs were dropping, but luckily none in our direction.

My Mum and Dad and myself, and all of our neighbours were looking upwards and shouting and cheering for our fighters blasting hell out of the Germans. Unfortunately some of ours were being shot down too, but not as many as the Germans. All of a sudden there was a German bomber flying right towards us. It was a Dornier, so low we could see the pilot flying it and we could see the gunner in the nose of the bomber pointing his machine gun at us. Suddenly an RAF fighter was on his tail blasting away with his guns shooting right into the back and top of the bomber which then took a nose dive and crashed. There was a tremendous thud, a massive explosion and the ground shook, and there was a big red flash and we saw the tail of the plane go up in the air. We could hear the machine-gun ammunition exploding within the burning bomber. Everyone was excited, cheering and laughing... The fighter that had shot it down roared up into the sky, rolled over backwards and came diving down very fast and then turned over into a beautiful victory roll. We all jumped up cheering and waving to the pilot.[4]

John Ellacombe is the son of Gilbert Ellacombe, a doctor who had served with the Royal Army Medical Corps in the Boer War. With some other doctors he had formed a health service in Livingstone, Northern Rhodesia (now Zambia). When the wife of the Governor of Northern Rhodesia asked her sister to visit, she met with Gilbert, a bond formed and they were married. In 1918 their first son, also Gilbert, was born and on 28 February 1920 John arrived in the world. When Gilbert senior retired he was determined not to go back to England, the climate being the deciding factor, and a move was made to Cape Town, where there was a good public school and John was able to play lots of sport, cricket, rugby and golf. Pastimes which would interest the military, where quick decisions under pressure are required along with leadership and physical fitness.

Through a friendship at school John became attracted to the idea of flying, in particular to be trained by the Royal Air Force. As John recalls:

It was obvious that there was going to be a war. There was a lot of talk of it and there was a lot of recruiting going on. We all felt it would be a very fine adventure. One of my friends at school had a brother in the RAF, Coastal Command and flying boats. We met him, heard all about what it was like and became very enthusiastic. There were various people in Cape Town who were looking for recruits to join on short-service commissions.

In 1938, following some initial flying experience in Cape Town, John was accepted into the RAF and prepared to travel to England.

It was all great fun. Well it appeared to me to be, my parents weren't very keen. I had a lot of relatives in England, my uncle was a Group Captain in the RAF, very experienced and he gave me a lot of help. I was absolutely convinced there was going to be a war and I thought the right place to be was in the armed forces. It was the thing to do. Above all there was a sense of adventure, and I wanted to fly.

John came to England, with his mother, by sea in May 1939. Just before the outbreak of the war he received his call-up papers and prior to the opening of hostilities he took his mother back to Southampton, from where she returned to South Africa. Meanwhile John travelled to Cambridge to begin his flying training amongst similar raw recruits.

I was largely among men from overseas, Canadians, New Zealanders, a couple of Australians and another South African. We went to Jesus College, a course of about thirty-eight people, where we did preliminary training in navigation, armaments, other stuff of that sort.

From here John went to 10 Elementary Flying Training School at Yatesbury, 'on Tiger Moths, and we were there during that awful winter of 1939. A very nice place to fly from and very good instructors and we thoroughly enjoyed ourselves.' He accumulated just over one hundred hours flying before a posting to 2 Flying Training School at Brize Norton, to fly Harvards where...

...we did a lot of gunnery. They were a splendid crowd, the esprit de corps was superb. We had a lot of good rugby, our course was the only one to beat RAF Brize Norton. We were joined by a couple of other chaps, one of whom was Billy Fiske, an American, who was an absolute charmer. A most delightful man. His one aim was to fight. He said, 'America is not going to join for years and I want to fight the Germans.' He was a great bloke and everybody loved him. One day we were rather alarmed because he came back, he had been up to the American Embassy, and he said 'Britain is going to lose the war if we don't manage to hold on after Dunkirk.' That was the first sort of warning.

John completed his training on 12 July 1940. His abilities were clearly recognised. The top seven men from his course were to be sent straight to an operational fighter squadron. Pilot Officer John Ellacombe was immediately sent, along with his good friend Irving 'Black' Smith (so named because of his darker complexion as compared to R L Smith, who was also on the squadron at the time), to 151 Squadron at North Weald, along with Robert Beley and James Johnston. John's flying experience to date consisted of 65.40 hours dual, 105.00 hours solo, 5.00 hours dual at night and 2.25 hours solo at night. On arrival at North Weald, aged twenty, he was certainly anxious.

We were taken into meet the station commander, Wing Commander Victor 'George' Beamish. He said, 'I have no knowledge of you. Nobody sent me a signal but I am delighted to see you. We'll have you converted on this station. I've one pilot wounded, not fit to fly at the moment, Barry Sutton [56 Squadron], and he'll convert you on a Master and then on to the Hurricane. I reckon in three weeks I'll have you in operations. I'm going to work you jolly hard.' He had the sort of personality that personified leadership.

Beamish would soon earn the respect of the squadron's new recruits:

He always flew. He would take off with either squadron. Whoever was going. If he was in the ops room and saw the raid coming he would run down to his aircraft, which was kept outside the control tower, and as we took off you would see this other Hurricane joining us – he was certainly a very aggressive, very tough chap.

He was one of the great men that I met in the war. He was a big man with a loud voice. Very cheerful, enjoyed company. He had been a great rugby player and he led by example. He already had a DSO, because he had shot down several aeroplanes already, and he was a bloke you could look up to. I felt this from the very first meeting with him. Instead of saying 'go to hell, I don't know who you are.' He said 'right, here we are and we will convert you.' That was great, and his whole attitude was let's get on with it. He was an inspiring leader.

Later on the day of his arrival John met the squadron Commanding Officer Ted Donaldson whose manner and appearance were testament to the experiences of the squadron in the preceding weeks. Squadron Leader Donaldson had led the squadron during the air battle over France in May and June, including providing air cover for the evacuation of the BEF from Dunkirk. He had been in numerous air combats, claiming involvement in shooting down eight enemy aircraft. On 31 May 1940 the squadron diary recorded his award of the Distinguished Service Order. Donaldson had led his unit through a tough time, with numerous losses. But as June moved on and the overrunning of France became an inevitability the squadron received news of a change of priorities on 16 June, 'Information received that the squadron will not be required for French operations and the immediate future should be employed in preparing for Home Defence.' However that didn't stop an escort to Blenheims the next day to the south of Cherbourg, during which two aircraft were lost. On 30 June, whilst on an escort to six Blenheims to Vignacourt, Donaldson's aircraft was lost. He had fortunately been able to bale out, coming down in the sea, was picked up and taken to Ramsgate. Donaldson recalled the incident in a *Daily Telegraph* article written in 1980.

> My squadron was ordered to escort Basil Embry to destroy a large enemy fuel dump in France. We did not particularly like this assignment because Basil, absolutely fearless himself, took so long with positive identification of the target dump, for the Germans had so many dummies.
>
> Basil was not about to waste bombs on dummies so round and round he went with his Blenheim bombers being shot at from the ground while we were continuously attacked by Messerschmitts from above. But we did not leave him and this kept the Messerschmitts from attacking the bombers.

Eventually, flying home from this, Basil's squadron was jumped by Messerschmitts low over the sea and a terrific battle started. It was then that a particularly threatening Messerschmitt arrived and went straight for me. We fought for fifteen minutes ending up with head-on attacks on each other. Usually, Messerschmitts did not like this, for a Hurricane could turn more sharply, so it usually made off, which it could do so at 60 mph faster than the Hurricane.

In this case, on about the fourth head-on attack, shells and bullets started to strike my poor aircraft. The first shell knocked my oil tank clean out of the leading edge of the wing, so I knew the engine could not run much longer. Then the petrol tank blew up and my clothes caught fire and I became hot but still the bastard continued to shoot. My gloves were burning and my goggles 'frizzled' up but I took neither off – luckily!

I undid my straps and climbed on the wing, for the Hurricane was flying very slowly and I could actually see the burning wing bending upwards. Then I realised with alarm that I was only 800 ft off the sea. I thought this too low for a safe bale-out but at this time I fell off and it took me seconds to locate the pull ring, which I must have pulled, for, as I was about to hit the water, my parachute opened. I disappeared to the full extent of the cords and the wind got under the parachute and lifted me like a missile to the surface and started pulling me at about 5 kmh towards the French coast. Boulogne was two miles away, so I got rid of it at once, but then again shells started coming over, even when my head was under water. It certainly hurt my ears.

The Germans had been shooting at pilots in the sea at that time but my squadron flew over me as long as their fuel lasted. They were not going to let the Germans near me.

Later the Y [Listening] Service which listened to all R/T prattle told me it was General Galland who had shot me down.

I met him in London recently and I still don't think much of his conduct that day, for he must have known that my Hurricane was dead as far as fighting again, but he never stopped shooting. After this encounter neither did I.

Donaldson would leave 151 Squadron in early August, posted as a Chief Flying Instructor to an FTS. When John Ellacombe first met him, 'he appeared then to be in a rather shocked state.'

> The squadron had been involved in the Battle of France and at Dunkirk and suffered pretty heavy casualties. Quite a few of them were almost sort of 'battle weary', and Donaldson, who was a magnificent pilot and a very nice bloke, was obviously, in our view, past it. Shortly afterwards he went, and another squadron commander came in. Pete Gordon [arrived 29 July as a supernumerary, Donaldson leaving on 5 August] – a Canadian, a delightful chap. A wonderful leader and great character.
>
> They were a very experienced squadron. There were two of them, Dickie Milne and John Willie Blair, who had been with them throughout and they were very experienced pilots. They had both shot down about ten aircraft, and very charming blokes who never blew their top. They were always very good companions, and we were thoroughly at home and enjoyed ourselves.

In the days previous to John's arrival 151 Squadron had seen some action. On 9 July, the squadron had encountered a strong enemy force over the Thames estuary. Claims were made, two Me109s and one Me110 destroyed. One pilot, Flight Lieutenant Ironside was wounded in the face when his cockpit cover was shattered by a bullet. Another pilot, Midshipman Wightman was shot down into the sea, picked up by a trawler and returned to Sheerness. Wightman had arrived at the squadron only a few days previously.

On 12 July the squadron, operating from Manston and whilst on patrol over a convoy east of Orfordness, came across three Dornier 17s. Wing Commander Beamish would add one of these to his tally, the German bomber seen sinking in the sea. But the squadron suffered. Donaldson's Hurricane was riddled by enemy cross fire, yet he managed to land at Martlesham safely. Flying Officer James Allen failed to return, last seen to be gliding towards the Channel, his engine dead. He was never found.

Of course losses needed replacing, and so it was that on 13 July 1940 John Ellacombe arrived in a batch of new pilots. Indeed the next day a further three new pilots would join him. John would soon begin to appreciate the high level of morale on the squadron.

It was tremendous, absolutely. It came right down from the top – from the leadership, the other pilots and the tremendous spirit in Fighter Command.

11 Group's Keith Park and Fighter Command's Air Officer Commander-in-Chief Sir Hugh Dowding knew intimately everything in the make-up of their commands, the strengths and weaknesses, particularly those of their men, and they fought the fight utilising the strengths, minimising the exposure of the weaknesses. RAF recruitment, training and the operational culture also appear to have given confidence to their basic fighting unit, the pilot, in his ability and his weaponry.

John's first flight, on 14 July, consisted of thirty minutes dual on the Master, then thirty minutes solo. His next flight was forty-five minutes on a Hawker Hurricane I (L2005). This brought his total experience on a Hurricane to forty-five minutes. He had been posted to an operational squadron with no experience whatsoever of the combat aircraft it used. Perhaps a clear indication of the need to replenish squadrons following the losses incurred during the Battle of France.

The Hurricane was a very nice aircraft. Quite easy to land once you got the sort of feel for it. You had to land in your semi-stall position otherwise you would start bouncing, but once you learnt all that it was a delightful aeroplane to fly. Stable and you could pull a very tight turn, and we were told that we could out-turn the Messerschmitt 109 as long as you saw him coming. Another good thing about the Hurricane was that it had a big mirror above the cockpit. So if you looked at that when you were looking around you would, with luck, not get somebody on your tail.

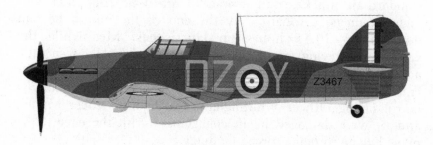

151 Sqn Hurricane

We were very conscious of the fact that our .303-in bullets were not enough, and I lost count of the number of times we sat behind bombers and saw our bullets exploding on them with apparently nothing happening. Sometimes you would set them on fire, but often we were very, very conscious that it would be nice to have a .5, or later on of course, the twenty millimetre cannon which we got in the Hurricane IIC. At least your Hurricane had sixteen seconds of ammunition, and the last three seconds were only tracer. If at that point you suddenly saw an aeroplane, you realised you had two more seconds to go, so you would make sure what you were shooting at was what you wanted to kill.

The guns had several settings. I remember my embarrassment the first time when I was being indoctrinated in 151. We were taken down to the range where they had a Hurricane and the guns were fired into the range background. I said to the Flight Sergeant, 'How often do the guns jam?' He said, 'Pilot Officer – in this squadron the guns never jam.' He was a very formidable bloke, and in fact I never heard of one gun ever jamming. The re-arming in a Hurricane was very efficient. You had two batteries of four guns and it used to take about three minutes to open the top, take out the old thing, and put in the new complete set with all the ammunition. It was superb. This was an advantage over the Spitfire, which took about eight or nine minutes to re-arm. Also the Hurricane was a more robust aeroplane. It could take more punishment.

Much of the rest of July involved John familiarising himself with his mount, formation flying, sector reconnaissance, practicing standard air attacks, combat practice, air-to-air firing, dusk and night landings, aerobatics. By the end of the month he had notched up 30.55 hours on Hurricanes. Meanwhile the squadron, carrying out shipping patrols, had in fact seen little action, although Pilot Officer Hamar was killed when his aircraft crashed on take-off on 24 July. On 29 July, whilst on a convoy patrol Flying Officer Whittingham and Flying Officer Milne's aircraft were damaged in an engagement with the enemy, the pilots having to make forced landings.

Later that summer the Squadron ORB was able to record what it was like to be on the receiving end of a 151 Squadron attack in July 1940. An extract from the diary of a German pilot, who was killed on 15 August, is recorded.

It is of particular interest to the members of the squadron as it describes a combat between members of the squadron and a large force of Me110s attacking a convoy. He states that there were two Hurricane squadrons, but in reality there was only one. This action took place on 29 July 1940.

'My second war flight. A Do17 reports English convoy of sixty ships proceeding northwards from the Thames estuary. Zerstorergruppe 210 starts from St. Omer at 1735. Eight Me110 bombers of the 2nd Staffel and three Me110 C.6's of the 1st Staffel fly over Dunkirk and meet thirty C.2s of Z.Ct.26 who are acting as fighter escort on account of probable clear skies. Thirty minutes later flying northwards at sea level then ten minutes northwards climbing to clouds at 4,000 feet. At 1815 hours the bombers attack just off Orfordness in position 1219. At the same time two Hurricane squadrons turn up from the left, one below and one above us. The chief makes a tight climbing turn and I fall back a bit, then it is flat out climb. I have to abandon the idea of getting onto the tail of the lower lot of Englishmen because the covering formation comes on to me from above and to the right. Coming out of a curve I fire a short burst at a Singleton [single-engined aircraft] who goes past. He does not fall. In the next second my W/T shouts out something unintelligible and a hail of fire sears through the whole aircraft, from the right. The inter-communication packs up immediately. Another two seconds and I would have been in the clouds. I circle in the clouds and take stock and decide to beat it. Outside the clouds I come across three Me110s, the Chief and two supports from Z.Ct.26 who want to go in again to attack. When I want to tack on to them my W/T calls out, "I am wounded! Let's go home." So I head for the Dutch coast flying low. The trimming tabs are shot away and I have to hang on like grim death to maintain height. Oil spurts from the starboard motor and it looks as if I am in for a bath. The W/T bravely remains silent in spite of his pain. At last at 1905 hours I land at St. Omer with tyres shot through and through. My bus is in a shocking state. I had colossal luck. It has about thirty hits from above and to the right. One shot went through the cabin and missed my head by a hair's breadth only because I was crouching forward; another went through my cushion. The W/T operator only just escaped a bullet through his head. All the W/T apparatus was completely smashed. One shot landed in an M.G. drum and exploded all the cartridges; starboard engine three hits, oil sump, engine cowling, and the lighting circuit destroyed: bullet through the sump centre, other holes in both wings and landing flaps. Result of the attack – one hit on a 1,000 ton ship, one hit on a 8,000 ton ship. Z.Ct.26 bagged four Hurricanes without loss to themselves.' [FC only had 3 losses for the entire day.]

On 1 August John's logbook records a fifteen-minute flight from North Weald to Rochford, an entry that would be repeated many times in the next few weeks. From 29 July 151 Squadron began using the more easterly base, from which patrols could be carried out as far as Dover.

Here we would wait all day, fly sorties, escort convoys or scrambles. It was purely a dispersal airfield, wooden huts and some tents. We sat at dispersal all day having tea and sandwiches. We would wait for the phone to go and that became a very nervous matter. We were two rings. You would have one ring, then the second and you would tense up. Do we go? Then if the third ring came we could relax, it was for someone else. It was an emotional and tense moment. You didn't know – are we about to go to war or not? But you all wanted to get into the action. You all wanted to kill some bloody Germans. We hated the bastards. We were taught to and adopted the attitude very quickly anyway because you heard of losses, and some chaps being shot in their parachutes.

Esprit de corps creates a unity of aggression against what can be perceived as an inhumane enemy. In 151 Squadron's case there was plenty of opportunity to demonise the foe. John took a very personal line towards his adversary, no doubt influenced by the squadron's, his peer group's, experience of the enemy to date. One incident which was recorded in the squadron ORB is worth recounting here as no doubt it also had an effect on the airmen's stance towards the enemy. Flight Lieutenant Ives had not returned from a Blenheim support operation to the St. Omer area on 25 May 1940.

> *151 Squadron ORB 5 June 1940:* The following is an extract from a letter received by our CO from Pilot Officer Muirhead, an ex member of the squadron.

> To O.C. No. 151 Squadron
> Dear Sir
> I am writing to give you news of F/Lt Ives who, unless he was picked up by the motor boat which torpedoed us, is, I'm sorry to say, missing. He originally landed on the beach 12 miles S.W. of Ostend and I met him in Ostend after being shot down and jumping at the same place. We spent the next two days together dodging bombs and bullets and 'Ivy' spent a lot of his time helping the wounded. In fact he was everything anyone who knew him would have expected – and then some. We sailed in the 'Aboukir' at about 10 p.m. on Tuesday night. 'Ivy' myself and an Army officer were on top manning the gun as we expected to be bombed at any time. Eventually, however, we were torpedoed at point blank range and blown into the water. The motor boat that torpedoed us then went around machine-gunning people in the water. Only 24 people out of over 500 on board were saved and I was the only officer. Please express my heartfelt sympathy and admiration for 'Ivy' to his people – he was a brick.
> Yours sincerely,
> *J. Muirhead P/O*

It is considered unnecessary to add to the above about the squadron's feelings, for they are the same.

For 151 Squadron there was very little contact with the enemy during the first week of August. The only major incident being an engagement on 5 August during which a Me109 was claimed destroyed and a Ju88 as a probable. John still awaited his first operational sortie, which came on 8 August, in the shape of a convoy patrol.

> We did a lot of these, which we didn't like much as you were flying about 2,000 feet above ships and of course

109s could bounce you. We would normally fly down to Rochford, and we would be on readiness, there. We flew up and down, up and down one end to the other. Watching these poor wretched ships ploughing along, and we were told that a convoy of ships carried the equivalent of about 50 to 100 trains, so they were absolutely essential to get the goods from one part of the country to another.

His forty-minute flight went without incident. Two days later John would complete two further operations and this time he would see the enemy.

We were vectored by North Weald on to a large force of enemy bombers and I saw these things in the distance. Tiny little bees, and then much bigger, and they finally turned away. We did not engage, and when I landed I said to one of my mates, 'Why didn't the CO say he could see them.' He replied, 'You and I were the only two who could see them. You must have exceptional eyesight, and you are going to fly as my number two from now on.' That was a chap called John Willie Blair, a wonderful pilot, who had already had considerable success. Anyway Peter Gordon heard that and said, 'No he's going to fly as my number two!'

John was still to engage the enemy, but he wouldn't have to wait long. 'Suddenly things hotted up and a lot of attacks started to come in.' The Luftwaffe command had been busy preparing for *Adler Tag* and the intensity of the air battle was about to escalate. Fighter Command squadrons, particularly those operating in 11 Group, would be strained to the limit and 151 Squadron was no exception. On 11 August *Adler Tag* was postponed, nevertheless the Luftwaffe sent a large force to attack Portland, whilst fighters bluffed an attack on Dover. To the east convoys were attacked and 151 Squadron saw action. Pete Gordon and Jim Johnston, during a routine patrol, damaged a Ju87 and Me109 respectively, during an attack by a reported fifteen Ju87s and twenty-eight Me109s on an isolated ship.

The next day saw the Luftwaffe preparing the way for *Adler Tag* in earnest, with radar stations and airfields targeted. Harbours and convoys in the Thames estuary were also attacked. John would record in his logbook a convoy patrol and a fighting patrol (scramble) without coming across the enemy. Others in the squadron did. Pilot Officer Beley, who had come to the squadron with John, lost his life whilst on a convoy patrol, shot down into the sea, rescued, but later dying of his wounds in Manston sick quarters. Also on the patrol was Flying Officer Tucker who survived but was badly wounded from several bullet wounds, and Pilot Officer Debenham whose aircraft was damaged but who managed to return safely to Rochford. John remembers the effect on him of those lost:

> You would often land and say, 'Who's not here?' For example 'Beley', or whoever. You just had to shrug it off and hope it wouldn't be you next time. You were told never to show fear. The worst part of it was the fear of showing fear. You were quite determined to kill the next bastard who tried to shoot you. There was just a tremendous *esprit de corps* and determination. I think it was a hatred of the bloody Germans, they had just ravished France and made a mess of everywhere. One remembered what happened in the first war, we had been taught that at school, and we knew if they landed and occupied the country that was the end of Great Britain.

Despite a faltering start, owing to a postponement order that was not received by all units, *Adler Tag* was launched on 13 August with heavy attacks on airfields, Portland and Southampton. The RAF station at Eastchurch was hit hard in the morning but the attacking Dornier 17s met RAF fighters, including 151 Squadron on their return route to France. At the end of the day John entered in his logbook, 'Fighting patrol, engaged Dorniers'. John came out of the encounter unscathed and without success, but others in the squadron took advantage of the lack of enemy fighter cover and claimed four Dorniers shot down, but for the cost of Sergeant Atkinson, who baled out, was picked out of the sea and, 'ended up in hospital suffering from shock.' The next day John remained on the ground but the squadron was scrambled to counter a large formation of Me109s, claiming two destroyed and one probable.

The 151 Squadron diarist would record 15 August 1940 as 'a busy day'. Indeed this was to be one of the most decisive of the battle. A poor weather forecast had initially postponed any major Luftwaffe incursions, but a considerable improvement later in the morning allowed operations to go ahead. Radar stations and fighter airfields featured as targets in the Luftwaffe plans; Hawkinge and Lympne airfields were first to come under attack late morning, then Me110s attacked Manston. Meanwhile a major raid had been brewing far to the north-east, but RAF fighters scrambled and inflicted severe losses. More Luftwaffe attacks developed in the afternoon, to the south, with the fighter airfield at Martlesham Heath targeted. 151 Squadron's busy day was about to begin in earnest. Eighty-eight Do17s, one hundred and thirty plus Me109s crossed the coast near Deal, and seventy Me109s headed inland between Dover and Folkestone, with Rochester and Eastchurch the targets. Me109s swarmed the area, many protecting the bombers, others carrying out sweeps. The 151 Squadron diary records that the unit's Hurricanes, including John Ellacombe's, were scrambled, taking off at 1530 hours. A few miles west of Dover they ran into enemy fighters. Pilot Officer Debenham pursued a Me109, which crashed in France. Pilot Officer Rozwadowski and Flying Officer Milne would also claim a Me109. John Ellacombe also saw action as was recorded in his combat report:

> Number of enemy aircraft – 100+
> Type of enemy aircraft – Dornier, Me110, Me109
> Time attack was delivered – 15.30
> Place attack was delivered – W & SW of Dover
> Height of enemy – 10,000 – 30,000 feet
> Enemy casualties – 1 Me109 probably destroyed , damaged
>   by me
> P/O Ellacombe – Nine Hurricanes of 151 Squadron were patrolling at about 18,000 when we were attacked by Me109s. I chased one who had unsuccessfully quarter attacked the leading Hurricane. I fired my first bursts at 400 yards and closed to 200. After firing about 3 bursts I got a 5 second burst in a turn, after which black smoke issued from the 109 and he rolled over on his back, diving. I finished my ammunition at 100 yards when large volumes of black smoke issued. I was over the French coast, I turned back leaving the 109 diving vertically towards the sea. My wireless aerial damaged.

Shortly afterwards another enemy formation was engaged by the squadron, with little result, 'owing to the unwelcome attention of the 109s'. Debenham's aircraft was, 'shot up a bit'. The air battle was also raging to the west over Portland and the Solent area, but as evening drew on there was no let up as more bomber formations approached. At 6.45 pm 151 Squadron was again airborne, the diary noting that, 'In this action we faired badly', although 'Black' Smith claimed a Me 109. Squadron Leader Gordon, 'was peppered with shrapnel from a cannon shell and was slightly wounded in the back of the head and leg.' Four pilots failed to return. Rozwadowki was missing, Beggs was wounded and ended up in hospital. Jim Johnston came down in the sea, losing his life, his body recovered. John Ellacombe was one of the pilots that did not return.

> We used to fly in threes in 'Vics'. The four formation didn't come in until much later and I found flying in threes to be quite suitable and very manoeuvrable, and when I flew number two, most of the time either to John Willie Blair or then to Pete Gordon, it was a very good formation and you could turn and manoeuvre very easily. Pete Gordon had said 'Buster – Buster' [Full speed]. So we pulled the knob and I went into twelve pounds of boost, and after half a minute my engine blew up. All I had was a cockpit full of glycol. I had to pull out and went down and tried to land on a golf course which, as I got nearer, I saw was absolutely covered in iron bars to prevent landing, which meant I had to force land in a tiny little field which happened to be a brigade headquarters for anti-aircraft guns.
>
> The Hurricane was a very good aeroplane because it had this large radiator underneath, that if you force-landed in a field all you did was bend the propeller. If the radiator was changed the aeroplane could fly again forty-eight hours later, unlike the Spitfire, which was always severely damaged.
>
> When I got back to North Weald I found to my horror that in the combat that I had missed we had lost two killed including my mate who had trained with me, Jim Johnston. In fact Pete Gordon the CO had a bullet through his leg, but he ignored that, just bandaged it up and flew again two days later.

151 Squadron was now right in the midst of the battle for control of the skies over south-east England. The Luftwaffe, in seeking to destroy Fighter Command, had mauled the RAF on the ground

and in the air, with thirty-four aircraft lost, seventeen pilots killed, sixteen wounded. But the German units paid a higher price. The RAF reported claims totalling 182 German aircraft shot down, more than twice the actual figure of seventy-five. Nevertheless Fighter Command remained as a potent defensive force. But for how long could this be sustained? The Luftwaffe was under the impression that the RAF was on its last legs. Fortunately over the next couple of days 151 Squadron had very little contact with the enemy, although there were fierce engagements on 16 August involving other units, the RAF losing twenty-two fighters, eight pilots killed. The Luftwaffe lost forty-five aircraft. 18 August was another of those momentous summer days in which German and RAF airmen fought for their lives. Huge enemy formations went mainly for airfields again. 151 Squadron would enter the affray that evening. Earlier the squadron's pilots completed some uneventful patrols from Rochford, before returning to North Weald. Then at 1700 hours the squadron was brought to readiness and took off to intercept a large enemy formation heading for North Weald. John Ellacombe would once more be part of an aerial melee.

> Combat is so rapid you overcome any fear. The first thing you do is look in your mirror and make sure there is no 109 coming up behind you. You're scanning all over trying to get at them and kill the bastards. There was such a tremendous hatred. Adrenalin was rushing. It was often so quick. You would break, perhaps see tracer coming at you. Heave back and flick roll and when you came to there was often nobody in sight.
>
> Following combat there's a reaction. You look around to see what damage there is to the aeroplane. Who's not there, has the place been bombed, what information is there? The excitement was enormous. We had a marvellous Intelligence Officer Frank Marlow, who stayed with 151 throughout the war, even after he became a squadron leader – he refused to be posted. He was a wonderful chap to come and talk to and I think Frank Marlow had a great effect on everybody. He would rush round and tell you what had happened, take your report, write everything down. He was a permanent figure, always there when you landed.
>
> You developed a twitch, everybody was tensed up, two,

three, four sorties a day. Fatigue was a factor, you would have a couple of pints of beer, go to bed and pass out completely. Sensibly, when we had enough pilots, you would get every fourth day off and you were told to go to London, get off the base.

On 18 August Peter Gordon attacked some bombers and he was set on fire, but managed to bale out. I followed him down and circled around. He landed in the river Crouch in Essex and as he walked out of the water he was shaking his hands and I thought he was taking his gloves off. It was actually his skin and he was horribly burnt. We all learnt a lesson from that and from then on wore our gauntlets.

The pilots of 151 Squadron came across the enemy formation appearing through cloud just east of Chelmsford. Blair claimed a Me110 and reported leaving another with black smoke pouring from its starboard engine. Milne reported blowing up a Ju88. Debenham sent a Me110 into the sea, as did Czajkowski. Beamish, although shot about a bit, left a Ju88 with smoke streaming behind. A successful encounter but again at a cost, Peter Gordon burnt and John Ramsay failing to return. He had indeed lost his life, his body not found until 1983, and subsequently buried with full military honours on 25 October that year. Attrition had again taken its toll, not just on 151 Squadron, but also of Fighter Command, with twenty-seven fighters taken out, ten pilots dead. The Luftwaffe losses totalled fifty-three aircraft. Fighter Command despite Goering's assurances that its defeat was imminent, was still meeting the Luftwaffe in force and morale was suffering.

The next five days were very quiet indeed for the squadron in terms of enemy encounters, similarly, in comparison to the previous week, for the rest of Fighter Command. John Ellacombe completed five operational sorties. Squadron Leader King arrived at the squadron on 21 August to replace Pete Gordon. The only other incident of note took place on 22 August, as recorded in the squadron ORB:

Convoy Patrols from Rochford. F/Lt Smith's aircraft was slightly damaged when a 109 appeared out of the blue on his tail. The Squadron had been ordered to patrol Manston and there were a number of Me109s above us. We were unable to engage the enemy as we could not climb to their height, excepting the one 109 which attacked F/Lt Smith they were quite content to sit above us and watch our antics as we tried to get up to them. Otherwise the day was without incident.

However during this period John had another more sombre duty to carry out. On 21 August he flew via Abingdon to Hawkinge to attend the burial of Jim Johnston.

I took along Johnnie Comar, a Canadian, who had trained with me. We flew to Hawkinge aerodrome, where the local people had laid on a padre and a firing squad of six RAF airmen. While the good padre was saying the final bit of his service we could hear a scream above and looked up and saw these Junkers 87s heading down our way, shedding their bombs as they dived. The airmen disappeared in a flash. I told the padre to run like hell and Johnnie Comar and I jumped into the grave on top of Jim's coffin, which still gave us four or five feet of trench. The whole place thumped and banged for about a minute. When it was quiet we climbed out. We couldn't see the padre. We couldn't see the airmen. Even the gravediggers had disappeared. It was horrifying, that raid being mixed up with saying farewell to a friend.[5]

The general lull in operational activity was no doubt welcomed by the men of 151 Squadron, but ferocious air battles soon began again. On 19 August Goering had made his commanders aware that, 'until further notice the main task of *Luftlotten* 2 and 3 will be to inflict the utmost damage possible on the enemy fighter forces.' Poor weather delayed any but on 24 August the chance came and the critical stage of the Battle of Britain began. The squadron went into battle that morning and lost two more pilots, both men surviving, Sergeant Clarke with shrapnel wounds to the head, Pilot Officer Debenham with severe burns. That afternoon enemy bombers appeared to be heading for London but then turned towards Hornchurch and North Weald. 151 Squadron was scrambled, with seven pilots airborne. Squadron Leader King claimed a probable Do215, Wing Commander Beamish a Me110, Pilot Officer Blair a He111, Pilot Officer Smith a He111, Flight Lieutenant Smith a Me109 and John Ellacombe a He111.

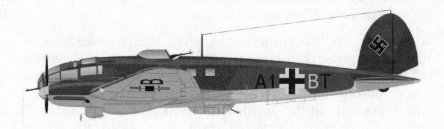

Heinkel 111

Pilot Officer John Ellacombe's combat report 24 August 1940
Number of enemy aircraft – 24 Heinkel 111s and 24 Me109s
Time attack delivered – 16.10 approx
Place attack was delivered – 6m west of North Weald
Height of enemy – 4,000 feet
Range at which fire was opened in each attack delivered on enemy aircraft together with estimated length of burst – 200 yards up to 50 yards, 3 sec, 3 sec, 5 sec, 5 sec.
    P/O Ellacombe – First burst disabled port motor, third or fourth disabled starboard, and the Heinkel glided down, forced-landing in a field... damaging both wings. The crew of 5 scrambled out, apparently unhurt.

John recalls the incident:

We attacked some 109s, drove them away, and we then found this formation of Heinkels. My particular one landed at Samuel's Corner in Essex. I had no ammunition left but I saw the aircraft land and three men climb out. Then a policeman rode up on his bicycle, put it down, and he ran up to these men pulling his notebook out. By then they had their sidearms out. I was circling round and if I had had any ammunition left I would have strafed them. I thought, 'you silly bloke, get out of the way.' But no, in two minutes they all had their arms round one another and he was writing down all their details. From then on it was such a joke I nearly spun in laughing. There were two other men in the aircraft severely wounded.

But despite the best efforts of the RAF's fighter pilots bombers did get through. The squadron diarist recorded thus, 'A portion of the enemy aircraft got through to North Weald and bombed the aerodrome but did very little damage.' In terms of the effect the attack had on the squadron this statement is fair, but with regard to the effect on the aerodrome, R.S. Heath who was a member of the ground crew at North Weald, gives another perspective.

At the time, it seemed that the aerodrome was having a charmed life because other airfields were getting heavily bombed. However, one morning an Me110 made several runs over the airfield at low level until it was chased away by 56 Squadron aircraft. Within two days of this sortie, the German bombers came and caused damage to accommodation blocks, cookhouse, officers' mess, and other buildings, also civilian buildings nearby including the 'Woolpack' public house.

Nine soldiers were killed these being all young men who had dashed into a shelter near one of the blocks, only for it to receive a direct hit from one of the bombs. Approximately 200 bombs were dropped, some of them being delayed-action.

Squadron Leader King had landed minus the aircraft propeller and its associated reduction gear which had been shot away in an action with an Me110.

I was in the hangar when the attack commenced and ran, complete with steel helmet and gas mask, and also a rifle with fifty rounds of ammunition towards a shelter near the boundary fence. To this day I can see some chaps pushing a Merlin engine towards our dispersal. They ran but the engine, which was on a wheeled mounting, began to go down-hill. They stopped, ran back and chocked it just as the bombs hit the camp. We all ended up in the entrance of the shelter, crouching down just as one bomb burst about five yards away and collapsed the shelter. Several chaps were dragged out covered in dust and badly shocked.

John Ellacombe: We landed back that day and my annex to

the officers mess had been destroyed, and I was left with not even a collar and tie because we used to wear a silk scarf, and I had to go into town next day to Mr Burberry's and get re-equipped. Your uniform allowance in those days was forty pounds and that was enough to buy you two uniforms, lots of shirts, several shoes and everything else. I think Burberrys was a very expensive place. You paid four pounds for a uniform. If you went to Alkits you got one for about two pounds fifty. Anyway I got re-equipped and set on.

Once more the structure of Fighter Command had been shaken. Once more the RAF lost men and aircraft, twenty-two fighters in total. But also, once more, the Luftwaffe had lost some of its weapons, thirty-eight fighters and bombers in all.

The 151 Squadron diary entries for 25, 26, and 27 August include, 'Nothing to report', 'The whole squadron was given the day off' and, 'Nothing to report' respectively. Other squadrons could not record similarly and there were major engagements and losses for both sides. A patrol, for 151 Squadron, on 28 August resulted in contact with the enemy who were still targeting airfields, and the loss of Pilot Officer Alexander badly burned, with Sergeant Davies having to force land at Eastchurch, wounded. On 29 August the squadron moved to Stapleford, where it carried out several patrols, to oppose further Luftwaffe attacks on airfields, John taking part in two. On one of the squadron's patrols another pilot was lost, Pilot Officer Wainwright being forced to bale out and ending in Epping hospital with fractured ribs.

On 30 August there was further intense combat, as the Germans initially carried out feint attacks on shipping and then later ventured inland to bomb airfields. 151 Squadron undertook numerous patrols. On the second of the day, on which the ORB recorded that no interceptions were made, Squadron Leader King failed to return, his body later being found in a burnt-out Hurricane, which had crashed and become engulfed in flames. Later in the day the squadron was airborne again to intercept a large formation of enemy aircraft. A Do215, Ju88 and He111 were claimed. Sergeant Gmur was killed. John Ellacombe also encountered the enemy.

On 30 August we were scrambled and, as we broke cloud,

we were bounced by an escort of 109s, and we broke. When you break, you pull as tight a turn as you can, then either climb or dive. I looked around and there was nobody in sight. Everybody had just disappeared. My base airfield 'Bengal' was calling. 'This is Bengal and there is a very large formation heading our way.'

I looked around and sighted twelve Heinkels. I had responded so I had no choice but to attack. They were about six miles away so I could do a head on. I closed to just 2,000 yards, flying straight at them, head on, rapidly closing in. I just pressed the trigger, about a three or four second burst, with my eight guns that was 160 rounds a second. I went for the leader and then flew underneath him. I saw all his perspex break off and two engines were hit, but as I went under my engine blew up. He had put one bullet through my spinner. I recovered the aircraft, found a very large field and landed. I was then attacked by a man with a pitchfork screaming, 'I'm going to kill you you ****
German!' He was soon disarmed by the army who appeared. They were from an anti-aircraft battery nearby and we watched the Heinkel crash in the next field. The army sergeant went over, came back, and said, 'don't go and look, they are in a filthy mess.' I was quite happy to sit back. It was during the harvest and whilst waiting for transport I was quite content to have a few pints of draught cider. Eventually a van came up and took me back to North Weald. I walked into the bar and there was Victor Beamish, my station commander. He said, 'John go and get a Hurricane. You'll fly as my number two. There's another raid coming in.' I said, 'Sir, I am as drunk as a skunk. I have had three pints of draught cider and my head is whirling.' He responded, 'How can you drink on duty?' I explained what had happened and he said, 'Oh well, never mind, let's not go.' I reckon that saved his life. Possibly mine too.

John also recalls the loss of Sergeant Gmur.

He was shot down the day that I landed in the field after shooting the Heinkel down. In fact going back to base I passed his Hurricane which was burnt out with his body in. I stopped and I could read the number. We had another Pole and we also had a Czech. They were very, very good pilots.

They hated the Germans. Absolutely hated them. In fact, I understand once or twice when Germans were shot down in parachutes they were shot at, but then the Germans would shoot any of us. Which was why we were all told, 'If you do have a chance don't bale out. Crash land your aeroplane.'

John's Hurricane was one of twenty-five fighters lost that day. The Luftwaffe lost thirty-six aircraft. By now the attrition rate had taken its toll on 151 Squadron, which was down to just six operational pilots. But the calls on their time still came in. On 31 August 'scramble' was called, 151 Squadron remaining in the aerial front line. A morning patrol led to the claims of a probable Me109 to Flight Lieutenant Smith and a damaged Me109 for John Ellacombe. Yellow section also claimed a Me109, which they dived on. Although the RAF pilots did not fire, the Me109 dived into the ground.[6]

Pilot Officer John Ellacombe's combat report 31 August
Number of enemy aircraft – about 15
Type of enemy aircraft – Me109
Time attack was delivered – 08.00 hours
Place attack was delivered – over Manston
Height of enemy – 15,000 feet
Enemy casualties – Me109 probably destroyed
Range and length of bursts – 150 yards, 100 yards, 5 sec,
    3 secs
General report – Took off about 0745 hours from Stapleford. When attacked by Me109s I dived after one, firing a 5 sec burst at 150 yards. The radiators were blown off and smoke poured from under the wings. I closed to 100 yards and fired a 3 sec burst, after which more black smoke and white smoke poured out, from the engine this time. The machine went into a spin and I broke off the attack. However, when close to the ground he recovered and made out to sea. I dived down to finish him off. He entered a low bank of sea fog or cloud about 3 miles from the coast, and I waited in vain for him to come out on the East side. I can only assume he crashed in the sea, as the clouds did not extend north or south, and the smoke was still pouring from him when he entered the cloud.

On landing John had little time for rest and would shortly be airborne, again feeling the heat of battle, as his next combat report testifies.

> Number of enemy aircraft – about 30 bombers, 25 fighters
> Type of enemy aircraft – Do's, Heinkels, Me109s
> Time attack was delivered – 10.20 hours
> Place attack was delivered – 10 miles east of Thames Estuary
> Height of enemy – 12,000 feet
> Enemy casualties – Me109 damaged
> Ranges and length of bursts – 200 yards, 5 secs
> General report – Took off about 10.00 hours from Stapleford. The squadron attacked the bombers, but I was intercepted by 109s. I got on the tail of one and fired a 5 sec burst at 200 yards. Petrol fumes or white smoke poured from his starboard wing, but I was forced to break off as he outclimbed me and I nearly stalled. Confirmed by F/Lt Blair DFC, my section leader.

Flight Lieutenant Blair would claim a Ju88 damaged and P/O Smith a Do215. Pilot Officer Czajkowski did not return from the operation, but he would survive, ending up in Shoeburyness hospital with bullet wounds, and later claiming a Me109. It was not just 151 Squadron suffering losses obviously. Indeed on 31 August Fighter Command would suffer its heaviest losses to date, thirty-nine fighters, with fourteen pilots killed (the Germans losing forty-one aircraft). Into the afternoon 151 Squadron would be making a further contribution to the statistic. On their return from the earlier sortie news came through to the pilots that they were about to move. John Ellacombe and the other pilots were told to, 'get packed and go to Digby. You are going to be replaced by another squadron.'

> Just then we were scrambled and the five of us got airborne to attack some Junkers 88s. I had completed one attack and during my second attack, the return fire, which I could see coming, hit my aeroplane.

> *Pilot Officer John Ellacombe's combat report 31 August*
> Number of enemy aircraft – many bombers and fighter escort
> Type of enemy aircraft – Ju88s and Me109s
> Time attack was delivered – 13.20 hours

Place attack was delivered – 15 miles inland over Thames
Height of enemy – 16,000 feet
Enemy casualties – Ju88 damaged
Ranges and length of bursts – 250 – 150 yards, 4 secs
General report – Took off with squadron from Stapleford,
13.05 hours, climbed to 16,000 feet, sighted enemy
heading east. Attacked in line astern. Did not fire in first
attack as position was unfavourable. I then attacked 3
Ju88s in close formation from rear. The right hand machine
received my burst of 4 secs at 250-150 yards. When I broke
away I observed that this machine's port engine had
stopped and it left the other two, gliding down in a south-
easterly direction.

I delivered my second attack from the beam on the port
Ju88, but just before I fired, an explosive bullet hit my
gravity tank, which burst. Burning petrol poured into the
cockpit and I jumped at once. I delayed opening my
parachute to get well clear of the enemy.

IMPORTANT. The shots that hit me were fired from
broadside, from the Ju88. This is I believe a modification in
their armament.

John continues the story:

My gravity tank blew up. My cockpit went, 'Wooph' and I
couldn't see anything for flame. Now fortunately I was
wearing my gauntlets, which came halfway up your arm. I
was wearing those because of what I saw when I was flying
number two to Pete Gordon when he was shot down and
burnt. From then on we all said, 'to hell with this, we are
going to wear our uncomfortable gauntlets.' That saved my
hands. The only part of my hand that was burnt was
through the zip, which burned into my skin.

I got out of the aeroplane very quickly and looked up. I
was going to delay my drop until all the Messerschmitts
were tiny little things in the sky. I was standing upright and
it was well, very nice, an incredible feeling, just going
down. I reckon I dropped about 6,000 feet. I then looked
down and realised I had no trousers on. I took my helmet
off and looked at that, but it was badly burnt. Stupidly I
threw that away but then tried to grab it again but couldn't
quite reach it. My eyelashes and face were burnt, as were

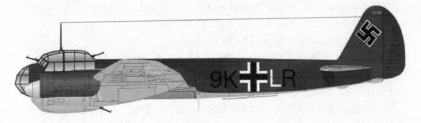

Ju88

my trousers. I opened my parachute. I was heading down towards an open field when I saw a Home Guard and he fired two shots at me. I was screaming out, 'Don't shoot, I'm British', but he obviously couldn't hear because I think I heard a second bullet pass quite close. I crashed into the field. There was strong wind and I was dragged across before I got rid of my parachute. The Home Guard came across and I again shouted at him. He was very apologetic, and took me to a farmhouse. I could walk, but not very well as I had a bullet in my foot. The farmer said, 'Sit down. We'll keep you here. I'll phone for the police to come and collect you.' His wife wanted to pour vinegar on my burns but I said, 'No, no, please just give me an old sheet to keep the air off.' I was very thirsty and my lips were slightly burnt or dry. I asked for a drink of water and he got a large glass and put a bit of brandy in it. He said, 'You know that'll be good for you.' Foolishly I drank it, but I shouldn't have knowing in shock you don't take any drink.

Then the door burst open and in came two young policemen. The first one came up and took a great big swing trying to hit me on the head, 'You bloody German'. The Home Guard man hit him and said, 'Can't you see – he is RAF, look at his wings.' So the policeman was most apologetic, and the thought struck me in two days I had had a farmer trying to kill me. Then a LDV trying to shoot me. Then a policeman trying to kill me, quite apart from the Germans, and I wondered whose side I was on. Anyway they took me to Southend General Hospital where I was met by a Dr Munro and a gorgeous out-patients sister. He looked in my eyes and face and said, 'Your eyes are alright. Your face is burnt. We can treat that alright. Do you young buggers always fly pissed?' He could smell the brandy on my breath and I assured him that I didn't drink when flying. Anyway when I came to they operated and sprayed all the burns.

Incidental to this episode, John has in his possession a copy of a police report.

Southend-on-Sea Constabulary
Leigh-on-Sea Section
31 August 1940

Sir,

I beg to report that at 1324½ hours today, a message was received from the Western Control that an aeroplane had crashed and was on fire at Rayleigh Road, junction of Southview Drive, Eastwood. At the same time I saw an airman descending by parachute over Eastwood.

With PCs 36, 38 and 108, I went in the direction in which the parachutist was descending and when near Kent Elms Corner the airman reached the ground. We proceeded on in the direction in which he had landed and found he had landed in one of Mr Rankin's fields about half a mile south of The Lawns, Rochford. We found the airman in the farmhouse of Blatcher's Farm – occupied by Frederick John Dean. He was suffering from burns about the face and legs and stated that his petrol tank had burst. I was informed that a Home Guard – George Edward Emeerson – of the Lawns Cottage, Ark Lane, Rochford, was the first to reach the airman and had assisted him to Blatcher's Farm.

We placed the airman in the police van and conveyed him to the Southend General Hospital arriving there at 1350 hours. The airman gave his name as Pilot Officer Ellacombe and added that he came from North Weald. He asked that North Weald be informed of his whereabouts. I telephoned Central police station and Rochford aerodrome was informed from there, and the parachute was removed by the RAF.

I returned to the farm where I was handed the following articles by Mr Dean

1 – Airman's yellow waistcoat
1 – Pair of gauntlet gloves
1 – Pair of crepe soled shoes

1 – White scarf

On the airman I found an Identity Card and note book. I spoke to Rochford aerodrome and was asked to hand the above property over to them and this I did.

The aeroplane fell on some waste land on the north side of Rayleigh Road, near Jones' Corner and was completely wrecked. Bushes in the vicinity were set on fire, but the outbreak was extinguished by the AFS from Kent Elms Corner section and Leigh Fire Brigade.

After some treatment John was placed in a small ward, in which Pilot Officer Frank Czajkowski, shot down that morning, was also recuperating.

Frank had a bullet through the shoulder and one through his legs. He was a lovely bloke. They had taken the precaution of moving the mirrors out of the room, so I couldn't see my extraordinary face, but Frank said, 'Here is my pocket mirror.' He pushed his chair across, to show me what I looked like. It was all black – the whole thing. Right round my face was a crust. I didn't look very good but I knew it wasn't serious. The doctor had assured me it was only second degree burns and it would all get better and the eyes were alright.

Czajkowski was an extraordinary chap. He used to get in his chair and wheel himself down the wards. He came back very excited one day and said, 'John, there's a little ward down there and there are about ten Germans in it. Two of them came from that Heinkel that you shot down and they are a bloody sight worse off than we are.' He would rub his hands with pleasure. The next day a doctor came in and said to me, 'Keep that man out of my ward. I am looking after these Germans. He is going there and telling them we are going to get them better, interrogate them, and then shoot them. Their recovery is not going well.' So poor old Frank was no longer allowed to go in there and blaspheme at these blokes. We were there for ten days and then because of the bombing of London we were moved up to St Luke's Hospital in Bradford, and there we were looked after marvellously and eventually recovered.

After several months convalescing John returned to 151

Squadron, but by then, of course the Battle of Britain had run its course. The day after John had been shot down, attrition rates finally enforced a move for 151 Squadron, to Digby to reform. On 1 September 1940 the squadron was down to just four operational pilots. Between 11 August and 31 August, 151 Squadron lost six pilots killed, eleven wounded and eight unharmed, who had baled out or force landed. In return Frank Marlow, the squadron's intelligence officer, reported 35 enemy aircraft destroyed. Fighter Command, as a whole at that stage, was suffering, the losses of pilots becoming excessive and fatigue for those surviving was mounting. Finding suitable replacements was proving difficult. But find replacements Dowding did.

John Ellacombe's time in the day battle had ended. John's next combat experiences would come at night.

151 Sqn Defiant

Chapter 4

Nightfighter

In September 1940, as the Luftwaffe's night offensive escalated, a high ranking meeting was called to discuss how to counter the growing threat from the Luftwaffe in the hours of darkness. Calls were made for a commitment of single-engine fighters. Dowding was reluctant but his hand was forced and he had to allocate three Hurricane squadrons for night-fighting duties. One of these was 151 Squadron.

Group Captain Smith, then a Pilot Officer with three months experience on the squadron recalled the change in the operational requirements of 151 Squadron, and reflects that, like Dowding, they did not see a future in single-engine nightfighters.

Early in October 1940 we were told that the squadron was, in future, to specialise in night fighting. We all lacked night flying experience. For example, I had 8.30 hrs in my logbook, J.W. Blair had about 15 and R.L Smith just over 20.

At about this time the Air Ministry published the L.M.F. (lack of moral fibre) Orders and Instructions. I remember, we all roared with laughter and we all said that these instructions described our attitude to night flying to a 'T'. We all declared ourselves to be L.M.F and asked to be posted to 11 Group Hurricane squadrons. We were told not to be bloody silly and get on with it, and of course, that is what we did.

At first we had a fairly high night flying accident rate due to inexperience, but we gradually improved. Throughout October/November we kept a day readiness state and I recall being scrambled on several occasions but only once achieving an interception.

151 Squadron had a lot of new pilots. John Ellacombe rejoined the squadron at Digby and a few days later it moved to Wittering. John had carried out very little night flying to date, but the total in his logbook would now steadily rise.

On 26 January 1941 he was in the air again, forty-five minutes dual in the Magister, 'local flying practice over Wittering'. Through February there was further local flying and an introduction to the Boulton Paul Defiant. Through March further familiarisation with the Defiant, including night flying training and on 12 March with Sergeant Gazzard a patrol. During the rest of March four further patrols with Sergeant Wrampling. Only one patrol in April, in a Hurricane, and in May back in the Defiant, eight patrols all but one of which were with Sergeant Stewart who would now, with the odd exception, become John's regular gunner.

> We had a mixed squadron of Defiants and Hurricanes. The Defiant was a very nice aeroplane to fly. Very stable, very easy to land at night, very good visibility. A very wide undercarriage with the same engine as the Hurricane, and of course, a lot heavier with your gunner and his turret at the back. So we felt it was not adequate as a fighter. I intercepted six aircraft at night and my gunner, Sergeant Stewart, would say, 'We can't shoot it down sir. It's a Wellington.' He had marvellous eyesight and sure enough when we got closer it was as he said. It was our wretched aeroplanes coming back, and I never shot anything down with 151 Squadron. It was maddening.
>
> The technique with regard night fighting with a Defiant was to get underneath, then look up until you saw the perfect silhouette, and we would spend hours in the darkroom looking at things objectively. To see where the radiators were and the exhausts were and the shape of, and how many tails and things, and what have you. So in theory you had very good identification, but there were mistakes made.

It was a frustrating time for John, 'unfortunately the Germans weren't coming very often so it became a bit boring' but others on the squadron did have some success, notably Richard Stevens, who by July 1941, flying Hurricanes, had become the RAF's top scorer by night. John recalled him as a bit of a mystery man, with a determination to shoot down Germans based on a deep 'hatred'.

> We finally found out that his wife and kids had been killed in a bombing raid. If there was a raid coming in he would get airborne and throttle right back so that he was using minimum fuel. One day he returned and said, 'I shot down two aeroplanes', and somebody asked if he could prove it. There was blood and guts on his wing and he would not let the airmen clean it off. The filthy stain remained there.
>
> I knew Steve fairly well, and one day, we had a ghastly experience. Steve had shot a Heinkel down not very far from Peterborough, and he said, 'John I want to go and get some souvenirs.' So I drove him out in a little van, which we had stolen from Digby when we had come down in convoy. The army was at the crash site, and the crew were still in the aircraft dead. The rear gunner had the machine gun through his stomach and out of his back. Steve said, 'Hold his shoulders while I pull it out', which I did. I then went and puked in the hedge while Steve washed the machine gun in the river.
>
> Generally he was very pleasant, a normal delightful bloke. He was older than most of us, about thirty, and we were all in our young twenties. He enjoyed his parties, was very good company but when it came to killing, my God he was a bloody killer. His hatred was unbelievable.

Through the summer months regular operations continued. In June there were six Defiant patrols, one Hurricane and a co-operation with a Havoc. In July, flying the Defiant, two patrols, one Havoc co-op. During August John took part in numerous Havoc co-ops, both in the Defiant and Hurricane, day and night. September, October, November, December, January resulted in similar logbook entries but mainly at night. Between all this there was daylight practice, formation practice and familiarisation with gun cameras.

On 22 February 1942 Squadron Leader Smith put John's name forward for a Distinguished Flying Cross. His recommendation read:

This officer came straight from an FTS to No. 151 Squadron in July 1940 and took part in the Battle of Britain, in which he was shot down. He displayed a high standard of courage and initiative in his engagements with the enemy. After five months in hospital recovering from wounds and burns, this officer immediately wished to rejoin his squadron on operational duties, and since then has carried out 52 night operational sorties under all weather conditions. He has at all times shown the greatest keenness to engage the enemy and has set an example to the rest of his squadron. He has destroyed two (confirmed) enemy aircraft, probably destroyed two others and damaged a further two.

Station commander Group Captain Basil Embry added to the recommendation, which was duly awarded.

This officer is one of the outstanding pilots who has done so much to build up the well deserved reputation of No. 151 Squadron as a nightfighter unit. If the weather is bad and if there is any enemy activity, Flying Officer Ellacombe is one of the first to fly. When in action he shows a complete disregard for his own safety and a sense of duty up to the highest standard of the Royal Air Force.

This officer was badly wounded and severely burnt in the Battle of Britain, and I consider his return to operational flying and his determination to remain in his present unit, in itself shows courage and a fine resolve. His good work over so long a period of operations deserves recognition, and I strongly recommend him for the DFC.

On 19 February 1942 John was posted to 253 Squadron at Hibaldstow, now a Flight Lieutenant and a flight commander.

They had recently been put on to night fighting, and quite frankly they did not like night flying. It was very difficult because a lot of the chaps would say things like, 'Oh, I can't take off. I'll taxi out. My aircraft has gone u/s.' I would go in, take it airborne, check it, bring it back again, and gradually they realised that I was determined and I knew a lot more. They were good blokes but frankly they were under-confident in their own ability. By then I had at least one hundred hours night flying on Hurricanes. Their morale did pick up. We had a lot of funny jobs to do. I was sent off to do a lot of things over the steelworks at Scunthorpe. I was told the hours that the blast furnaces were going to open and asked if I could record how easy it was to see from the air. They were worried about bombers. We did a lot of special jobs like that, which was all very interesting.

Now, just flying the Hurricane John's operational duties continued mainly at night, Havoc patrol, searchlight co-ops. There was also some daylight army co-operation practice and ground strafing. Included in all this was some brief experience on the twin-engined Mosquito on 11 and 12 July, as second pilot to Wing Commander Smith.

Some of his sorties during this period involved supporting RAF Bomber Command's escalation of the strategic bomber offensive in May and June of 1942.

When the big raids were going off, 1,000 bomber raids, we would fly out with them right up to the Dutch coast because it was still almost light by then. This was in the summer of 1942, and we had our long-range tanks on in case any Messerschmitts were coming out, but we never saw anything. It was a very impressive sight to see these chaps going out still in fairly light conditions. It was not going to be very good for them once they got over.

Whilst at 253 Squadron John also continued to take part in co-operation patrols, notably in partnership with Havocs. The main problem at night was obviously locating and identifying the target. One method tried was to kit out the Havoc aircraft with a Turbinlite, a powerful light, and when a contact was made with an enemy the Havoc pilot would illuminate the prey for his 'parasite' fighter.

The Hurricane would take off first, circle round, and watch the other chap taking off. There was a thin strip down the outside of each of his wings painted white with a little light shining down. Because of this you could see the back of his wing, you would come down, and as he got airborne would formate on it. You would fly alongside until the Havoc pilot, with his radar operator, would have a contact. He would then give you a code word that he was about to illuminate, and the theory was that you would go down and there would be a beautiful enemy aircraft fully illuminated, ready to be shot down.

Of course one problem with this method was the effect on a pilot's night vision which could be, 'completely ruined. So if he went out of the beam you were in trouble.'

Night vision is a funny thing. The RAF expert on night vision was a Group Captain Livingstone. He came to Wittering and we all sat in a darkroom with this machine he had, which was about three feet square, up to eight feet high and there were lots of little things that you could look at. We had to stand in a circle and record what we saw. I recorded twenty-nine of the thirty objects there. He said, 'you have cheated', and I said, 'Why?' He said, 'Nobody can see more than about twenty. So you must have exceptional night vision.' I had to go and do the damn thing again. He thought somebody had told me what was there. He changed everything and again I got about twenty-eight or twenty-nine. Some chaps couldn't see a bloody thing. They never saw anything at night. Stevens got the lot right. He had the most exceptional eyesight. There was nothing you could put up he wouldn't see and of course, he proved it with all the things he found.

On a number of occasions, at night, John thought he had made promising contacts, crept right up on what he thought was a suspected enemy aircraft only to find out, 'they were bloody Wellingtons. Fortunately I recognised them and I didn't shoot them down, and the gunners didn't see me.' But on the night of 28/29 July 1942 John's luck would change as demonstrated in his combat report.

Number of enemy aircraft – one
Type of enemy aircraft – Do217
Time attack was delivered – 01.25 approx
Place attack was delivered – 15 miles west of Mablethorpe
Height of enemy – 10,500 feet
Enemy casualties – Do217 probably destroyed
General report – I was airborne at 00.45 hours and joined up with Squadron Leader Winn at 00.47 hours. We proceeded on a vector of 110 degrees to 10,000 feet where

we were handed over to Partington GCI at 00.55 hours. Partington GCI put us onto a bogey which turned out to be friendly. We were then put onto a hostile at 01.23 hours and were ordered to increase Angels to 11,000 feet. At 01.23 hours Havoc obtained AI contact. At 01.24 hours Hostile identified as a Do217 by Squadron Leader Winn and I saw it as soon as he called out. Enemy aircraft was above us and passed over us to starboard. I opened up fully and flew down moon of enemy aircraft which then saw Havoc and also dived down moon. I fired a short burst in a dive at 200 yards range experiencing return tracer from top turret. Enemy aircraft climbed steeply to port where he again apparently saw Havoc and half rolled to starboard and dived vertically. I followed and fired again, more return fire. I fired another short burst and when he fired a third long burst back at me I hit the turret with a big flash. From then on there was no more return fire. The enemy aircraft then pulled in sharply to port towards the Havoc. I did a beam port attack closing to 40 yards firing a long burst. There were strikes on the port inner plane and fuselage. I had to pull up sharply to avoid ramming, climbed up and half rolled to observe enemy aircraft. The enemy aircraft rolled on his back and fell vertically towards ground. I then lost visual contact. The last attack took place at 4,000 feet. The combat started over the sea and the enemy aircraft was driven about 15 miles inland. I circled round expecting to see a fire on the ground but only observed a huge yellow flash which might have been enemy aircraft striking ground and failing to ignite. In view of the subsequent GCI plot of enemy aircraft which disappeared after final attack and a report of a heavy explosion in this area it seems evident that the enemy aircraft dived vertically into the ground.

I was flying a long range Hurricane IIC but jettisoned the tanks about 15 miles out to sea in order to keep up with the Havoc after AI contact had been made.

John carries on the story:

We were flying alongside one another and Charles Winn, the Squadron Leader, said, 'I have a contact.' I said, 'Somebody has just flown over the top of us.' I followed him and identified it as a Dornier and Charles sat back. I had a four-cannon Hurricane and I hit him several times. He rolled over and dived down. We followed him but I had to pull out because otherwise I was going to hit the ground. Wherever it landed we never found the damn thing. It was right on the beach so they called it a probable. I am convinced he went in. I had to absolutely heave out, and I got down to within about 500 feet. It was very frightening. I thought I had left it too late.

Into August and the squadron began preparations for involvement in one notable event, Operation Jubilee – the raid on Dieppe. Prior to the raid John had attended a briefing outlining the need for the use of Hurricanes.

We knew what was going to happen because I had been to the briefing at Tangmere by Air Officer Commanding Leigh-Mallory. He said, 'I have got ten Hurricane squadrons. I am prepared to lose half. We must knock out these guns.' Just like that, as he stood there holding his papers. We Hurricane flight commanders and squadron commanders just said, 'Oh yes – jolly good.' He said, 'the defences will be 190s and 109s. Their base is there, there and there. We have done away with the bombers to knock the guns out. The Hurricanes and the Hurricane bombers are going to do that.' We didn't think very much of this. We lost more aircraft that day than we lost in any one day in the Battle of Britain, and 50% of those were Hurricanes. It was not a good day for Hurricanes.

On the morning of 19 August 1942, 253 Squadron duly prepared for the attack on Dieppe. On the first sortie John recorded in his logbook, 'flak intense'. That didn't deter him or the squadron from a further sortie across the Channel, however.

We had cannon-armed Hurricanes and twelve-gun Hurricanes. We were supposed to attack the guns on the west bank, which we did. As we flew in my number two, a chap called Seal, just blew up and smashed into the ground, and I thought, 'Well, he's dead', it looked so horrendous, but he was actually thrown out of his aeroplane and just badly bruised. We lost one aircraft that sortie. I didn't fly in the second sortie because we reckoned with a CO and two flight commanders, we needed one to survive. We didn't know how many sorties we were going to do, but on the third sortie the convoy was actually withdrawing.

They were about four miles off shore and as we crossed in we were bounced by FW190s. They were slightly faster than the Hurricane and we all broke viciously. My number two stuck with me, Pilot Officer Dodson, an Australian. We flew inland and we saw a gun battery. They were, I think, 88 millimetres. We saw them firing, we attacked and could see our shells exploding on men. You would suddenly see a great big flash as a chap's shoulder was probably knocked off.

Now Dodson had his twelve machine guns and he was on my starboard side. Somebody shot my throttle out and hit my engine, and obviously hit a lot of other things as well. Glycol was coming out so I knew I had about 20-30 seconds before the engine stopped. I thought, 'I'm going to get out to sea as quick as I can.' I turned right and flew straight through Dodson's cine-camera line, and he was firing his twelve machine guns. He took a perfect picture. He must have hit the aeroplane but fortunately not me. He had to duck down to avoid me and he hit a high tension cable, which he brought back to Friston. I reached the coast and then my engine blew up. I managed to get up to about 600 feet, jettison the hood and the panel, fall out of the aeroplane and open the parachute. When I looked up all I could see was tracer bullets. I thought the parachute was on fire and I realised it was all the gunners on the coast shooting at me. I landed in the sea, kicked my boots off, jettisoned my parachute and set off to swim to Newhaven. It was only sixty miles and all these bullets were smashing into the water all round me! Fortunately they turned their attention elsewhere and I was swimming away happily, thinking I had made quite a lot of distance, when a little assault landing craft came and picked me up. They pulled me in, I had hardly swum anywhere. They then nearly killed me. They said, 'Drink this', and gave me a mug. I wasn't used to drinking neat whisky and I almost choked. They had been there all day bombed and shot at and they were absolutely punch drunk. They were beyond any more fear. They were as calm as anything and were wonderful blokes. We were making about four knots and we were being fired at by these gun batteries. I said, 'Can't we increase the speed?' The reply came, 'We have only got one engine left.' We were chugging along, taking a slight diversion, and then, thank heavens, we saw a steam gunboat coming. They came and threw us a rope and towed us at high speed to the rest of the convoy.

On return to shore John had time to reflect on the risk the navy men had taken.

They were lost from the convoy because they only had one engine left. Yet when they saw me come down they very, very gallantly turned back to pick me up. I tried to get the chap a decoration but I don't know where the thing went. We went back into Newhaven and I climbed out on the wharf in my bare feet. One of the army officers said, 'Would you like some boots?' I said, 'Yes, please.' He said, 'Well, we've got 600 bodies. What size boot do you have?' I said, 'Oh about size eight.' He said, 'Come along with me.' We found somebody, lifted their feet up and took the boots off. You know one was beyond any sort of feeling when I had got these boots on, and ultimately they took me back to my base at Friston.

Shortly after the Dieppe raid John moved squadrons, an assessment pasted into his logbook recording 'well above the average' as a nightfighter pilot. On 1 September he took up duties with 538 Squadron, where operations, at night, remained much the same as before, numerous Havoc co-ops and numerous black-out inspections. But John was clearly not satisfied and on 20 February 1943 left the squadron to enter a new phase in his flying career.

I had then completed just over two years of operations on and off and had had a fairly unpleasant time over Dieppe. Frankly my twitch was getting rather bad. I was actually given the choice to go to an Operational Conversion Unit to be an instructor. I told them I'd like to go back to 151 Squadron, who were now on Mosquitoes. I was granted that privilege.

John started accumulating hours initially at 12 AFU Grantham, flying the Blenheim and hence further twin-engine experience. In mid April 1943 he was posted to 54 OTU at Charter Hall, initially building up hours on the Beaufort and the Beaufighter and developing a relationship with his navigator/ radar operator. At the end of the course he was assessed as above the average as a nightfighter pilot.

> I had a wonderful navigator. When I went to Charter Hall I was a Flight Lieutenant with a DFC, and a Pilot Officer, a fairly elderly chap, came up and said, 'My name is Bob Peel and I would like to be your navigator. I am a very good sportsman. I am very good at squash and golf and hockey.' It turned out this was Wing Commander Peel, who was an accountant officer, and to fly he had to drop a rank and become a pilot officer. Anyway I agreed. He seemed a sensible chap, and apart from being a very good navigator, a very conscientious chap, he saved me a lot of money because he knew every fiddle there was to making claims. He taught me a hell of a lot about finance and he stuck with me.

On 20 July 1943 John and Bob arrived at 151 Squadron, then at Colerne. Squadron Leader Bodien took John up on 22 July to give a demonstration of the Mosquito. The next day John would take the twin-engined fighter up himself and over the next few weeks would build up experience, and come to appreciate the aircraft.

> A lovely aeroplane. Light on the controls, a pleasure to fly. It wasn't as tight manoeuvring but it was a good stable aeroplane with plenty of fuel. It was also comfortable for your navigator to work in.

Over the following months patrols came and went but there was little action for John and Bob. On 16 April 1944 they were to move squadron again. John summed up the reasons for his next move thus:

> We went down to Colerne and covered some of the Baedeker raids. I never intercepted anything, and we were then posted down to Predannack to go and do long-range patrols helping Coastal Command, but by then 2 Group had started up with the Mosquito fighter-bombers. Smith was a CO at 487 and he rang me up. I mean we had been great friends. He rang me up and said, 'Would you like to join my squadron?'

Basil Embry was then AOC 2 Group and he had been my station commander so he knew me very well. We did a bit of a fiddle and I was posted to 487 Squadron.

487 Squadron was part of 140 Wing under the leadership of Group Captain Peter Wykeham-Barnes.

A fine man. Quite outstanding, and very approachable. I had tremendous respect for him. He had a very keen sense of humour. He was always prepared to listen to your point of view, but was a very strong-willed man.

Through April, John and Bob completed a lot of low level cross country and low level bombing practice. During May it was time to test this training out on operations. Starting on 3 May with an intruder operation to Juvincourt. On 6 May there came a special operation to counter the German secret weapon threat that was developing in north-west France. The Allies had been closely monitoring the construction of launch sites for pilotless flying bombs, the V1s, and the campaign of bombing these sites had been running since December 1943. 487 Squadron added their weight on 6 May with an Oboe formation attack on a Noball site, i.e. a V1 launching site. Oboe was an electronic bombing aid whereby signals sent from England were picked up on the Oboe equipped aircraft guiding it to the target, over which another signal was received prompting the release of the bombload or target markers. 9 May brought another Oboe formation attack, on a rail target, John entering in his logbook, 'brought bombs back, 7 aircraft damaged'. John was certainly enjoying the opportunity to fly the Mosquito at low level.

It was tremendous. Absolutely tremendous, especially when Bob Peel would say, 'there is a river coming up', and the river would come up. If you got lost that was tricky because there were certain parts of the coast that you did not want to come out over because they were absolutely packed with guns and searchlights.

The assault on the beaches of Normandy, and the breakout into France and beyond, would be the main Allied land campaign for Western Europe in 1944. An immense amount of detailed planning had occupied Allied staffs in the run up to D-Day and the air forces had been set their respective priorities and objectives. Air superiority was key for the protection of the seaborne troops and supply lines, and to provide the umbrella beneath which the army could fight for territory. In addition emphasis was placed on the air forces hindering the movements and deployments of enemy troops and armour. To protect the Atlantic coastline the Germans had to spread their forces relying on redeployment through internal road and rail networks once the point of Allied assault was identified. Of this the Allies were aware and they would use their air weapon to attack such networks and enemy concentrations in the form of railyards and road junctions. The versatile Mosquito, in its fighter-bomber role, could reach and attack these targets, flying from airfields in England so such tasks would be allocated to 487 Squadron. Not that the pilots knew at that stage, although John felt something was coming, 'because it was all terribly hush hush at that time.'

On the nights of 5, 7 and 8 June John set about making his contribution to disrupting enemy communications, as his logbook shows:

> *5 June:* 2.30 hours. Night road patrol, Argentan – Lisieux – Falaise – Rocquancourt – Putanges 4 x 500lb on road junction ¹/₂ NW Falaise.

> *7 June:* 2.25 hours. Night road patrol. Argentan – Putanges – Falaise – Sées. 4 x 500lb road junction Trun.

> *8 June:* 2.30 hours. Night railway patrol. La Haye – Coutances – Folligny – Villedieu – Les Poeles. 4 x 500lb in wood in Villedieu rail station. Explosions and large fire on presumed enemy dump.

On D-Day and in the next few days, members of the SAS were parachuted into occupied France, detailed to disrupt and hinder the relocation of enemy troops to the battle area in Normandy. Early in the evening of 11 June a signal was sent to England reporting a build-up of eleven trains carrying petrol, at Châtellerault. 2 Group was contacted and the Mosquito bombers of 140 Wing (six crews) and 138 Wing (six crews) were called upon. At 487 Squadron Group Captain Wykeham-Barnes marshalled his most experienced airmen.

> Wykeham-Barnes came out and said, 'Smith, come here quickly. We have just got information from the SAS that there are petrol trains pulling into this marshalling yard.

Get three aircraft airborne as quick as you can.' That was the briefing. Bunny Smith grabbed me and Wally Runciman, and said, 'We're going off. Instantaneous bombs.' Ronnie Marsh was his navigator. He handed over his target map to have the flight put on but he took off without it. Smith had arranged always that we had bombs on the ground by the Mosquitoes, instantaneous or delayed action. It must have been about an hour and a half after they called us that we hit them.

As we crossed the Loire I could see them arguing but Smith had remembered that once you had crossed the Loire there was a bridge. Then you had to go about ten miles. Anyway we found Châtellerault. We were the first three Mosquitoes and nobody shot at us. There were the trains lined up. We did one attack and dropped our bombs as we went across. There were huge trucks loaded with high octane fuel and as the bombs went off you could see the mass of flames. We didn't go back for another attack because we knew there were others coming. There was absolute chaos, and that place was bombed right until the evening. More and more Mosquitoes came and bombed it. Within a couple of hours the message came in that we had hit it.

John and Bob were next operational on the night of 20 June, the ORB recording, 'bombed 6 lights moving S of railway. Lights doused results not seen. Strafed Immeauville a/f while aircraft taking off. Results not seen.' The two airmen would complete fifteen further night patrols up to the end of July, behind the battle area, attacking railyards, airfields, bridges, road junctions and strafing directly onto enemy troops.

Sometimes we would attack an airfield. Sometimes we were given a road to follow. Sometimes we would follow a railway line just on spec. to attack any train you could see, and you could always see a train because they were mostly steam trains and they made a hell of a mess what with the smoke and flame. Sometimes it was just targets of opportunity. You would be given an area to attack and you would just patrol it and sometimes you wouldn't see a thing, but most of the time you would find something useful to attack.

We had the navigational aid Gee, which was very accurate, and sometimes during night sorties we would go into an area and would fly down a Gee line. [The aircraft received pulses sent simultaneously by transmitters from England. The navigator, using a Gee chart, plotted the arrival of the pulses and calculated their position.]

On one occasion a Mosquito came past ten feet underneath me. I said, 'Wally, was that you?' I knew Wally Runciman was also going to this particular place. And it was him. That showed you the accuracy. We were both absolutely on the bloody thing.

The main opposition to these types of operations at this time came from ground defences. John very rarely came across any aerial opposition.

I saw one German fighter flying low in moonlight. Bob Peel suddenly said, 'I think there's an aircraft over there.' It was a Me110. I got into a very tight turn. Bob had undone his straps to have a look and, poor bugger, once I really pulled he was just smashed down onto the floor. The Me110 couldn't catch us and pushed off. In daylight we never saw any enemy aircraft.

John's next operation was as a result of intelligence received from the SAS behind the enemy lines. On the morning of 1 August 2 Group received details of the target, the Caserne des Dunes barracks at Poitiers. Responsibility was passed on to 140 Wing, and twenty-five Mosquitoes (two of which were reserves and not used in the attack) and crews were prepared. Peter Wykeham-Barnes led the attack with ten Mosquitoes from 21 Squadron. 'Black' Smith would follow in behind leading 487 Squadron.

We were briefed that the SS were moving into the barracks that evening at six o'clock, and there were going to be a lot of troops moving in. We knew this lot were absolute bastards and we were tasked to drop the bombs from about 500 feet and then pull up. I was leading the second section of four.

122 Wing provided a Mustang escort, and the Mosquitoes sped to the target unhindered by any aerial opposition. Surprise ensured the success of the raid.

The I.P. [Initial Point] was Mont St Michel. The navigation was perfect, and absolutely nobody saw us coming. Amazing to think of twenty-three aircraft flying nought feet. It makes a hell of a noise, but there wasn't a gun fired at us. We were well below radar, flying so low. We went straight to it and straight out again. As we attacked, the three-storey buildings, the whole bloody thing, just collapsed. Strangely enough, I flew over there two years later, and they hadn't even dug the bodies out. The destruction was such that they had to move on because of the attacks that were coming. The briefing, using the SAS information, was very good.

All 487 Squadron aircraft returned. One 21 Squadron aircraft was lost, force-landing, the two airmen successfully evading capture. A few days later Air Vice-Marshal Basil Embry passed on his appreciation to the crews who took part in the operation.

Reconnaissance photographs have since shown that this was a very clean attack; only three bombs have fallen outside the barrack area and these have not damaged civilian property. Nearly all the bombs have found their mark in barrack buildings. Of three large barrack blocks, one is $3/4$ destroyed and the other [sic] is completely destroyed by high explosive at its western end and the western part has suffered severe fire damage, causing partial collapse of the roof.

Seven other buildings and [structures] lining the walls of the barracks have been destroyed or gutted by fire, containing possibly 40 or 50 motor transport vehicles. The activity of the barracks is confirmed by the presence of horse exercise rings and ambulances are seen at the main entrance, some twelve hours after the attack. It has been reported that 150 enemy troops were killed and more than that number again injured.

For the remainder of August 487 Squadron continued to harass the Germans on the ground. John and Bob completed twelve more operational sorties. Notably they flew and operated above the carnage of the Falaise pocket and disrupted the German retreat across the Seine by attacking bridges.

Detailed below are some of 487 Squadron Operations Record

Book entries recording the night activities of its airmen. Included against some of the entries are further details of John Ellacombe's contribution.

12 August: The approach of a climax in the battle area called for an increased effort on the part of the Squadron. For the first time since 'D Day' we did 'turn rounds', and during the night 29 sorties were flown. Three aircraft went for railways in north-western France, the other attacking road and rail transport in the rear of the enemy lines. Results were good, many fires being started in woods and marshalling yards.

16 August: A stand down was given late in the evening but this was subsequently scrubbed, and 14 aircraft attacked bridges and crossings over the Seine. Weather over the target area was very bad, violent thunderstorms were encountered.
John Ellacombe's sortie: Bombed 4 bridges – no results seen. Strafed fire on road – large explosion and 6/7 burning MET [Mechanised Enemy Transport].

17 August: A maximum effort was called for at night, and our previous record of 34 sorties was improved upon, as the Squadron did 'turn rounds' and 35 sorties were flown. Targets were river crossings and transport of the retreating German 7th Army... The night's work constituted a record for the Wing as a whole, for 104 sorties were flown by three squadrons.

18 August: ...for the night's operations 19 aircraft bombed and strafed crossing on the river Risle. Many fires were started and lines of MET. were effectively attacked.
John Ellacombe's sortie: Strafed burning MET – flashes seen. Strafed MET – no results seen. Bombed lights in wood – no results seen.

20 August: Fifteen aircraft operated at night, harassing the retreating enemy and bombing road junctions and railways with good effect.
John Ellacombe's sortie: Strafed 6 MET – no results seen. Strafed 2 rows of trucks – hits claimed. Bombed north side of river [Seine] at Duclair. Bombs hit south side, terrific explosion.

John Ellacombe: We were given a lot of information that the Germans were pulling out – evacuating. During the time of the Falaise Gap battles we had two bombs and two flares, and we worked out which roads they were going down towards the Seine. We would fly out and drop a flare one side of the target. Then you would turn round never flying into the light of the flare, which was very bright. The light was shining down but you didn't fly into the light, because the anti-aircraft guns were so terrifically fierce. You would brief your chaps and would sometimes have four Mosquitoes going round the thing keeping the flares going. You would probably hit up to a hundred vehicles and god knows what. You would attack and you would see your cannon shells exploding on men. It was a horrific sight, bullets exploding on a man, but you would see this time and time again.

It was pretty horrendous. That is where the hatred came out and you would say, 'Got them, all those bastards'. You had your four machine guns, four cannons, a hell of a blast. I hated bloody Germans at that time and all of us had the same sort of attitude. We had all had so many of our friends killed.

At the end of August John's third operational tour came to an end. At this stage a new CO had arrived at 487 Squadron and he asked John what he wanted to do now he had completed his tour.

I just felt relief. I had reached the stage where fatigue, the twitch, really was overcoming me and I was very happy to finish. I had flown virtually three operational tours. He said, 'Where do you want to go? What would you like to do? Why don't you go and do a nice quiet staff job at the Air Ministry?' I said, 'Not bloody likely.' Smith went to the FTS at High Ercall with number 60 OTU, which had Mosquitoes. We pulled a fiddle to get me there, and I joined Smith with a lot of other chaps who had been in the Wing with us. It was a very happy station. We were converting all these blokes, very experienced pilots, who had come from Canada and had no idea how to fly at low level or do low level navigation.

On 30 September 1944 Wing Commander Smith put John's name forward for a Bar to his DFC. The recommendation recorded to date 315 hours 10 minutes on operations (182 hours 10 minutes since his DFC), 37 + 168 Fighter Patrols (37 + 73 since DFC).

This officer has completed a large number of operational hours and sorties, in the course of which, he has been shot down 3 times. He has always displayed a ferociousness and a keenness to engage the enemy that is of the highest order. Examples of which are the following:

During August 1940, S/L Ellacombe was shot down, and unable to bale out, he crash-landed in a field. He rejoined his squadron next day and carried out several operational sorties before he was again shot down a few days later. He was forced to abandon his burning aircraft and he suffered severe burns. He returned to his squadron within 3 months and continued operating until shot down for the 3rd time during the Dieppe attack in August 1942 whilst leading his flight on their third sortie that day against gun positions. After his rescue from the sea he immediately volunteered for training as a Nightfighter Pilot and completed 8 months in a Nightfighter Squadron where finding it too dull he volunteered for service with a Mosquito squadron of the TAF.

Since receiving his last award this officer has destroyed one enemy aircraft and has successfully attacked a large variety of targets by day and night. He is an excellent leader and flight commander and his personal example of perseverance, skill and courage have been an inspiration to all who came in contact with him.

I most strongly recommend him for the award of a Bar to the DFC.

Group Captain Wykeham-Barnes added his comments.

A completely dependable Flight Commander, S/Ldr Ellacombe has time and again proved himself a fearless and skilful pilot. I can back the squadron commander's opinion at all points, and strongly recommend this officer for the award of a Bar to the Distinguished Flying Cross.

Air Vice-Marshal Basil Embry's comments read, 'This officer has a really first-class operational record. He at all times shows an exceptionally high standard of efficiency and courage, and he very well deserves the award of a Bar to the DFC.' Air Marshal Coningham added 'Recommended' and the Bar was duly awarded. On 8 October John arrived at 60 Operational Training Unit, High Ercall, where he would remain until March 1945, mainly giving low level flying demonstrations to trainee Mosquito pilots. He then transferred to 13 OTU Finmere, continuing to fly the occasional low level demo on the Mosquito. During his time here the war against Germany ended. However despite the fact he was on leave, he wasn't able to celebrate VE Day – being in bed with measles, 'Missed the best party of the lot'. He summed up his feelings about the war thus: 'I was very pleased to have survived but I lost a lot of friends. It was nevertheless a great experience.'

John made the decision to stay in the RAF after the war, receiving a permanent commission. He went on to have a most distinguished career in numerous positions, rising to Air Commodore and Commander, Air Forces Gulf 1968-70, after which he became a CB. Prior to retirement in April 1973 he was Director of Operations (Air Defence & Overseas) at the Ministry of Defence. John then took up the role of Director of Scientific Services at St Thomas's Hospital, London. His final thoughts on the summer of 1940 are as follows:

I think people realised that if we had lost that battle within three months we would have been finished. We had to win. There were thirty-two pilots at 2 FTS, six survived the war. It should be remembered as one of the turning points of the war. The Battle of Britain saved Britain of that there is no doubt.

Chapter 5

The Battle for Survival

Hazel Roberts was seven years old during the Battle of Britain, and she recalls watching the air battles with her brother, from their home in Writtle, Essex.

As we all looked skywards we watched as wave after wave of German Heinkel and Dornier bombers headed over our houses towards London. Suddenly I shouted to my brother, 'here come our boys', as I saw our fighters emerging from behind the clouds. They roared in, there were only a small number of our planes against all the might of the German Luftwaffe. We saw lots of what we called dog fights. Our fighters doggedly kept up their ferocious attack against seemingly overwhelming odds, with great bravery. We saw planes blown to pieces, both German and British. Wreckage was strewn all over a large area.

It was thrilling that I witnessed with many others this extraordinary battle. It would appear at first sight to be as futile as David fighting against the mighty giant Goliath.

This experience made me feel proud to be British, and grateful to our pilots who had driven the enemy away.[7]

Tony Pickering was born in Foxton, Leicestershire on 25 August 1920, and went to school at Market Harborough Grammar School. In 1937 he became an apprentice engineer with British Thompson Houston & Company.

As a young boy of seventeen or eighteen years, we used to see aircraft flying over. In those days we were really interested in things like that. I had seen pictures from the First World War. I vividly remember seeing *All Quiet on the Western Front*, a terrific picture, and from 1937 onwards I think most people realised the war was coming. Churchill had warned us even when he was out of government. I, with other apprentices, we had a thousand at Rugby, all different types of trades, belonged to the Apprentice Association, a lively organisation. We used to talk about wars and things like that. We were all saying, 'where are we going, what are we going to do? Army, navy or air force?' An apprentice colleague, Bryn Willis said to me that a friend of his was in the Royal Air Force Volunteer Reserve and was flying Tiger Moths at weekends, being taught how to fly, and being paid. Well, gosh, what an inducement for someone to join. Two shillings an hour. As an apprentice I was only getting a meagre sum of money. My father even had to pay for my digs in Rugby.

Tony gained his first 'air experience' in a Tiger Moth flown by Flying Officer Morris on 29 July 1939 and went solo on 26 August.

I got into an aircraft fairly quickly. I was given a little talk, about forty-five minutes, was taken out and shown the controls, and then an instructor took me up and showed me around. After a couple of trips he took me up again and handed the machine over to me to do manoeuvres, teaching me how to take off and to land. After about twelve hours you were allowed to go solo. Most people survived, we were fairly well trained. I enjoyed it, every minute of it. It was lovely to fly around, see what was going on below, and being paid to do it.

We realised that we were being prepared for war. Everybody knew what was happening and some bright politician decided to expand the RAFVR. There was a very large number of us when the war started, we were an embarrassment. For the first two weeks of the war I sat on my bottom in Rugby.

Then following a few months at 3 ITW Hastings, away from flying, Tony became airborne once more, in a Miles Magister, the day he arrived at 15 EFTS Redhill, 22 November 1939. He now increased his hours and experience, and by 26 April had flown 46.40 hours dual, 39.00 hours solo, his proficiency as a pilot being assessed as average. Then came a move to 5 FTS at Sealand and three months training exclusively on the Miles Master, maintaining the average assessments. In addition the CO of 5 FTS added against *Any special faults in flying which must be watched* 'Slightly over confident'.

I realised I needed further training. I wasn't ready to get into battle. I was still very much a learner. We were all issued with pikes in case we were invaded. 'If the Hun paratroopers land', we were told, 'defend yourself.'

Whilst at Sealand the decision was made as to what kind of aircraft Tony would be flying operationally, and early one morning Tony's course was told to report to the flight commander's office.

We were paraded by a flight sergeant who lined us all up and said, 'shortest to the right, tallest to the left'. The flight commander was instructed that we were all standing to attention. He came out, walked down to the centre of us, put his hand down the middle and said, 'Right. You, the tallest, will go onto bombers. You, the shortest, will go on to fighters.' That's how I became a fighter pilot. I was picked because I was the right height.

Tony soon felt at ease within the RAF.

It was magnificent. We felt we were all in it together. We would fly and fight for each other. We wouldn't let each other down. We had comradeship. We felt confident we could hold the Germans.

One mode of passing from trainee to raw combatant took place between the operational training unit and the operational squadron. But in the case of Tony Pickering the CO at 32 Squadron was not satisfied with the raw 'combatant' he received. 32 Squadron had been involved in the Battle of France, operating from England. It had had its successes. It had had its share of losses. The same could be said of the opening stages of the Battle of Britain in July 1940. Pilots had been lost and needed replacing. When Tony arrived at 32 Squadron, equipped with Hurricanes, towards the end of July 1940, he had not even sat in a Hurricane let alone taken one into the air. On 29 July he managed fifty minutes 'experience on type'.

Three of us arrived at Biggin Hill, as sergeant pilots from training school. We reported to the squadron commander. He looked at me and said, 'Pickering. How many hours have you done on Hurricanes?' I replied, 'I have never seen one before sir.' He responded, 'Well tomorrow morning you'll be in action. There's a Hurricane out there, Pilot Officer Flinders will take you and he'll show you the controls. You'll do three circuits and bumps and then tomorrow morning at half past three you'll be awoken, have a cup of tea, then meet at dispersal at quarter past four and take off and we'll go down to Hawkinge. We'll sit there until the Hun comes over. You'll fly as number two to a Flight Lieutenant Proctor and he'll tell you what to do.'

I did not meet Hector Proctor until the following morning. He said, 'Pickering you'll fly as my number two. You'll sit directly behind me, you will not be more than about ten or twelve feet from me at all times whatever I do. You won't put your gun button on fire. I don't want you to blow me out of the sky. We'll attack the Hun.'

In the event I just followed him around. We arrived there

early, it had just got light. We were sitting around until about 9 o'clock and then we were scrambled. Down we came again, refuelled and again sat and waited. Then we were off again and then back to Biggin Hill.

But Tony's stay at the squadron was to be very short lived indeed. His considerable lack of experience was something that the squadron could not and would not be prepared to accept. The Battle of Britain was still in its early stages and Fighter Command was coping with the current level of operational activity. Thus there was the opportunity to take inexperienced pilots out of the front line for training.

When we came back from our first ops the CO said, 'It's hopeless, you chaps are no use to me whatsoever. I'm going to send the three of you to Sutton Bridge, to an operational training unit for a course.' I was sensible enough at that age to realise that I knew nothing about a Hurricane. I had plenty to learn and I had no experience whatsoever. It was ridiculous that we were asked to take off. We were just making up the numbers.

Tony duly arrived at 6 Operational Training Unit Sutton Bridge on 3 August and began to get to grips with one of the RAF's principal fighter weapons, so much so that by 23 August he had been able to inscribe a total of 31.55 hours of Hurricane time in his logbook. He was then sent back to 32 Squadron at Biggin Hill, arriving on 25 August, but his stay with the unit only lasted two days and he only managed one operational patrol with no enemy aircraft encountered.

The CO called us all together and said, 'The squadron is being taken out of the line, we're moving up to Acklington. Pickering, you and your other two comrades [Ray Gent and Tony Whitehouse] don't need a rest.' I thought, 'no we don't.'

Posted to 501 Squadron at Gravesend, arriving on 27 August 1940, Tony describes his first impression:

501 Squadron did not suffer from lack of confidence, there's no doubt about it. They had six or seven highly experienced pilots. Not necessarily from wartime, although they had had some experience in France. But they were five

to eight years older than me. We were young lads of nineteen but we took it upon ourselves to drive those Huns off the coast. We were not worried at all, the older people had an influence on us, men like Morfill, Farnes and Ginger Lacey. And of course there was Squadron Leader Hogan. He was a gentleman and I knew of his history. When I was sixteen years old I had read of his flight in a Wellesley from Egypt to Australia. He was a first class man, a good leader who could really understand men.

Tony's initial impressions also centred around a quite basic need.

The food was terrible. We were fed by the army and they did their best, but it was just terrible. I couldn't eat it and I remember one night going to a hotel in Gravesend and having a meal there. As soon as I ate it I was sick. My stomach couldn't take good food. We had a very good flight sergeant pilot, Morfill an ex-RAF boy, Halton. He spoke to Squadron Leader Hogan who realised we were being underfed and responded by inviting all the sergeants into the officers mess every night to have our evening meal. Fed by RAF cooks, it made all the difference.

Tony had arrived at Gravesend at a crucial moment in the battle. Goering's Luftwaffe was seeking to destroy Fighter Command and in the two weeks preceding his arrival the statistics were giving great concern to Dowding and his Group commanders, particularly Park, commanding 11 Group. Experienced pilots were being lost, injured or killed. And the pilot's individual battle against fatigue was ever present.

Initially Tony put in some 'service training' flights on arrival at 501 Squadron, and was involved in one patrol on 28 August. Early on 30 August he made the flight to the forward base at Hawkinge and on his third patrol of the day contact was made with the enemy and Tony would later commit to his logbook the fact that he had damaged a Dornier 215.

We damaged quite a few Dorniers, but of course when you arrived back people were making claims and I was a very junior pilot. I was more or less pushed to the back. Everyone else was claiming so I thought all I'd put in my logbook was damaged. But I will be honest the more advanced chaps were better pilots than I was. They were experienced pilots and did the claiming. I could have recorded another half a dozen damaged, but never bothered putting them in the logbook as other people were claiming. We would do these attacks, pouring eight machine guns into the enemy, then break away and probably one would go down. One of the senior pilots would claim it. On these sorts of occasions I never made any claims because more senior pilots did more damage than I did. We all fired our guns at the enemy and I may or may not have made hits. I'm not upset that I didn't claim. After all I was very junior.

The Luftwaffe had kept up the pressure on Fighter Command on 30 August with large attacks on airfields in the south-east. 501 Squadron would get amongst the attackers and take its toll, contributing to the Luftwaffe's losses. But the 'Hun' had got through. Notably German bombs had fallen on sector station Biggin Hill, causing considerable death and destruction. Biggin Hill would be hit again during the next two days. Such attacks were striking directly at the sinews of Fighter Command's control system. Below is the 11 Group summary of the raids on Biggin Hill.

30 August 1940: Low level bombing attack. Very serious damage to buildings and equipment. 16 large H.E.s dropped rending workshops, transport yard, stores, barrack stores, armoury guard, meteorological office and station institute completely useless. 'F' type hangar also badly damaged. All power, gas and water mains were severed and all telephone lines running north of the camp were out in three places. Casualties – 39 fatal, 26 injured.

31 August 1940: High level bombing attack. Extensive damage to buildings and hangars. The operations block received a direct hit and caught fire, while the temporary lash up of telephone lines and power cables was completely destroyed. The officers' married quarters and officers' mess were also damaged.

1 September 1940: High level bombing attack. Bombs fell among the camp buildings without doing much further damage, but shaking buildings and making them unsafe. One aircraft was destroyed, but the aerodrome remained serviceable. Practically no buildings were left in a safe condition and the road running through the camp was blocked by 3 large craters. All main service and communications were destroyed. As a result, it was decided to disperse sections in the vicinity of Manston, chiefly because of the damaged buildings which made it necessary to salvage all equipment and transfer it elsewhere.

The resulting disruption led to some improvisation on 501 Squadron's part.

I can remember when Biggin Hill was bombed. We had a pilot Sergeant Crabtree who had been injured, who sat on the control tower roof at Gravesend, with binoculars, and he was directing us as Biggin Hill control was out of operations. He could talk to us and tell us where the Huns were. By that time they were coming over in such large numbers that the sky was black. It looked like thunderclouds – it was fairly easy for him to direct us.

It is interesting to note Tony's use of the word 'Hun', which was in common usage amongst all fighter pilots of that time. The enemy was grouped under a term which had become associated with barbarity and evil. The Hun had started the war, were the aggressors, the violators of international law, the threat to democracy, murderers and criminals. So in the air the men flying the aircraft in the sights of a Spitfire or Hurricane pilot were not in general fellow aviators undergoing similar human stresses and pressure, who may also have started their flying careers because they too were just interested in flying. They were the Hun in Hun machines that had to be knocked out of the sky.

With the Battle of Britain now at its peak a planning conference was held at the headquarters of 11 Group on 30 August, chaired by Keith Park and including all his sector commanders. Park opened the conference.

...by stating that it was the considered opinion of Higher Authority that the enemy must make his attempt at invasion within the next three or four weeks, taking into account factors of weather, economics etc. It was also definitely imperative for the enemy to establish air superiority before attempting such an invasion, which would indicate a continuance and possibly an increase of the present air offensive over this country.

Our object, therefore, for the next month was to prevent the enemy gaining any measure of air superiority, and at the same time and with our present equipment to prevent, as far as possible, his night attacks on our aircraft factories and other vital industries.

Fighter Command was not prepared to relinquish any superiority in the air, maintaining the daily pressure of life or death on the pilots. Tony Pickering's logbook now stands as testament to the intensity of operations during the early days of September 1940. From 31 August to 10 September inclusive, eleven days, he would record twenty-five operational patrols. On the first day of the month Fighter Command airfields were again heavily bombarded. Similarly the next day, which was a day of notable activity for 501 Squadron and Tony Pickering. The first patrol required a 0750 hours take-off, prompted by the presence of the enemy approaching Gravesend. The squadron found its German counterparts in the air but not before a few forty-pound bombs had dropped on the edge of the aerodrome. Two pilots were injured, Sergeant Henn and Pilot Officer Skalski. That afternoon there was another encounter near Ashford and as the squadron diary recorded, 'most pilots engaged the superior forces of the enemy.' Pilot Officer Rose Price was later recorded as missing believed killed, but the squadron would record in its records four destroyed confirmed, four damaged and four probably destroyed. Tony Pickering recalls what it was like operating against the bomber formations at this time.

We did head-on attacks, fired our guns as we went through and then carried straight on. It was get in there, fire your guns and then get out quickly. Some of the more experienced pilots would mingle around a bit. I don't think we had any fear, but we did feel weary at times. We were doing three or four trips a day, sitting by our aircraft for hours.

Invariably we would go in as a squadron, probably three of us in line abreast, in a vic about fifty yards apart. As soon as you had fired your guns and gone through them you'd be split up. Often you would suddenly look around and you wouldn't see any aircraft. Incredible.

You would get through the bombers, tearing along, and

watch for the 109s coming after you. You would manage to get out of their way and lose them, or they would lose you. Then you would circle around and not see an aircraft. Then the CO, Hogan, I recall on virtually every occasion, would call up and say, 'Mandrel Squadron, angels 15', or angels 20 or 25, and he would give you the code name of a place. I would say on about two thirds of the occasions, after going through the bombers, you were able to reform. But it took time and by the time you had got the squadron together again, the Hun was on his way back to France. So very rarely was there a second opportunity. Personally I can't recall ever going back into action again.

Tony also recalls another hazard of operational flying.

I did have problems with my ears once when I was chased by about three Me109s and I had to go into a vertical dive. I came down from about 28,000 feet to 2,000 feet almost vertically. When I got out of the aircraft I was rolling over in agony from my ears, which felt as if they were bursting. I went to the Medical Officer and he had a look and gave me a tablet and said I would be OK. I came close to bursting my eardrums, though.

The 3 and 4 September were relatively quiet for 501 Squadron, although not for other Fighter Command squadrons, but on 5 September the enemy was found again in force as German air power maintained its desire to eliminate British air power. Ordered to patrol over Canterbury, at 0915 hours at 22,000 feet, Me109s and enemy bombers crossed 501 Squadron and Tony Pickering's path. One Me109 was claimed destroyed, one probably destroyed and one damaged. Pilot Officer Skalski fell to German guns and he ended up in Herne Bay hospital. At 1450 hours 501 Squadron was again ordered up, to patrol over Maidstone, returning with a claim of one destroyed, two destroyed but unconfirmed. The squadron diary records pilots returning between 1555 and 1615; Tony landed at 1600 but had little time on the ground. The squadron was ordered up again at 1620 hours. It appears from the diary that the squadron was unable to take off as a unit, rather as pairs or threes as and when they were ready after returning from the previous engagement. However no interceptions were made.

The 6 September saw no let up. In the morning at 0840 Tony and his colleagues were airborne to intercept an enemy formation over Ashford, and the pilots would later report seeing approximately one hundred enemy aircraft ahead of them. One Me109 was later claimed as falling to the guns of 501's Hurricanes. But the squadron suffered severely, Sergeant Adams and Sergeant Houghton were killed and Sergeant Pearson originally recorded as missing believed killed, had indeed lost his life. In the early afternoon 501 was sent to patrol Gravesend but little of note happened and the same could be said of an interception attempted later in the early evening.

When the day battle ended on 6 September, although Fighter Command and its pilots would not be aware, a significant moment had been reached in the battle. The strength of Dowding's force had been steadily drained, a result of the direct campaign against the RAF's fighter pilots, their aircraft, the airfields and the factories in which their weapons were made. Wood and Dempster's *The Narrow Margin* records that from 24 August to 6 September, 295 fighter aircraft were destroyed, 171 seriously damaged. To replace these came 269 Spitfires and Hurricanes. And of course Dowding was losing his airmen, 103 killed or missing, 128 wounded. But what was apparent to the Luftwaffe command was that Fighter Command was still opposing their incursions over England, in force. The impression was forming that Dowding's command was nowhere near the defeat that the Germans thought would be forthcoming, and the requirement for the planned invasion – that is control of English skies – would not be achieved if current tactics were maintained. So pressure in German circles mounted for a change in policy, and those who had always suggested targeting London received greater voice. Indeed when the RAF, in response to a mistaken night bombing of London on 25 August, started to fly over Berlin, the clamour for retaliation rose. Perhaps an attack on London may crack British morale, it was argued. Consequently 7 September was the date the Luftwaffe changed tactics. Londoners were about to suffer. But, and significantly, RAF airfields were also about to receive a much needed respite.

On this momentous day in 1940 Herman Goering broadcast to the German people.

I now want to take this opportunity of speaking to you, to say this moment is a historic one. As a result of the provocative British attacks on Berlin on recent nights the Führer has decided to order a mighty blow to be struck in revenge against the capital of the British Empire. I personally have assumed the leadership of this attack, and today I have heard above me the roaring of the victorious German squadrons which now, for the first time, are driving towards the heart of the enemy in full daylight, accompanied by countless fighter squadrons. Enemy defences were as we expected beaten down and the target reached, and I am certain that our successes have been as massive as the boldness of our plan of attack and the fighting spirit of our crews deserve. In any event this is an historic hour, in which for the first time the German Luftwaffe has struck at the heart of the enemy.

501 Squadron's diary would record conditions during the morning as 'sky cloudless, weather fine', and late morning the pilots would complete an uneventful patrol. At 1600 hours RDF stations began to pick up formations assembling over Calais. Soon it was realised that this was something out of the ordinary. Three hundred bombers with six hundred Me109s and Me110s in support, in two waves, set course for London. It's not surprising, considering the course of the battle to date, that the RAF fighter squadrons were mainly being sent up to cover the sector stations. Because of this the thunder cloud of German

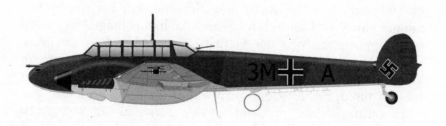

Me110

bombers and their escorts reached London relatively unmolested, to rain down their explosive cargo. Tony would later witness the tribulations of the capital's people and their reaction.

> We would have a day's leave occasionally. The CO, Hogan would say, 'OK, you can go home at 8 o'clock tonight and have 24 hours off. But I want you back tomorrow night, ready for business the next morning.' What impressed me was that at the time London was being bombed – and I always remember travelling through on the underground with my sergeant pilot's uniform on, and seeing all these elderly ladies who were laying on the underground platform, where they had to sleep – they would get up and put their arms around you and kiss you and say, 'Oh wonderful, wonderful you chaps'. I'll always remember those London cockneys, they really felt something for us. I also remember going through Euston station. There was bombing all over the area. But you would see lady volunteers who ran the canteens on the station. They were about seventy to eighty years of age and they gave us cups of tea. We thought we were brave, but these women were doing just as important a job as we were. I have never forgotten those people.

The 7 September afternoon entry recorded by the 501 Squadron diary opens simply with 'At 1640 hours the Squadron took off to intercept the largest formation of the War. Four waves of bombers, each escorted by a strong force of Me109s. The squadron formation was broken up but Flight Lieutenant Gibson damaged a Me110.' Tony landed at 1750 hours from the patrol. Five minutes later he was again airborne, but his twenty-five minute patrol was uneventful. The RAF had managed to put up some opposition, forty-one German aircraft had been cut from the sky, but at a cost of twenty-eight fighters. Numerous German airmen would return and report minimal opposition. Possibly, it was surmised, Fighter Command was at the brink of defeat.

In terms of the previous week's activities 8, 9 and 10 September could be classed as fairly quiet for 501 Squadron and on the afternoon of the tenth the squadron moved to Kenley to give better protection to London. The station provided somewhat different conditions to Gravesend as Tony recalled, 'It was like walking into the Savoy Hotel, the food was marvellous, the accommodation was good, and we were looked after by young eighteen or nineteen-year-old WAAFs – our age!' In the meantime Goering had made the decision that targeting London was indeed the key to success and during daylight and at night the English capital's trial by air bombardment was to continue.

Keith Park, in response to the new tactics of mass raids had ordered that paired squadrons were to be used by controllers if possible, and this would be reflected in the operational activities of 501 Squadron. On 11 September the day started quietly, the lull continuing past midday. Then mid-afternoon attacks developed on London and the Portsmouth – Southampton area. Fighter Command immediately sent up nineteen squadrons in response, one of those being Tony's whose battle experience was about to widen. He was airborne with the squadron (eleven Hurricanes) at 1520 hours to patrol Maidstone. In response to Park's orders 501 Squadron was accompanied by 253 Squadron. A large formation of Heinkels and Dornier 17s were found and the RAF pilots attacked.

> We went in on a head-on attack. I had been firing my guns at the bombers as they were approaching. A bomber came into my sights and I pressed my gun button. I suddenly felt a horrible bang. The front gunners of the bombers were all firing at us and somebody had hit me and destroyed my sump. The oil pressure fell immediately. I turned over and came down vertically away from the bombers, we were at about 18,000 feet. We were just south of London at the time, over Kent, approaching the city. I knew where I was and it was a clear, beautiful day. 'This aircraft's had it', went through my mind. So I switched off the fuel, I didn't want any coming into the engine, and switched off my ignition switches. Nothing was going into the carburettors. I did not want to catch fire. I looked out and below and I could see Kenley aerodrome. I decided to opt for a force-landing, which we had been taught to do without an engine. Apart from the sump being shot away the aircraft was fully controllable, although smoke was pouring from out of the engine. I got down to about 3,000 feet and I was just thinking about getting my wheels down, which you could pump down in an emergency, or blow down with a gas bottle. Anyway I didn't get as far as that because flames suddenly appeared from the engine. Something ignited and

suddenly there were flames all down the side of the cockpit. I was out in about two seconds flat. My cockpit was already open. All I had to do was pull the pin on my harness and just stand up. As soon as my head was clear, above the cockpit cover, the slipstream pulled me out. I pulled the parachute cord and landed safely in the guards depot at Caterham. I was picked up by two Irish guardsmen. I had no badge of rank on, just a shirt and a pair of slacks and my Mae West. I don't think they had seen my aircraft crash as they approached me with their rifles, and bayonets. I identified myself but they were a bit suspicious. They took me to their CO, a colonel, with a black patch over his eye. He took me into the officers mess and gave me a couple of whiskies. Then he arranged for a car to take me back to Kenley.

Tony's downed Hurricane was one of twenty-nine RAF losses that day (seventeen pilots had been killed, six wounded), which exceeded the German losses of twenty-five for the entire day.

Tony was not back on operations until 16 September. In the period he was non-operational the most important events took place on 15 September with heavy attacks directed on London. That day 501 Squadron's morning engagements with Do17s and Me109s yielded a claim of three enemy aircraft destroyed, three probables and one damaged at a cost of Squadron Leader Hogan, who managed to bale out unhurt, and Belgian Pilot Officer Van den Hove d'Erstenrijck who had only arrived at the squadron the day before, lost his life. His Hurricane had been hit in the cooling system, subsequently exploding at 200 feet. In the afternoon 501 was again thrown into the midst of the battle and 'dogfights ensued again', the squadron returning two enemy aircraft destroyed for no loss.

At the end of the day the score sheet provided a terrific boost to the morale of the nation as a whole. One hundred and eighty-five German aircraft were claimed shot down, the news filling the front pages of national newspapers. Subsequent historical investigation since reduced this to an actual loss of sixty. Even so these losses were deemed excessive by the Germans and were further proof that Fighter Command was maintaining its defensive potency. Goering would instruct his airmen to return to a policy of defeating Fighter Command directly. Whilst still targeting London, smaller bomber formations would have considerable fighter escort with a view to taking as many of Fighter Com-mand's pilots and aircraft out of the battle as possible, although mass formations could still be used in good weather and the aircraft industry would remain on the target lists.

The heat of battle died off on 16 September but the next day 501 Squadron's Sergeants Ginger Lacey and Eddie Egan fell during an afternoon engagement with Me109s.

I was quite friendly with Eddie Egan. We were both about the same age. We liked music and liked going out to have a quiet drink together. Perhaps walk back with a couple of WAAFs. I was a country lad. My life consisted of ringing church bells and studying hard as an apprentice to get qualified. I had a quiet life and came from a family who were quiet. We didn't go round trying to impress our neighbours and Eddie was very much like me.

On 17 September we had been attacking bombers and Eddie and I, as usual, went straight through. Diving through them, firing our guns all the way. They were so closely packed it was strange that we did not collide with them. Eddie and I were together and we were waiting for orders from Hogan, to get back together as a squadron. Four Me109s came up from behind and picked Eddie off. Why him and not me I don't know. Eddie went down in flames. I pulled up towards them and they just pulled their sticks back and disappeared. Eddie didn't bale out and I saw him hit the ground in a wood. When I got back the CO asked, 'How's everybody? What happened?' I told them what had happened to Eddie, where he went in, which was recorded by the Intelligence Officer. About three months after this I was asked again what had happened because they hadn't found Eddie. Then a year later I was asked yet again. They still hadn't found him. We were getting casualties then. I realised I had a job to do and got on with it. You just had to do that.

The whereabouts of Eddie Egan remained a mystery for just over thirty-six years until the remnants of a buried Hurricane, which contained the remains of a pilot, was discovered in September 1976, in a wood at Bethersden, Kent. Also discovered was a parachute pack holed by 7.9 mm bullets. Further investigation suggested that the remains were in fact those of Eddie Egan. The

Coroner accepted this, but the Ministry of Defence did not. As such the remains of 'an unknown airman' were interred at Brookwood Military Cemetery, with Eddie Egan's relatives in attendance. In November 1979 a further investigation of the crash site unearthed the Hurricane's identity plate. Now with irrefutable evidence that the remains must have been those of Eddie Egan, the headstone at Brookwood was replaced and Eddie's sister made an addition to the basic inscription on the headstone, 'In Treasured Memory of a Much Loved One of the Few.'

More 501 Squadron airmen fell on 18 September, Sergeant Saward and Squadron Leader Hogan, both men managing to bale out. As Tony Pickering recalled, 'We certainly knew we were taking punishment, and we were getting tired. But I don't think we thought for one minute that we were going to lose. Typically British. And we did have a good CO.'

From 19 to 26 September there were further engagements, but nothing like on the scale of those in the first half of September. During this time 501 was brought back up to strength as new pilots came in. However the massive pressure placed on the pilots remained, Tony Pickering's experience being typical. During the fifteen days leading to 30 September, he carried out twenty-four operational patrols. Three of these days involved three patrols and on one day, 24 September, he flew four.

At dawn on 27 September 501 Squadron was placed on fifteen minutes availability up to 0900, then along with the Hurricanes of 253 Squadron twelve of 501 Squadron, including Tony Pickering, took off and gained 15,000 feet to counter a reported fifteen enemy bombers. An estimated twenty Me110s appeared. One was claimed destroyed and Sergeant Ekins was forced to bale out, ending up in Sevenoaks hospital. At 1115, an hour after returning from the previous patrol, Tony was again in action with his squadron. Me109s engaged the squadron as they were attacking Dornier 17s. Two Me109s were claimed destroyed and one Do17 damaged. Pilot Officer Gunter lost his life, his parachute failing to open after baling out. Whilst the enemy was sighted on a further patrol in the afternoon, no interception took place.

On 27 September Tony recalled being involved in the shooting down of a Me110 probably destroyed.

We were attacking Me110s head on. One peeled off with

smoke pouring out of him and went down. I was then attacked by Me109s, which were sitting up above and I had to go onto the defensive. I couldn't stop and look. So all I could claim was a probable. We damaged quite a few. You would be putting a few rounds into these bombers and bits and pieces would fly off. Three or four of your chums would be doing the same. Those with more experience than me claimed them.

27 September went down as another momentous day; Churchill would place it with 15 September and 15 August, 'as the third great and victorious day' for Fighter Command in the Battle of Britain. Fifty-five German aircraft were not to return to their units that day, against twenty-eight Fighter Command losses.

There was considerable action for 501 Squadron again on 28 September, twelve pilots, including Tony Pickering, taking off at 1000, alongside 605 Squadron. Me109s engaged the RAF pilots and dogfights broke out. Pilot Officer Rogers survived after baling out. Pilot Officer Harrold, who had arrived at the squadron on 26 September, lost his life. Pilot Officer Jones crashed on landing, without injury. A further engagement that afternoon fortunately resulted in no losses, with no claims. An engagement with Me109s on 29 September passed without loss either. Then 30 September saw further patrols. Flying Officer Barry force-landed at Penbury and Sergeant Farnes came across a Ju88, from which white smoke was already billowing. He sent the enemy aircraft in to the earth near Gatwick. By the end of the month Tony's squadron had lost twenty-two Hurricanes and eleven pilots killed or wounded. 501 Squadron, like many others that summer was certainly subject to the stresses of the intensity of battle.

I do remember around the end of September, early October that AVM Park must have made a decision to put an awful lot of aircraft into the air. We were getting weary and most of the chaps were feeling tired. There was talk amongst the sergeant pilots about wishing we could get to bed earlier. Up until this time we had either been airborne with another squadron or on our own. But on this occasion Park decided to put about twelve squadrons up together and he flew us up and down the railway line between Ashford and somewhere near Croydon. A long straight stretch of railway, which we had often patrolled. It was a beautiful late Saturday evening, you could see for miles and there wasn't a Hun that came anywhere near us. All you could see was a squadron of Hurricanes here and a squadron of Spitfires there. A squadron above you. A squadron below you. The morale of the pilots, I don't suppose Park ever realised it, leapt up when we realised we were still in command of the sky. It absolutely amazed me and my morale went up one hundred percent. I have never forgotten that incident.

Of course there were also other tried and tested ways to boost morale.

There hadn't been much socialising at Gravesend because we would be flying then a meal and then it was time to get your head down because you would be up again early the next morning. When we got to Kenley in September, and then into October, the nights came in and we were day fighters. So we weren't starting quite so early and we finished earlier at night. So we'd go down to the pub. The girls would come with us, the WAAFs. They were great. Kenley had been bombed, as had Biggin Hill. We were off the ground, but those girls had to take the bombing. Being a sergeant pilot, of course, I was allowed to mix with them. Discipline was such that the officers were not allowed to mix with other ranks. That's where I had one up on the officer pilots like Ken Lee. As a pilot officer he had to mix with WAAF officers. There were one or two nice WAAF officers but there weren't many, very few in actual fact. Most of them were comparatively elderly. But ours were young and we sergeant pilots mixed with them quite freely.

The start of October brought about a major change in the nature of Luftwaffe operations. 1,653 aircraft had been lost since the opening of the Battle of Britain, but to what end? Air superiority had not been achieved and postponement after postponement of the invasion had resulted. A bloodied Fighter Command had stood resolute against the onslaught. Goering, preserving his bomber forces for the night offensive, switched mainly to deploying fighter-bombers at height in the daylight hours.

The first day of the month is notable for a change in tactics for 501 Squadron. On an afternoon patrol Me109s were sighted but an instruction to look out for bombers prevented an attack, and the squadron diary recorded that, 'on this occasion the squadron flew in pairs for the first time.'

> I was still a sergeant pilot and we were not in conversation with the flight commanders and the squadron commander. By September time we weren't flying much after seven o'clock. In the evening the officers would get together in the officers' mess and talk tactics. But as sergeants we were kept away from the discussions. There was no class distinction or anything like that. But the sergeants were kept in the dark, you just weren't in with the discussion with the officers.

There were only minor engagements, and poor weather, over the next three days. But there was further action on the morning of 5 October. Eleven Hurricanes took to the sky at 1115 in company with 253 Squadron. Ten Me109s, from 20,000 feet came down to meet them. Two of these fell to the Hurricanes' guns and one was damaged. Poor weather curtailed any flying on 6 October. On the morning of 7 October approximately twelve Me109s were engaged north-west of Ashford, with one claimed shot down and Flying Officer Barry killed. That afternoon, with 605 Squadron, Me109s were again engaged, two claimed destroyed, one probable. Pilot Officer Mackenzie then found more Me109s and attacked from the rear. Damaging one Me109 he then, 'forced it into the sea by ramming its tail with his wing tip.' He was then attacked and with no ammunition all he could do was evade, force-landing badly shot-up just north of Folkestone. By now the German bombers were transferring their focus to night time. Me109s started to carry bombs in daylight, which Tony reckoned, 'was most unfair. We RAF fighter pilots did not involve ourselves in bombs until later in the war.'

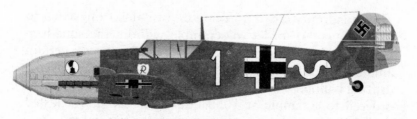

Me109

Over the next four days the 501 Squadron diary recorded little activity of note in terms of engagements. What is worth noting however is the way the entries reflect the change in Luftwaffe tactics. Single enemy bombers are reported or small formations of Me109s. On 12 October, numerous small engagements resulted in some German aircraft failing to return to France.

The 13 and 14 October saw little action, but Me109s were again engaged on 15 October. One claimed shot down for the loss of one pilot, Sergeant Fenemore, killed and one pilot Sergeant Jarrett wounded and Pilot Officer Dafforn landed at Rochester with glycol damage. On 17 October during one patrol, whilst at 25,000 feet, the 501 Squadron pilots saw two enemy formations at 30,000 feet. That evening a stick of bombs was dropped on the aerodrome damaging five Hurricanes.

From 18 to 24 October enemy incursions, what there were, remained elusive and poor weather curtailed operational activity. Tony Pickering had taken part in patrols on 18 and 20 October, but he would not be in the air again operationally until 28 October. Meanwhile his squadron colleagues had duties to perform fighting Me109s. On 25 October the enemy was at last found. At 1111 hours 501 Squadron was airborne patrolling base, climbing to 25,000 feet. Twelve Me109s were seen and two were claimed. That afternoon a further patrol led to the downing of another two Me109s. But a collision between Pilot Officer Mackenzie and Pilot Officer Goth resulted in the latter's death, Mackenzie successfully baling out. The next day a further Me109 was claimed and one damaged. And on 27 October yet another Me109 fell to a 501 Squadron Hurricane's guns.

28 October proved uneventful but the following day would bring the 501 Squadron pilots and their Luftwaffe adversaries together again, but not until the afternoon. The day started fairly uneventfully for 501, as recorded by the squadron ORB:

The squadron were at 15 minutes available from dawn to 0840 hours. An order to scramble without the squadron being called to readiness was received. This caused a certain amount of confusion and delay. Sergeant Lacey destroyed a drifting balloon which fell into the sea. The squadron were ordered to scramble at 1050 hours and the patrol lasted until 1200 hours, but no enemy aircraft were sighted.

However the Luftwaffe presence over south-east England was about to grow again. Early in the afternoon RDF reported twenty plus enemy aircraft at 26,000 feet ten miles north-west of Le Havre. This was later surmised to be an enemy fighter sweep to the Portsmouth area. A similar raid would develop later in the day, both raids believed to be diversions for raids developing to the east in the early evening. At 1415 hours 145 and 213 Squadrons were ordered to take position 20,000 feet over Tangmere and then to intercept the raid. 501 Squadron along with 253 Squadron, then on patrol in the Biggin Hill area, at 1444 hours were also ordered to reinforce their Tangmere colleagues and intercept the raid. The enemy proved elusive for 501 Squadron and the other squadrons did not fair much better. 501 Squadron returned to Kenley, but shortly afterwards its services would be called upon again.

At 1601 hours RDF picked up the first plot of an enemy build-up over the Pas de Calais coast. RDF and the Observer Corps information led to eight raid plots being kept. As it turned out, approximately 200 enemy aircraft were to cross the channel in three waves. The first wave of about thirty enemy aircraft crossed the English coast at North Foreland at 1624 hours, followed by a further twenty enemy aircraft which traversed the Thames estuary. Some penetrated to North Weald, which was dive-bombed. The second wave came no further inland than the Dover-Deal area. The third wave, which included some Italian aircraft, headed for Biggin Hill.

The information coming in from RDF and the Observer Corps was processed and filtered and 11 Group responded accordingly. The deployments are detailed below, providing an example of the use of Park's new pairing tactics.

1607 hours: 17 and 46 Squadrons are sent to patrol North Weald, and twelve minutes later to proceed to the Maidstone patrol line at 25,000 feet.
1615 hours: 501 and 253 Squadrons are ordered to patrol Brooklands at 15,000 feet, and fifteen minutes later to patrol Biggin Hill patrol line.
1621 hours: 222 and 92 Squadron are sent to patrol Hornchurch at 15,000 feet.
1626 hours: 74 Squadron are ordered to patrol Biggin Hill to protect the airfield.

1631 hours: 229 Squadron are ordered to patrol Northolt.
1636 hours: 249 and 257 Squadrons are ordered to patrol over North Weald at 15,000 feet to protect the airfield.
1711 hours: 41 and 603 Squadrons are ordered to patrol Rochford at 20,000 feet. .

11 Group also requested 12 Group squadrons to patrol Maidstone-Sheerness and then to counter the raids that were droning over the Thames estuary on the way to North Weald.

Park had positioned his pilots and their weapons to meet the penetrations. He had however left his eastern flank exposed somewhat, but he had put in a call to 12 Group for support.

The 11 Group summary of the fighter squadrons' action that evening is somewhat critical of 12 Group's contribution. An inability to make R/T communication with the Duxford Wing resulted in a failure to intercept the enemy raids heading for North Weald, although 11 Group squadrons met the attackers on their return.

Park's controllers had marshalled his squadrons well and many of the 11 Group squadrons did engage the enemy. 501 and 253 Squadron were airborne at 1623 hours and 1630 hours respectively, and they too found the enemy. Tony Pickering was prepared for combat, as his report testifies:

Time attack was delivered – 1715 hours
Place attack was delivered – Cranbrook
Height of enemy – 10,000 feet
Number of rounds fired – 2,400
We were vectored onto 2 waves of enemy aircraft at 23,000 feet, which seemed to be engaged by Spitfires. I heeled off after one Me109 but he easily outdived me and I lost him before I could get within range. I circled around for ten minutes at 10,000 feet looking for the squadron, when I saw 2 Ju88s at 12,000 feet going east over Tonbridge. I climbed to attack but could not get within 800 yards and they were steadily drawing away from me.

Tony now carries on the story:

I had been chasing some Ju88s by myself. I had my throttle fully open and almost bent double, up to the stop and then bent. Trying to get a bit of extra power. Stupid really. These two Ju88s still went away from me with at least 50 mph to

Ken 'Hawkeye' Lee

Left: Ken Lee stands with a Tiger Moth, January 1937.

Middle: 111 Squadron Hurricane IIs, with fix pitch two-blade airscrews, February 1939.

Bottom left: At Filton during the phoney war, October 1939.

Bottom right: 501 Squadron billets at Anglure, France. Left to right: Pilot Officer Hairs, Pilot Officer Cridland, unknown, Flight Lieutenant Griffiths, Flying Officer Malfroy, Pilot Officer Lee, Pilot Officer Holden.

NB: All photographs are from the relevant pilots' collections except where stated.

Top: A Flight 219 Squadron, RAF Catterick, 15 August 1940. Terry Clark standing fourth from right, Dudley Hobbis sitting third from left. In the background is a Blenheim IF.

Bottom: Terry Clark's logbook showing his successful flight with Wing Commander Pike on the night of 16/17 April 1941. *(Steve Darlow)*

Top: 488 NZ Squadron, Bradwell Bay, May 1943. Doug Robinson third from left seated. Terry Clark standing behind.

Bottom left: Terry at Bradwell Bay in the summer of 1943, ready for the night flying test with 488 NZ Squadron.

Bottom right: Terry Clark DFM 1943.

Top left: Terry pictured bottom right at RAF Epinoy, April 1945. Cheers.

Top right: In the foreground at the No.1 GCA unit – RAF Prestwick. Late summer 1945.

Bottom: Memorials like the one at Capel-le-Ferne Kent keep the memory of the Battle of Britain alive. *(Steve Darlow)*

spare. It absolutely amazed me, they were so fast, my poor old Hurricane couldn't keep up. After a while I gave up, they just disappeared.

He then saw on his starboard side and about mile in front an aircraft which proved to be an Me109. 'I thought, right, you're not going to shoot me down chum.'
Tony's combat report stated:

I closed in to 300 yards and saw it was yellow with large black crosses on the upper surface of the wings. I immediately opened fire from dead astern and he went into a dive turning and twisting to evade my fire. I followed him down firing short bursts all the time and when he was at about 500 feet diving towards the ground I gave him my last bursts which set fire to his starboard petrol tank and he dived into the ground at the corner of a wood and immediately blew up. The pilot did not bale out. The aircraft crashed at Ham Street approximately 15 miles North West of Dungeness.

It may be interesting to note the use of the term short burst, frequently used in combat reports. This short burst of course meant unleashing eight machine guns to spray the air ahead with metal, each piece of which could kill a man. Behind the basic language of the combat report lies the ferocity of a life and death struggle.

The only thing he could have done was open his taps and get away quickly, but I think I had some height on him. If you've got height, you've got speed. He tried to swerve, but never tried to out turn me. Perhaps he was running short of fuel, so wasn't able to start any combat flying. He probably wanted to get back to the channel fairly quickly. Nevertheless he went in. Whether he got out, I don't know.

Tony felt no compassion for his fallen adversary, 'A lot of my chums were being shot down, so that was that really.' The entire day had been successful for Fighter Command, nineteen enemy aircraft accounted for against a loss of seven.

The 30 October brought more combat, two Me109s claimed destroyed, one probable, 'our own casualties were nil'. October fizzled out with an uneventful day.

The last day of October is now officially recognised as the end of the Battle of Britain. The strain on Fighter Command had been immense but the enemy air force had been kept from its goal. 501 Squadron pilots had certainly played their part, made their sacrifices, eighteen pilots had been killed, and claimed their successes. At the time they were not to know that the daylight Battle of Britain was effectively over. However it was certainly apparent that there was a lessening of enemy activity in the shorter days of November. The main requirements placed upon Fighter Command's day fighters was about to change, moving from defensive to offensive. Before Tony Pickering would make his own personal contribution to these offensive operations, he had other duties to perform.

Chapter 6

A Mention in Despatches

Tony Pickering carried out ten operational patrols in the first week of November 1940, the fifth being the most intense, comprising three sorties. Following a solitary patrol on 8 November, his services would not be required again until 17 November and until the end of the month he undertook only five more operations. December followed much the same pattern, with nine patrols in the first twelve days.

On 19 December Tony was posted from 501 Squadron to 601 Squadron at Northolt where he saw out December with some squadron formation practice.

> 501 Squadron moved from Kenley to Filton. I was on leave at the time, a few days. The assignment then was to protect Bristol but 601 Squadron at Northolt asked 11 Group if they could have some pilots from 501 Squadron to reinforce them. The CO, in his wisdom or otherwise, decided that Tony Pickering and a couple of others should be transferred.
>
> They picked three sergeant pilots, they didn't send any officers. Some of the officers I'm sure would have told the CO they weren't going! But we had to. I know what went on, if we had to make a transfer, because I became a flight commander and carried out similar procedures.

There were only two entries in Tony's logbook for January, some further formation practice. In February he would complete just two further flights. His last was as an escort to Blenheims on 2 February, and on 13 February he left, posted to the Maintenance

Wing 57 Operational Training Unit. His first flight was on 16 February, 'experience on type' – airborne in a Spitfire.

> I was pleased. I think I had had enough. I was lucky because just before I was transferred I had a very bad dose of influenza and went on a trip over France. It was February and it was cold in the Hurricane and we struggled along. I felt terrible but being a young lad I hadn't wanted to say to the flight commander, 'I can't go on this trip sir, I don't feel well.' You were scared to do things like that in case they thought you were a coward. So I went on the trip and I felt so terrible. When I got back I went to see the doctor. He stuck a thermometer in my mouth, recorded a temperature of 104 and sent me to bed for a week.
>
> Subsequent to this they decided I should have a rest so they sent me to be a test pilot. It was certainly something new as here I was climbing into Spitfires. The Hurricane was a good old steady horse, worked hard, could take a lot of punishment. Whereas the Spitfire was like a racehorse, could flash past the post.

Over the course of the next year Tony's logbook filled up with records of his many flights, mainly testing aircraft, 675 flights in all (107 in each of April and June) and 335.50 hours (154.20 hours on Spitfires, 2.30 hours on Hurricanes, 78.35 hours on Masters, 51.45 hours on Magisters, 6.25 hours on Tiger Moths and 42.15 hours on Fairey Battles).

> These were repaired aircraft, such as ones that had landed with their wheels up. It wasn't uncommon for an under-training pilot at the operational training unit to land his aircraft forgetting to put his wheels down. In fact they put a man at the end of the runway with a Verey pistol and if the fellow was coming in with his undercarriage up they would fire off a red light at him.
>
> I enjoyed my time there. Certain things happened but I never had to bale out. I had to land a Spitfire on one wheel on occasions, instead of landing on the runway I landed on the grass alongside. That was exciting because there would be a crash wagon waiting to put the aircraft out if it caught fire, and an ambulance to put me in if I crashed. You'd see them there as you were coming in to land, waiting. I

disappointed them all the time thank goodness.

Tony now became a pilot officer, and as the establishment for this specific test pilot job was a sergeant pilot, new duties were on the horizon. He now completed a course at Central Flying School Upavon, flying Masters, carrying out the Chief Flying Instructor test on 13 March with Wing Commander Donaldson and receiving an average assessment as a flying instructor with the added comment, 'should make a useful instructor, v. keen'. Over the course of the next year Tony imparted his experience to the new pilots who came through 57 OTU, and he certainly seemed to enjoy his time there.

> When trainees arrived they had never flown a Spitfire before, so before they did I had to take them up and make sure they could land a Miles Master. So it was two or three hours in a Master and then off in a Spitfire. They were good, about half had been in the ATC [Air Training Corps] and were trained with good discipline. We had no problem with them.
>
> I really enjoyed flying the Spitfire. Sometimes you could take off by yourself, and if you felt like going up to about 35,000 feet on a lovely day you could. In those days you could burn the petrol, nobody seemed to worry and I wasn't paying for it.

Included in this was a four-week course at the Central Gunnery School, Sutton Bridge, from which Tony was assessed as 'above the average', as a marksman air-to-ground, on a drogue, in combat, and as an instructor.

On 19 February 1943 he was posted to 131 Squadron, Castletown as a flight commander, B Flight.

> I knew I was due to go back to operations. I had been made an acting flight lieutenant at the OTU and the wing commander arranged a position as a flight commander. I had at least two sergeant pilots in my flight, who had flown in the Battle of Britain. I made sure they got their commissions.

One noticeable requirement for Tony after a couple of months at the squadron was to practice landing his aircraft on a ship. In the Mediterranean preparations were underway for the seaborne invasion of Sicily, and a call may be made on the pilots in the United Kingdom to transfer if necessitated by losses. Early in April Tony practiced deck landings (on land) in a Spitfire. He then moved to Fleet Air Arm Station Machrihanish managing to get three flights in a Seafire prior to a test on his abilities on 13 April. A note in his logbook recorded the outcome, 'This is to certify that Flight Lieutenant T G Pickering has completed four deck landings with an assessment on HMS *Argus* – above average.' As it was however his assistance in the Mediterranean was not required, and much of May and June was taken up with training flights and a move to Exeter at the end of June.

In 1943 the Allies were in no position to open a land front in the West. But the sky provided the theatre in which the enemy could be engaged. Indeed such a battle was necessary in order to gain the air superiority which would be paramount to the success of the Allied entry into Western Europe through Normandy in 1944. The American bomber forces based in England, whose numbers were steadily growing, were gradually extending their reach in daylight, penetrating into Germany, and demanding an answer from the enemy air force. However, their heavy losses on deep unescorted flights emphasised the need for fighter accompaniment. This both the RAF and United States American Air Force would provide.

Tony's squadron would be one of the RAF squadrons employed in supporting the daylight air offensive over Western Europe. From July he would play his part in such escort duties. Over the course of the next seven months Tony would participate in eleven Rodeos (fighter sweeps into enemy airspace), a considerable number of Circus's (escorting bombers into enemy airspace) and Ramrods (attacking enemy land targets), two Rhubarbs (operating in small formations in enemy airspace, acting freelance) and one Roadstead (attacking enemy shipping at low level). With respect to these operations Tony would receive a Mention in Despatches.

> We were flying Spitfire Vs and most of our trips were made escorting bombers; American Marauders, Mitchells, Fortresses and Liberators, bombing the ports on the Bay of Biscay.
>
> The enemy didn't attack us. Our friend the Führer was engaged with Russia and had taken a lot of his squadrons

from France to Russia. So there weren't so many of the Luftwaffe in France as there had been earlier, by any means. And they didn't want to mix it with us. We, the Spit Vs flew close escort to the bombers. About three or four miles away. You didn't get too close to American bombers for obvious reasons. Above us Johnnie Johnson with his Canadians, had his Spit IXs, operating from Kenley. Any Me109s or FW190s that appeared were chased away by Johnson and his crowd, which were about 50 miles an hour faster than we were. So we didn't see a lot of action.

Some extracts from the 131 Squadron diary give an indication of the nature of operations at this time.

3 August 1943: At 1925 hours the Exeter wing took part in 10 Group Circus No. 49. They were acting as part of the target cover for Whirlwind bombers attacking Brest/Guipavas aerodrome. The wing flew in three groups of 8 aircraft arriving over the target area at 2027 hours, stepped up from 10 to 14,000 feet. They orbited for a few minutes while the Whirlwinds went in and bombed, and then started back home. About 8-10 FW190s and at least 23 Me109s were encountered on the way back between the target and 10 miles out to sea. Individual combats resulted during which F/S Parry probably destroyed 1 FW190. It was last seen going down steeply at 500 feet with much black smoke coming from it after having been hit on three occasions by bursts from the Spitfire's cannon and m.g. Also 5 FW190s were damaged by the CO, P/O Luckhoff (2), F/S Turnbull and F/S Tate. But against these claims, gratifying as they are, has to be set the sad loss of F/O E Smith (Australia).

11 November 1943: The big item of the day was 11 Group Ramrod No. 311 in which 162 Marauders were bombing a 'hush hush' target at Martinvet, a few miles inland from Cherbourg. 3 separate formations of bombers went in at 5 minute intervals. The Church Stanton Wing was part of the second fighter 'umbrella' of seven Spitfire Squadrons. They were airborne at 1200 hours, arrived in the target area at 1230 and patrolled Pte de Barfleur – target – Cap de la Hague at 20,000 feet for 20 minutes until the last of the bombers had left. Enemy reaction was negligible – no fighter and little flak – and the whole formation of 162 bombers and fighters returned safely.

An entry in Tony's logbook following his last flight at 131 Squadron on 7 January 1944 records, 'off for a rest from flying duties after 4½ years continuous flying'. His operational flying career had come to an end. The squadron ORB recorded:

F/L Pickering 'B' Flight Commander is posted to Exeter for Controllers duties. He joined the squadron 11 months ago, when he commenced his second tour of ops. He was an experienced fighter pilot and a good instructor who organised his flight extremely well. He was popular with the whole squadron and will be missed by all who came in contact with him.

Tony then spent a relatively short time in hospital, having his tonsils out.

Which was quite a serious operation in those days. Then they decided I should be a sector gunnery officer at Exeter. I had been on a gunnery course, and had received a good assessment. I had completed two tours, and in those days it was considered that you had done your operational flying.

Subsequent to this Tony took up duties as a controller on 4 December 1944 at Exeter and then on 10 February 1945 at Colerne. He then received a posting to the Middle East and the gunnery school at RAF El Ballah.

616 Squadron were flying Meteors from Colerne. The wing commander, an intimate friend and comrade, was a man called Watts, whom I had met as a fighter pilot early in the war, and I also knew one of the flight commanders. We used to meet in the officers' mess at Colerne. They said to me, 'Pick, do you want to come back [onto operations] and fly Meteors?' I reminded them that Fighter Command had issued an instruction to all stations that no one was to use any influence to get on this first jet squadron. The old pals act was out! If found doing this then severe disciplinary action would be taken. Anyway Wing Commander Watts said, 'I can get you on Pick, don't worry. Come and fly Meteors with us.' It was like offering somebody gold, to get onto this Meteor squadron. Everyone wanted to. So I

agreed. It would have meant a third tour but I wanted to fly Meteors. Within forty-eight hours of Wing Commander Watts saying he could get me on, I got a call from the adjutant of the station, a WAAF officer, who said, 'Flight Lieutenant Pickering, you are posted out to Egypt.' Why was I posted? No reason was given.

When I arrived in Cairo I was asked what I was doing there. I said I didn't know, I had been posted. They said, 'Well we didn't know you were coming. What are you? A fighter pilot?' I replied, 'Yes, done two tours.' I was told I wasn't wanted and that I was to be sent up to the Eastern Mediterranean Air Force at Alexandria.

After a train journey the next day I reported to a WAAF officer and was asked, 'What are you doing here?' I said, 'I don't know.' She said, 'What were you doing in England?' I replied, 'I am an ex fighter pilot.' 'Oh', she said, 'that's fine. In the office at the end is Wing Commander Proctor.' 'Wing Commander Proctor!' I exclaimed. 'Yes', she said, 'he looks after all the fighter pilots. Go and have a word with him. He might find a job for you.' I went to see Proctor and he looked at me and I looked at him. He said, 'We've met before haven't we.' I said, 'Yes we have.' He was the 32 Squadron flight commander I first flew with at Biggin Hill, sitting on his tail with the gun button off. He got me a job at El Ballah, where I finished the war, training people on Hurricanes and Spitfires, gunnery and dropping bombs and firing rockets.

There was an air war going on over Italy and here was Tony Pickering sent out to Cairo, nobody knew I was coming. But, although no reason was given, I have a feeling I know why I was sent out there. My friends at Colerne were outgunned by Fighter Command.

Tony stayed at RAF El Ballah until November 1945. An assessment of his abilities on 25 June 1945 records his development as a fighter pilot as 'exceptional'. He then left the RAF and embarked upon a successful career in engineering, designing and then selling steam turbines, which would take him all round the world. Now retired and living in Rugby with his second wife Christine, sixty-six years on from the events of 1940 Tony recalls his postwar feelings about being involved in the

Battle of Britain, and how those momentous events should be remembered.

We who had taken part and were civilians really, forgot about the Battle of Britain for a few years. I didn't realise how important it was as I was so involved in educating myself as an engineer and securing a position. That was most important in my life, I had a wife and son and a daughter followed later and I was much more interested in getting my life organised.

The press have played their part in promoting the Battle of Britain, and the publishing companies. Over the last twenty years, since I have been retired, I have been very much involved.

I was very young and played a most insignificant part probably. Nevertheless we were there and youngsters of my age group came forward and took part in the battle and kept the Hun at bay. People should remember that a lot of people lost their lives, killed in the bombing of London, and the aerodromes. It wasn't just about the pilots. There were also the fitters and the armourers who kept us in the air. Whenever we go to dinners I can assure you every member of the Battle of Britain Fighter Association will always say it was down to the people who kept us in the air. The WAAFs in particular, the young girls who did a magnificent job. We just flew the aeroplanes. They were the ones that got bombed, we didn't. We certainly do appreciate that we were part of a team. There were one or two pilots who made a name for themselves. They were that kind of a person. There were others who did their little part, like myself. We kept the ball rolling. We as fighter pilots also remember the heavy losses suffered by Bomber Command and other services serving our country 1939 to 1945. We don't want any glamour. We did our best.

Wing Commander Peter Olver DFC

Chapter 7

The Value of Experience

As a child Audrey Middlemas, living in Mitcham, Surrey, witnessed the Battle of Britain, 'and I'll never forget it, never...'

We watched the German planes come over and the Spitfires would go up, outnumbered to no end they were, but they'd go out up there, fighting and my brother would say 'You are not going to send me to Canada and miss all this!' You weren't sort of thinking about the pilots in the planes and that people would die. To him I suppose it was just an exciting game. But it was the 'Battle of Britain', when the outnumbered Spitfire pilots saw off the Germans.[8]

There could not be anything much more perilous for a pilot, during the air war in Europe, than his first engagements with the enemy during the Battle of Britain. Inexperience accounted for many a combat-fresh pilot. And if lack of experience was combined with bravado, the already small odds against surviving diminished considerably. Peter Olver would enter the main air battle in October 1940, and his experience, or lack of it, would provide a case in point.

> I was shot down on my first engagement, which was the best thing that ever happened to me. It really taught me a lot. I wanted to be good and I kept getting above average assessments. But that didn't make much difference to a German. They had had experience, in Spain, which we had not. True Spain wasn't much of a battle for them but it meant they had *some* battle experience. I got all my battle experience in that one business of being shot down.

Peter was born in Leamington Spa on 4 April 1917. There were two things in life that grabbed his imagination as a young man, 'I wanted to be a stockman. I thought God had given me a special arrangement with livestock. Then when the war came along I wanted to be a fighter pilot. I think everybody wanted to. I wanted to fly.'

As the situation in Europe worsened Peter was living in digs in Derby, working in the electricity industry and whilst there he joined the Royal Air Force Volunteer Reserve.

> There was a great big notice in the post office saying join the Derby VR, which was wrong, it should have been the Nottingham one there. When I pointed this out to them they were quite upset. Anyway I couldn't get in for a long time and there was a tremendous waiting list, thousands from the Rolls-Royce works who were pretty good mechanics.

Peter aspired to be at the controls of an aircraft, 'I wasn't prepared to do anything else. I wanted to fly a Spitfire.' But his youthful enthusiasm met with frustration.

You just couldn't get a trip for flying. All they did was get you to clear up after people had been sick in the machine. If you got a trip you were lucky. There were too many people and not enough machines. I really was as keen as hell.

He had been in the air before the war, in a Tiger Moth, 'a ten bob ride in a ropey old aeroplane tied up with string.' Late in 1939, having been called up just before war began, Peter started accumulating hours on less ropey Tiger Moths and really began to enjoy the experience, although his first dual flight was not so enjoyable, 'The chap I was with put it into a spin and I could see a bloody great stone on the ground. I thought we were bound to hit it.'

Peter's training took him from Initial Training Wing to Elementary Flying Training School and then to Cambridge in early 1940, and Marshall's flying school where he completed a course on Miles Masters. From here he went to Sealand completing an intermediate and then advanced training course. At the time, Peter was frustrated at not being pushed through to the front line. 'There was a sense of stopping us entirely as far as I could see, I couldn't get through, I wanted to, everybody wanted to. It was training, training, training' but flying was certainly coming naturally giving him a lot of confidence in his abilities. He also recalled that morale was good, 'I thought we were going to win the war. I never thought the Germans would beat us. I thought they were just bloody impertinent.' His next post was to an operational training unit (7 OTU) to notch up some hours on operational aircraft, in preparation for entry into the battle. But with few serviceable aircraft available for training Peter only managed seven hours on Spitfires before he was posted to an operational unit, 611 Squadron, part of 12 Group.

On 29 September 1940 five pilots had left 611 Squadron, posted south to 11 Group, replacing the high losses of the previous month. In came seven new pilots, one of which was Peter Olver. The squadron was operating from two bases at the time, Digby and Ternhill. Digby's 'strength' was recorded the next day as, 'one effective operational pilot... two operational pilots sick with sore throats and temporarily off flying... and 9 non-operational pilots, 7 effective aircraft, and two other aircraft awaiting new engines, and this assortment has been running today as an Operational Training Unit, styled "611 FTS" [Flying Training School].' The ORB stated that the squadron, 'as a fighting unit' was operating from Ternhill, 'with 10 operational pilots and one nearly operational pilot, and 9 effective and one broken aircraft'.

The 611 Squadron diarist recorded activity at Digby over the next few days:

> *1 October:* 'No. 611 FTS' continued in full swing with 20 hours practice flying.
>
> *2 October:* Another 20 hours practice flying.
>
> *3 October:* Fair morning, but low cloud and drizzle after midday caused a suspension of the 'FTS' work.
>
> *4 October:* The 'FTS' continued in full swing and 4 pilots were assessed as day operational.
>
> *5 October:* The 'FTS' has produced results. Moreover the weather is reported clear at Ternhill. Accordingly Squadron Leader McComb took off at 1150 hours with five of the new pilots (known as 'weakies') for Ternhill, to bring the squadron there up to strength.

The use of the term 'weakies' appears somewhat condescending to the new pilots. Certainly the ORB gives the impression that the squadron was not happy carrying out an 'FTS' role. Clearly the squadron's hierarchy were either not aware or unappreciative of their responsibilities within the grand scheme. The requirement on squadrons such as this within 12 Group, to hold a pilot reserve, was an important element of Dowding's approach to the battle. Beyond the range of enemy fighter-escorted bombers he could control this strategic reserve, rotating pilots and squadrons in and out of the main battle in the south-east when required.

Peter Olver was one of the pilots who had been assessed as day operational on 4 October and flew to Ternhill the next day, taking part in two uneventful patrols on 7 October. On 8 October came another patrol, again without enemy contact. The rest of the squadron was similarly noting the absence of the enemy in their airspace. 11 October served up another fruitless patrol for Peter but other 611 Squadron pilots did encounter small numbers of enemy aircraft whilst on two separate patrols, ending up claiming three destroyed, one probable and one damaged. Against this one 611 aircraft was damaged by return fire. Also Sergeant K.C. Pattison became lost as darkness set in and force-landed. Pattison, who had arrived at the squadron on 29 September and had flown to Ternhill along with Peter on 5 October, was seriously injured and would die two days later.

The next five days, although there were patrols, went without notable incident. When summing up the day's activity for 16 October, however, the squadron diarist would certainly have something to record. Early that morning a Junkers 88, at 1,000 feet, made its presence known, by unloading four 250kg high explosive bombs, incendiaries and spraying machine-gun fire everywhere. Flames devoured one hangar, approximately twenty training aircraft were written off and two Blenheims of 23 Squadron were damaged.

With respect to the frame of mind of one young airman, Peter Olver, 611 Squadron was not meeting aspirations. Peter's general recollection of 611 Squadron is also perhaps influenced by the squadron's attitude towards 'weakies'.

It was a bloody rotten old squadron. Just no good. I don't recollect doing anything much at all. I applied to go to 11 Group where all the action was. Morale generally was good, but it was all happening around 11 Group. I thought I'd win the war for them.

In the second week of October total RAF fighter losses, since the beginning of July, passed the 1,000 mark. Losses continued through October, although not at the same rate as the height of the battle, the second half of August and first few weeks of September. German losses up until the end of September surpassed the RAF's attrition and a shift in policy had resulted. Goering needed to preserve his bomber force for the night offensive that had opened in September. So to prevent losses fighter-bomber operations, carried out at height, became the feature of the daylight campaign. Countering high flying bomb-laden Me109s and Me110s thus required a change in Fighter Command tactics. Controllers had to identify which formations contained bomb-carrying aircraft and the squadrons detailed to intercept needed time to climb.

Whilst the new Luftwaffe tactics were difficult to counter, they were not going to achieve the overall objective – defeat of the RAF. On 12 October Hitler issued a communiqué which effectively accepted Fighter Command's defensive daylight victory, '...from now until the spring, preparation for Sealion shall be continued solely for the purpose of maintaining political and military pressure on England. Should the Invasion be reconsidered in the spring or early summer of 1941, orders for a renewal of operational readiness will be issued later. In the meantime military conditions for a later invasion are to be improved.'

Of course Dowding was not on Hitler's distribution list. Fighter Command had no inkling at that point of the strategic success and there would be no immediate diminishing in the scale of daylight Luftwaffe operations. The packet fighter-bomber attacks continued. Park's response developed accordingly, and on 17 October he issued instructions, 'The general plan is to get one or two Spitfire squadrons to engage enemy fighters from above about mid-Kent, in order to cover other Spitfire and Hurricane squadrons whilst climbing to operating height at back patrol lines east and south of London.' One of the RAF's Spitfire squadrons that would be used to counter the high flying fighter-bombers was 603 Squadron, based at Hornchurch, and it was with great relief that on 18 October 1940 Peter Olver was sent south, along with Pilot Officer Maxwell, arriving at Hornchurch, both men joining up with this squadron.

603 Sqn Spitfire

603 'City of Edinburgh' Squadron was an Auxiliary Air Force unit. Prior to its move to 11 Group it had been based in Scotland, where it had met with some success. But the attrition rates in the south in August 1940 had led to it being called to the south-east, to be based at Hornchurch, later that month. It was replacing 65 Squadron, which was down to five aircraft and twelve pilots. The pilots of the time welcomed the move. One of them, Richard Hillary, would receive notoriety writing about his experiences as a fighter pilot in his book *The Last Enemy*. He commented on the excitement when news of the move south came through.

> Broody [Noel Benson] was hopping up and down like a madman, 'Now we'll show the bastards! Jesus will we show 'em!' Stapme [Basil Stapleton] was capering about shaking everyone by the hand, and Raspberry's [Ronald Berry] moustache looked like it would fall off with excitement. 'Eh, now they'll cop it and no mistake', he chortled.

On 27 August 1940 603's pilots flew their Spitfires down to Hornchurch. Station commander Group Captain Cecil Bouchier DFC met them on their arrival. A few years later he would recall his first impressions.

> It was my great good fortune throughout 1940 to command a large Fighter Station adjacent to the East End of London, and whose task it was to protect London, the Thames estuary, and Kent. It was there at Hornchurch, that 603 Squadron came to me on the morning of 27 August 1940. I shall never forget their coming! Could this really be a Squadron, I thought, as I went out to meet them on the tarmac on their arrival. The CO, on getting out of his Spitfire, had his little 'side-hat' perched on the back of his head; he meandered towards me with bent shoulders, hands in his pockets, followed by, what seemed to me then to be the motleyest collection of unmilitary young men I had seen for a very long time. I was not impressed. Good heavens! (I suddenly remembered) it's an Auxiliary Squadron. Ah! I thought that explains it, but what have I done to deserve it?... The RAF Station at Hornchurch was always my spiritual home, and I was very proud of it. I had grown up there in peacetime with 54, 65 and 74 Fighter Squadrons – those early 'Regular' Squadrons which were the first to bear the brunt against the German Luftwaffe,

and who fought so valiantly during Dunkirk and afterwards. They were truly magnificent. One by one, battered and weary they departed from my Station in a blaze of glory to quieter parts of the country to recuperate and fill up their ranks again, and thus it was that there came to Hornchurch other 'Regular' Fighter Squadrons, eager and fresh for the fray, to take their place. Into this line of succession... there suddenly dropped No. 603.[9]

Bouchier would later qualify this first impression stating, 'How wrong I was', even making the statement, 'They were, I think, the greatest squadron of them all.' Over the course of the next six weeks 603 Squadron was in the thick of the action. Pilots such as Brian Carbury, Basil Stapleton and Ronald 'Ras' Berry, to name just a few, were building up sizeable scores and opportunities to celebrate decorations arose with relative regularity. But there were losses. On 28 August, the squadron's first full day at Hornchurch, three pilots were killed. On 31 August three of the ground crew would lose their lives when the airfield was bombed, others were injured and one pilot was killed. There were six further deaths up until the end of the first week of October, and of course numerous pilots were injured. These losses needed replacing and in came new pilots, not all of whom came from the Auxiliary Air Force. Included was a certain Peter Olver of the RAFVR. Peter recalled his initial impressions of 603 Squadron and the welcome he received.

> I wasn't particularly a German hater but at that time I was worried that the war would be won before I could assist in causing them to eat their words about us all being so decadent. George Denholm was the CO and he didn't seem overjoyed at my arrival saying that I was too inexperienced in flying hours and would just lose another aircraft for him, but consented to give me a trial flying as his No. 2 whilst dropping some pilot's ashes in the Channel. This attitude was galling to me.[10]

From 18 to 24 October, when weather allowed, the Germans sent over the fighter-bomber raiders, but the general intensity of battle was nothing like on the scale of a month previous. The same could not be said of the hours of darkness however, where the night Blitz was exposing the RAF's under-developed night defences. However it is important not to understate the daylight battle, as there was still a large commitment for both sides. On 25 October, for example, the Luftwaffe lost twenty aircraft. Fighter Command pilots would fly 809 sorties for the loss of ten aircraft. One of these pilots was Peter Olver and now he would finally get his chance to engage the enemy and gain that all-important, indeed crucial, combat experience.

11 Group would later identify three phases of enemy attacks that morning and RDF would give good warning. Squadrons were sent up in pairs, twelve in phase one (0830-0930), eight continuing to patrol into phase two (0930-1045), along with four fresh squadrons, which would also patrol into phase three (1145-1230), supported by six fresh squadrons. 603 Squadron would be one of four squadrons that made two sorties. The 11 Group analysts would later summarise the resultant air combats thus:

> The enemy tactics were an intensification of previous raids by high fighters, some carrying bombs. The raids were larger in number and spread over a wider front than hitherto, and necessitated the employment of a large number of squadrons, many of which had successful engagements.

Not that the engagements went all the way of the RAF, as Peter Olver can testify.

> We were out on patrol and saw a tremendous lot of German aircraft making vapour trails high up above us. After one abortive attack the whole squadron disappeared and flew for home. I didn't want to fly home after achieving nothing. I'd merely shaken off the odd Messerschmitt that was after me, so I thought I would carry on. I went climbing up on to a circular ring of vapour trails, which was a sign of the Germans waiting for you. And after a bit one obliged, came down and shot me down. I didn't see him coming, he started on the starboard wing, on the outside, and worked in and knocked the aileron off. And he flew alongside, looked at me and then flew off. After a while the aeroplane stopped being a flying machine, it became a lump of metal. I was going down with it and I couldn't get out at first. I broke the seat by standing on it. The pressure throwing me into the bottom was terrific. But I used all my strength and managed to get out. The army

picked me up and thought I was wounded, as I had a lot of blood on my face, but I had merely hit my head on a tree coming down. I wasn't wounded at all. They got me drunk on whisky. The army always had those bloody great tankards and some chaps filled it with whisky. I drank that and that really fixed me.

Peter would receive the support of one of the more experienced members of another squadron as he came to terms with his first combat experience.

There was a chap called Shorty Lock, in 41 Squadron, [Eric Lock DSO DFC] and he was an ace, absolutely. I told him that I had been shot down that day. He said he knew I would, 'but you've got to look on the bright side you're still alive' and many weren't. He said until you've been shot down and baled out three times, and landed in the sea three times, and force-landed three times, then you're not even experienced. I didn't go as many as that but I know what he meant. He was very kind and told me a lot about what to do. It was unusual for an ace to take so much trouble with anybody but he did.

Peter would be back onto operations on 27 October, 603 Squadron sending twelve aircraft out on an early afternoon defensive patrol. South of Maidstone Me109s surprised the RAF pilots, resulting in the loss of two aircraft and death of the pilots. In addition Pilot Officer Maxwell crash-landed but escaped unhurt. In return one Me109 was claimed as damaged. The next day 603 Squadron redressed the balance somewhat, one Me109 claimed destroyed and two damaged on an early afternoon sortie, two Me109s probable and one damaged early evening. Peter took part in the second sortie and he was rapidly gaining crucial combat experience. Prior to an operation he recalled, 'a lot of anticipation and excitement' but fear was something that appeared not to trouble him.

I wasn't often afraid. I could tell when things were starting to go adrift, and rather than become afraid, it would make me rather cross. But when you have had experience of dogfighting and know what to do, it's not the same as when you are starting out. For an inexperienced pilot it's a real problem because you are bound to get shot down.

Peter's attitude towards the enemy was also developing.

> I didn't hate them particularly. I used to rather admire them. Although of course whilst some were alright, some were bloody awful and used to shoot people on parachutes. But only a few and you'd have the same amongst the RAF. I didn't see it happen but I knew some people that did.

31 October is officially stated as the last day of the Battle of Britain. As the month was closing the Luftwaffe had steadily withdrawn from a major commitment to the daylight offensive. Fighter Command and the RAF pilots were certainly now becoming aware of the change, indeed welcoming the opportunity to rebuild, to rest, to recover. But no one told them on 1 November that the Battle of Britain was over. Fighter Command still had to be ready for deployment against any raids that did develop. And in November calls would be made on the fighter squadrons to continue the life and death aerial struggle. 603 Squadron was no exception.

Peter Olver took part in a defensive patrol on 5 November, and whilst Me109s were spotted only one pilot was able to fire, with no results seen. One other pilot was wounded. Peter was next sent out, one of eight pilots, to defend a convoy on 7 November. The squadron's pilots came across a Me110, which had little chance as they took it in turn to come in, shoot and break away as the next pilot came in. Each pilot was credited with an eighth of a kill. Peter was back in action again on 11 November, one of seven pilots on a convoy protection patrol.

11 Group had contested three attacks in the morning, then as midday approached further enemy build-ups were detected, two attacks forming on convoys in the Thames estuary. On the first of these the 'Y' Service, listening in on enemy communications, gave advanced warning to Fighter Command, which allowed the early positioning of squadrons. At 1135 hours RDF picked up the raid at 8,000 feet ten miles west of St. Omer. 11 Group sent in eight squadrons to break up the raid. 253 and 605 Squadrons were ordered to the Maidstone line, covering London, but would not be used when the attacks on the convoys developed. 17 and 257 Squadrons were detailed to patrol the convoys, and at 1136 tasked with engaging the bombers. 64 and 603 Squadrons, at 1134 were told to gain height and patrol high over the convoy seeking out any enemy fighters. 615 and 229 Squadrons flew to

the Croydon line at 1142 and were later sent to the Manston Patrol Line to try and intercept the returning raiders, although in this they had no success. Nevertheless the RAF tactics paid off. 17 and 257 Squadron were soon amongst the Ju87s and Me109s, sending some into the sea. 64 and 603 Squadron, including Peter Olver, also met with success, enemy aircraft were engaged and fell to their guns. Below are extracts from his squadron's combat reports.

Pilot Officer Stapleton DFC: I was Guard 2 underneath my squadron when I sighted enemy formation ahead of us. I directed my squadron to them and attacked the last Me109 of a formation of 7. I gave him two deflection bursts. Black smoke appeared for about ten seconds. The Me109 did a controlled landing in the sea and disappeared after about 15 to 30 seconds. He landed 2 miles ahead of the outgoing convoy.

Pilot Officer Prowse: When on patrol as Red 2, with 603 Squadron, I attacked an Me109 which had left four other Me109s directly the squadron caught up with them. I chased him down from 20,000 feet to 2,000 feet and when he flattened out fired a three second burst from dead astern at a range of 300 yards. Immediately a trail of white vapour came from the undersurface of his port wing root. He began to twist and turn and I was only able to fire an occasional short burst at him. By this time I had closed to 100 yards. He straightened out and began to climb. I fired a three second burst from dead astern. He did a half roll and dived towards the sea. He pulled out at 500 feet and immediately executed another half roll from which he dived into the sea.

Flying Officer Pinckney: Patrolling as Blue 3 I attacked an Me109 from the quarter closing to dead astern and saw bullets going into the machine. I broke away as I was attacked by four other Me109s. Last saw the enemy in a very slow shallow dive heading towards France, with black smoke coming out.

Squadron Leader Denholm DFC: I was leading 603 Squadron when in the mouth of the Thames at 20,000 feet I saw four yellow-nosed Me109s flying towards me in a

North Westerly direction. On approaching them they turned round towards France. I fired about a 3 sec. burst at one which half rolled and dived, then fired at another from 250 to 50 yards, firing all my ammunition, very dense smoke issued from the Me109, my windscreen became covered with oil and he slowed down considerably. As soon as my ammunition was finished I broke away and thought I was being followed by another a/c. I then landed at Manston.

Pilot Officer Olver's combat report stated: I was Blue 4. When in Patrol with 603 Squadron I delivered a stern attack on a Ju87 (the nearer of a Group) firing a continual burst from 300 yards range closing to 15 yards (approximately 1,800 rounds)... The Ju87 went down in a shallow dive with intense black smoke pouring out.

Sixty-six years later Peter remembers:

It was quite easy to shoot down. They had been bombing the shipping. I got onto one, I just had one short burst at it, and it went straight into the sea. I probably hit the pilot.

Pilot Officer Olver's combat report again: I passed over the top of the Ju87 and turned simultaneously sharply to the right and was immediately attacked by an Me109. I got onto his tail and fired the remainder of my ammunition in 3 short bursts at 150-200 yards range.

And sixty-six years later:

The Me109 pilot was useless. If he was trying to shoot me down, he made a bad show of it. I've never known such a poor pilot. I chased him around, he didn't know what to do. He went into the sea. I felt a bit sorry for him because he seemed so useless. But we were there to shoot each other down. He would have had me given the chance. I felt it was very important not to watch them go down because that's when you get shot down yourself. You wouldn't last two seconds, there was always a lot of them. You had to keep weaving and watch your tail.

As often happened after combat the pilot could suddenly find himself all alone in the sky. For Peter this initially proved a

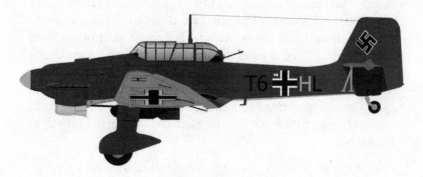

Ju87 Stuka

problem, as he had not had the opportunity to carry out sector reconnaissances on arrival at 603 Squadron. But he soon learnt to use a loop in the Thames as a landmark which would take him to Hornchurch, obviously avoiding the balloons on one side of the aerodrome, 'you made a point of not flying into those'.

The Ju87 engaged by Peter on 11 November, was to be his first full credited claim. Many more would be put against his name during the war, but he remains quite philosophical regarding claims.

> No claim is correct as a rule. If you are going to watch aircraft go down you wouldn't be alive today. You wouldn't last five minutes if you watched. But every time you shoot at something you think you shoot it down. Sometimes you can shoot one little burst and the aircraft goes down. And another time you can use all your ammo and they won't go down. It's hard to say why.

In the middle of December 603 Squadron was sent north to Scotland, and Peter went with the other pilots, but he wanted to get back to where the action was, 'I, and three other chaps with me asked if we could go back to 11 Group. We went to see the CO, it upset him, as he wanted to keep the pilots he knew.'

Nevertheless, his wish was granted and he joined 66 Squadron, at Biggin Hill, on 23 December 1940, along with Pilot Officer Maxwell and Sergeants Brice and Thomson. As Peter recalled, 'It wasn't a good squadron. It had been knocked about a bit and got very much worn down.' For the first five days there was no operational flying, but on 29 December Peter was in action.

66 Squadron combat report:
Approx 1015 – 1020 hours
Dungeness to half way across Channel
Height of enemy – 3,500 feet
Dornier 17 damaged
Flight Lieutenant Christie DFC and Bar – I was one of 2 aircraft of 66 Squadron ordered to patrol Dover-Dungeness area. We took off from Biggin Hill at 0945 hours. When approaching Dungeness I saw a single Do17 flying 2 miles out to sea from Dungeness to Dover at approximately 3,500 feet. I climbed to attack and opened fire with a 2 second burst at 200 yards and circled round delivering deflection bursts from above and below the enemy aircraft and both sides finally closing to point blank. I saw the lower rear gunner lolling in his cockpit obviously dead. I had to break off the engagement as I had used all my ammunition. I returned to base where I landed at 1030 hours. My plane was hit three times by enemy aircraft but not damaged.

Pilot Officer Peter Olver – At 0945 hours on the 29.12.40 I took off on a Dover-Dungeness patrol as Blue 2 of a section of 2 aircraft. At 10.15 when travelling south while just north of Dungeness we saw a Do17 which came just out of the cloud (4,000 feet) and continued towards land. On sighting us it jettisoned its bombs and turned and climbed for the clouds. Blue 1 attacked first and I attacked climbing very steeply firing short bursts from 300 yards to 50 yards. I observed my tracer bullets entering the Dornier, but without visible results.

At the commencement of the attack the return fire was considerable but died away later. I lost the Dornier in mid-channel in the clouds and returned to my base at 1050.

[11 Group intelligence patrol report]... the enemy aircraft was damaged, but apparently not very seriously as it was still flying normally towards some Me109s which were coming out from France to escort it back, when the engagement was broken off 20 miles south of Dungeness.

Throughout January there was very little operational flying, though Peter took part, with two other pilots, in one patrol on 4 January. One pilot lost his way and crashed into a balloon, he survived but the aircraft was written off. Into February and there was an increase in operational activity cover to offensive raids over enemy territory, and patrols. Peter recalled his experiences on one of his first sweeps over enemy territory.

> I was lucky to get back from the first one, because my engine started to pack up and a Spitfire by itself doesn't stand much chance. The Messerschmitts would fasten on to that. But I had to come down because the engine wasn't working and I wondered how far I was going to get across the Channel. I was just going to get it across as far as I could go and land in the sea. But it picked up the lower I got and I just crept across to a landing ground on the English side. I didn't get picked up by the Messerschmitts, I was lucky.

Into 1941, despite the diminished daylight activity from the Luftwaffe, there was still nevertheless a threat. On 14 February, during an interception patrol over Dover the squadron was jumped by Me109s. Peter along with two other pilots had his aircraft shot-up but all three came out of the encounter unharmed. One other pilot was wounded in the arm. One pilot failed to return.

> A friend of mine David Maxwell, who had trained with me, got killed by the sods. He didn't even see them. There was a group of about twenty of them flying around the south coast and they shot him down, killing him. His body was never found, which was rather tiresome.

Peter was now hardening his attitude towards losses. Similar to many pilots, building a barricade of indifference proved the best method.

> I was not too pleased about them obviously, but you have to get on with it. If you start worrying about losses you'd be a dead man yourself in quick time.

On 24 February, 66 Squadron was sent west to Exeter and 10 Group.

> There we started having a lot of new pilots, inexperienced but new and we kept posting the ones we didn't like and keeping the ones that were going to be good. Ultimately it became a good squadron again but it took time for that to

happen. A good squadron's like a good school really, the headmaster's got something to do with it, the squadron commander, but it's also down to the experience and the ability of the pilots. Some have got the right attitude, some mean well but they aren't any good. Not all people flying a Spitfire are any good. Some are devilishly bad really.

Into March and 66 Squadron began carrying out patrols. 'Nothing to report' and 'No action resulted' are frequent entries in the squadron diary. Flying over water has never been popular with fighter pilots. Peter's experiences at this time did little to endear him towards it.

I didn't like flying over the sea. I recall some terrible times when the waves were not just three or four feet high, they could be several hundred feet high in the Atlantic. You would fly for about an hour, orbit for an hour and fly back for an hour. You couldn't be at nought feet like you were told because you would be knocked into the sea. I hated it.

There was considerable operational activity in April but, 'no action' again featured against the diary summaries. But the enemy did come to Exeter, although using the shroud of night. The aerodrome was hit regularly in the first half of April. 66 Squadron aircraft were damaged and on the night of 11 April the 'billets of the airmen were shattered and men were evacuated to the village or dispersal points.' On 13 April another bomb and incendiary raid resulted in 'nearly all of our aircraft being rendered unserviceable by exploding bombs.' The next day accommodation was becoming scarce and 66 Squadron personnel began to live in tents and at the dispersal shelter. On 26 and 27 April the squadron was forced further west to Perranporth.

Operationally May was following the same pattern as the month before, numerous patrols without enemy encounters. On 27 May that changed.

Pilot Officer Peter Olver's combat report: At 2250 hours Pilot Officer Pickering Red 1 and myself Red 2 were approaching base on our return from a convoy patrol... when Red 1 led on to investigate shell burst on ship off St. Ives Bay. At this time I had 25 gals of petrol left only. On approaching the burning ship we saw tracer bullets sweeping the deck but could not locate the enemy aircraft due to poor visibility. Red 1 attacked on getting closer from quarter astern on one of the 2 enemy aircraft and on breaking away and climbing to port he drew the enemy aircraft fire and I was able to come up to within 200 yards unnoticed until I opened fire. Red 1 then left for enemy aircraft No. 2 and I broke to port at the same level (water level) as enemy aircraft and then gained in height and made a head on attack diving from 500 feet. There was no return fire from the port and some followed from the rear. I then flew towards land after enemy aircraft No. 2. I located him by his fire on Red 1 who had broken away by the time of my arrival and I was able to get in unobserved until I opened fire. Before my attack he jettisoned his bombs and was travelling very slowly indeed. I attacked from the port quarter to astern and broke at 100 yards. The return fire was accurate and as I broke I saw his wheels were hanging down – not fully I think. Enemy aircraft 1 meantime was seen to land in the sea and no one escaped before the aircraft partially sank. Enemy aircraft 2 was observed limping with wheels down from the ground.

Pilot Officer Pickering's combat report: I was returning with Red 2 from a convoy patrol 10 miles NNE of Trevose Head when I noticed a bomb explode about 40 miles ahead and when we had travelled half way I could see m/g fire at a burning ship. I set course south for the ship to cut off any returning enemy aircraft but did not see any, so I turned towards the ship and attacked an enemy aircraft, which had just broken off from an attack, opening fire from the quarter, range 300 yards and held the enemy aircraft in my sights until point blank range and dead astern. I did not experience any return fire until I broke away, and then it was not very accurate, but it enabled Red 2 to approach without being seen. After Red 2 had finished his attacks this enemy aircraft was seen to land in the sea west of St. Ives.

I then attacked enemy aircraft No. 2 which was flying NE along the coast towards St. Ives Bay. This enemy aircraft did not see me until I opened fire at 50 yards astern. Once again I experienced no return fire until after I had broken away. I then flew parallel to the enemy aircraft about 400 yards to port and 500 feet above, the enemy aircraft giving one short burst for quite a time which enabled Red 2 to attack again without being seen. As I had been flying for 2 hours I made for home base and landed at 2300 hours. This enemy aircraft was last seen crossing the coast between St. Ives and the barracks flying very low with its undercarriage down at a very low air speed.

Took off 2055, landed 2300.

Peter was credited with a half share of a He111 destroyed and a He111 damaged. Into June 1941 and the squadron had the better of further enemy engagements, but in July the enemy was either elusive or simply not present. The latter being the more probable, Hitler and the Luftwaffe's operational emphasis shifting over to the Russian front.

Now Fighter Command was gearing itself up for the offensive over enemy-occupied territory, operations designed to draw the Luftwaffe up, to maintain an aerial front in the west. On 11 August Peter Olver along with other 66 Squadron pilots flew to RAF Wattisham then to Martlesham Heath, from where, on the next day, they took off to join 152 and 234 Squadrons, accompanying Blenheims, setting course for the Dutch coast. Landfall was reached but there was little aerial opposition, the ORB recording, 'a number of enemy aircraft were seen... but only half-hearted attacks were made on the tail end of the squadron or on anyone who straggled. The attacks on the tail of the squadron were broken off if one of the sections turned to engage.' Peter Olver did manage to get in an attack, from 200 yards on an Me109F over the Schelde, 'but although confident he hit the enemy aircraft made no claim.' One 66 Squadron pilot, Sergeant Stevens, was recorded as missing from the operation. On 18 August Squadron Leader Forbes and Peter carried out a short patrol over France, 'and shot up an enemy controlled wireless station.' Two days later Peter took part in another incursion over enemy territory, attempting to force the issue with the Luftwaffe, as detailed in his combat report.

Number of enemy aircraft – approx 20 (109s)
Type of enemy aircraft – Me109s & Me110s
Time attack was delivered – 14.30 hours
Place attack was delivered – out to sea on return
Height of enemy – 109s 0 to 8,000 feet, 110s 0 to 1,500
    feet
Enemy casualties – 1 probable & 1 damaged
Our casualties – 2 Spitfire IIs long range
Personnel – 1 pilot
I was No. 2 of starboard section of 66 Squadron (8 a/c).
High escort for Blenheims. Sections of four weaving in line
astern. Due to dive after a 109 I had plenty of speed and
was able to climb and shoot while practically vertical at a
109, which commenced a head on dive. It turned away as
my bullets entered the fuselage towards its tail – Damaged.

Next burst at a passing 109 without sufficient deflection
– Missed.

Another 109 attacked No. 1 of S section Flight
Lieutenant Allen and myself head on. I was about 160
yards behind Allen, we both fired head on and as 109
turned to starboard our port, deflection shot. 109
continued on in dive and shortly a lot of bluish smoke and
oil started streaming out behind. Was unable to watch this
enemy aircraft longer due to presence of other enemy
aircraft – Probable.

Enemy aircraft unusually aggressive.

The September and October 66 Squadron diary entries record the
continuation of convoy and interception patrols and the odd
generally uneventful sweep. November 1941 had the squadron
carrying out convoy patrols and the occasional support to
Blenheims attacking targets in France.

It was around this time that Peter's 'operational tour' finally
came to an end, 'I did about 300 hours before they discovered. It
was so long it wasn't even an operational tour – it was just a hell
of a long time.' Peter, who had risen to the rank of flight
lieutenant, was posted to 'rest' and command at a Target Towing
Flight. Such a requirement had its own inherent risks.

You had a great long metal cord from the back, with a
drogue on the end. You would hope that the pilots would
shoot across it and not come in behind you. Some of them

didn't know what to do and would get in line astern and bullets would come whipping past you.

Peter was not satisfied with his lot, 'I wanted some excitement. I reckoned I was a pretty good fighter pilot.' As such he volunteered for service in the Middle East, 'I went by sea all the way round, round South Africa. It was a slow job because of the submarines. But there were a hell of a lot of us and they had a lot of cover.' He arrived in the Middle East in May 1942. Excitement was certainly going to come his way.

Chapter 8

Supreme Exertions

When Peter arrived in the Middle East, it appeared that he was not expected.

They weren't aware I was coming. I saw the AOC [Air Vice-Marshal Arthur Coningham] and said I was under the impression I was going to be a squadron leader there. They hadn't got any Spitfires at all, but they did have a squadron of Tomahawks. They stuck them together at the place where I landed. They were averaging a low number of hours because the Allison engines were no bloody good. I said I didn't want to fly a thing where I would be out of action after about five or six hours. He said he couldn't give me a squadron of Hurricanes, but he could make me a supernumerary flight commander on one. So I went for that. That's how I joined 213 Squadron.

The Hurricane was not as good as a Spitfire, but there weren't any. A Hurricane is a good old aeroplane there is no doubt about that. And also being made of fabric, a cannon shell going through it doesn't make much difference unless it hit a spar or something like that.

Peter arrived in late May 1942 and his first impressions were not favourable.

It wasn't a good squadron then. It was worn out. Too many people had been killed in it. It had done a lot of hard work, but they had lost too many people.

The Second World War North African land campaign is noted for the ebb and flow of the Allied and the German/Italian fortunes. By May 1942 the advantage lay with the Axis Commander Erwin Rommel. In January of that year he had launched a land offensive that had reversed previous British gains, taking the front to the Gazala line, beyond which lay Tobruk and the Egyptian frontier. Beyond that lay the strategic prizes of Alexandria, Cairo and the Suez Canal. The stakes were high. These Rommel would try and seize with further offensives.

The Gazala line defences were assaulted and outflanked at the end of May and in mid-June the British quickly retreated to the frontier, the defenders of Tobruk quickly over run. Military historian Basil Liddell Hart would record it as, 'the worst British disaster of the war except for the fall of Singapore'. On 26 June 1942 the Germans began the drive through British positions at Mersa Matruh, which lay mid way between the frontier and Alexandria. By the end of the month Alexandria lay only sixty miles ahead of Rommel's forces. Here on the Alamein line the tide was to turn once more.

Throughout the retreat the supporting RAF fighter squadrons were operating at full intensity. Those pilots who had previously seen action in the Battle of Britain would report that it was more intense than the operational requirements of the summer of 1940. The RAF was called upon to bomb enemy communications, positions and supply lines; the bombers needed the protection of the fighter squadrons to keep the enemy Me109s at bay. In addition the congestion on the ground, resulting from the retreat, needed protection from enemy air attack. The fight for the air was fierce and 213 Squadron was right in the midst of it. Peter Olver gives an excellent account of the nature of being operational at this time.

> We used to split our squadron into three, A flight, B flight and maintenance flight. When you took off from A flight you landed back at B flight and then you took off from that and landed back at maintenance flight and so on, and went backwards in hops all the time. You went and did your operation and landed back. You never landed at the same place when retreating because the Germans were advancing. Often you would see them coming in with their bloody motors and things across the landing ground, as you were taking off.

We were operational continually two or three times a day, advancing or retreating in the desert. Hard work and very tiring indeed. Mostly with the Luftwaffe but strafing, low down that sort of thing. The Italians were there but they were useless. Windy as hell. The Messerschmitts were the ones we had to watch out for and they didn't like attacking you because we used to fly as a squadron and turn into them. We knew that the enemy were faster, you couldn't doubt it. They were much quicker than we were and they were much better at altitude but they hadn't got the manoeuvrability that we had and also they weren't all good pilots. When they got the odd squadron back from Russia it took them a couple of days to alter the camouflage and it took them about two days to get used to not trying to dogfight us. Then they kept out of the way. I should think we had more aircraft but we would never even try to compete with them at altitude, you couldn't do it. You used to fly at 9,000 feet because their anti-aircraft guns were less effective at that height. They had very good guns indeed with good crews on them.

We had tents if you could find them, but even then if you are retreating fast you can't put them up. And when retreating you were lucky to get away with a parachute which you could use as a pillow, when you lie on the sand. You hadn't got any food or hadn't got a knife and fork or anything much. When I first joined 213 Squadron I didn't get anything to eat for some days because they were worn out as a squadron. But the airmen took me on and looked after me. I remember one night, we had the side of a tent up and I was lying with my head on a parachute. I got a great kick in the back, and a voice from the other side of the canvas asked if it was me. I said yes and they asked if I would like to have a cup of cocoa in their tent. They had tents, little ones. I went and they said there was something they wanted to ask me. I said ask away. My rigger and mechanic then asked me if I was married. I told them no. They said well you like girls don't you. I said yes I like them splendidly but not to marry them. They then asked if my mother was alive still. I said yes and asked them why they were asking me these questions. They told me that the last three times I'd gone up my aircraft had been hit in the tail and they didn't know what to say to her when they wrote home to tell her of my death!

We were losing pilots, but the chaps were pretty good by that time. The fighter pilots in the desert were the best in the world after they had been at it for a bit.

The day of 26 June 1942 gives an example of the nature of operations for 213 Squadron at this time, deadly encounters involving Peter Olver. Squadron Leader Young DFC led the squadron's twelve Hurricane IICs off from LG [Landing Ground] 012 at 15.15 hours, to carry out an offensive sweep over an area named Charing Cross. The pilots climbed up reaching 19,000 feet and setting a 290 degree course. After approximately half an hour, eight Me109s, in four pairs stepped in echelon right, were spotted three miles away at 14,000 feet flying east. The Hurricanes were spotted and the Messerschmitts turned to the west, and climbed into the sun, which is when 213 Squadron's pilots seized their opportunity. Pilot Officer Thomlinson sent one spinning down into the ground and then managed to get in a five to six second burst at another. Sergeant Ritchie in a beam attack saw his foe's tail unit disintegrate and the aircraft roll and plunge into the deck. Flight Lieutenant Temlett DFC witnessed bursts from his fire riddle the length of an Me109's wing, which crumpled and fell away. Flames streaked behind the aircraft and it plunged earthward.

Pilot Officer Henderson unleashed a two second burst and witnessed pieces flying off the engine and cockpit of his foe. Black smoke issued and the Me109 spiralled down. Henderson followed and at 4,000 feet saw the aircraft momentarily straighten out. Henderson from dead astern, at 100 yards, finished him off and the Me109 hit the ground. When a Me109 flew through Pilot Officer Sissons' line of sight at 200 yards, he put on full deflection and at virtually full beam sent off a two second burst, which resulted in strikes on the cockpit and pieces breaking away. The Me109 inverted, barrelled out, pulled up and then again half rolled. If the pilot was trying to regain control his desperate efforts failed and the Me109 smashed into the ground. Peter Olver was also in the action, as detailed by this combat report.

As Black 1 I was airborne at 1515. After the enemy aircraft had been sighted I saw A flight diving down on them, whilst the 109s tried to evade by performing steep climbing turns to the left. I heard the CO say he was going down. I followed after him, pulling across the top of him and performing an aileron turn. I picked an Me109 out on the extreme left, just as it pulled up to get away from A flight's attack. I outclimbed him and gave him a short burst as a result of which I saw bits flying off. He put his nose down and dived away down to the ground.

I then returned to base, landing at 1620.

Five 109s were claimed destroyed and one damaged.

As can be seen, the air fighting in the desert was intense, with the RAF making a valuable contribution to the overall battle. In acknowledgement, on 4 July, Prime Minister Winston Churchill dispatched a message to the commanding officer of the air forces in the Middle East, Arthur Tedder.

> Here at home we are watching with enthusiasm the brilliant supreme exertions of the Royal Air Force in the battle now proceeding in Egypt.
>
> From every quarter the reports come in of the effect of the vital part which your officers and men are playing in this Homeric struggle for the Nile Valley. The days of the Battle of Britain are being repeated far from home. We are sure you will be to our glorious Army the friend that endureth to the end.[11]

On 2 July Peter was posted to 238 Squadron taking up responsibilities as a flight commander. The land battle around Alamein in July saw attack and counter attack as both sides fought to exhaustion, but the British front held. During August the opposing armies received re-inforcement and at the end of the month and into early September Rommel tried to force the front open again. He failed, the defender came out on top and Rommel had to withdraw. The next to go on the offensive were the British under the command of General Sir Bernard Montgomery, and despite political pressure he would wait until preparations were complete. The last week of October would see the opening of the great, decisive, British offensive in North Africa.

In the desert the land and air battles were closely interlinked and what went on on the ground affected and was affected by what happened in the air. Throughout July 238 Squadron played its part in the fighting patrolling the battle area, over El Alamein. There were numerous engagements, victories and losses for both sides. On 15 July Peter Olver attacked and damaged a Ju88. The next day, an early morning patrol came across fifteen Ju87s with fighter escort. The Ju87s jettisoned their bombs and turned for home. Nevertheless the 238 Squadron pilots had had some success, six pilots claiming damage to one of the bombers, with Peter claiming a probably destroyed and one damaged. The lull in the land campaign in August was reflected similarly in the air. There were engagements however, and Peter would claim a Me109 damaged on 7 August. Taking off at 0930 hours, twelve 238 Squadron aircraft escorted Hurricanes on an army co-operation. Forty minutes into the flight four Me109s were seen as they dived on the squadron. 'The evasive tactics were successful and the squadron kept its position and height and continued to give protection to 127 Squadron who were close escort. Flight Lieutenant Olver was attacking a Me109, which shot away his tail light, he fired at it on the breakaway and saw pieces fly from the fuselage. Claimed as damaged.'

In early September 238 Squadron was again engaging the enemy air force over the battle area, but with Rommel's aggression spent, activity died off and the rest of September remained uneventful. Operational activity did pick up somewhat in October and the squadron went on the offensive looking for enemy targets behind the lines. Peter took part in one notable operation on 6 October, 'twelve aircraft led by Flight Lieutenant Olver left base at 1600 hours and flew at deck level to El Daba where they strafed the beach, railway, road and tented encampments. 4 MT [Motor Transport] were destroyed, whilst 20 MT and numerous tents were damaged and enemy troops shot up. Sergeant pilot Inder hit the ground with his starboard wing tip and has since been reported a POW.'

On 12 October 1942 Peter took over command of 213 Squadron. Preparations for the forthcoming British land offensive were dominating the strategic thinking in the first weeks of October. Tedder visited his units and, 'found them all in first class fettle. Morale was as high as ever and the standard of performance in the air most satisfying.' A case in point is 213 Squadron and if the squadron diary is anything to go by the recent retreat and air fighting had done little to diminish the morale of the unit.

13 October 1942: 'B' Flight beat 'A' Flight by 4 goals to 3 in an exciting soccer match.... The wedding party [who had gone to Alexandria to purchase a wedding present for a pilot] returned merrily, having acquired a magnificent (?) specimen of a palm tree, which now occupies a central position in the Mess.

14 October 1942: At readiness all morning, but no scrambles. CO discusses flying formations and tactics with the pilots.... At 1806 hours we were bombed and strafed. With probably two or three squadrons in the air, 'Jerry' impertinently intruded, and 80 Squadron, just moving in, caught the brunt of the attack, suffering 16 casualties, one fatal, and two more very seriously injured. Six Me109s came out of the sun, dropping bombs from a good height, others diving lower bombing and strafing. Ten bombs dropped amongst 80 Squadron, and only one near our Sergeant's Mess. This last blew down the latrine, and punctured the cab of one MT vehicle in two places. Those who were warned by the telephone exchange of the Red Warning, or heard the siren, made frantic dives into the nearest slit trenches or took what cover was available. Apart from abrasions, the Squadron got away free from injuries, and we hope our good luck will continue.

15 October 1942: ...News now comes through to us that we are not to take part in the show and everyone settles down again until excitement reigns as we learn we are definitely in on the show... [Following the return of pilots from a successful sortie covering a 6 Squadron attack on tanks]. Only 1 hour overdue for tiffin, we finally partook of our midday meal at about 1500, but only after we had listened intently to the AOC AVM Coningham, who talked first of all to the men of the squadron and then addressed the officers and pilots in the Mess. The AOC speaks confidently as to the result of the impending battle, and occasionally we think of what the future holds in store for us. Wishing us 'good luck', he leaves us to ponder over his 'pep' talk... In the evening Wing Commander J Darwen, Squadron Leader Marples, and the incomparable 'Willie' Allen, loathe to leave the squadron with whom he had for so long been IO, popped in for the odd spot. Some left early, but from reports received later of heads 'fat' and heads like 'boilers', the party was up to the usual high standard as enjoyed by the RAF.

On 16 October 1942 the wing prepared to receive one most notable RAF dignatory. The diary continues:

Not everyone is agreed that these parades are wise moves, influenced no doubt by the recent bombing and strafing. Most of us consider that a similar attack during this parade would be a feather in the cap of Jerry and would probably have a deleterious effect on morale. We ask ourselves whether the RAF would attempt to blot out a similar concentration behind Jerry's lines, and particularly the 'big shot'. We fell in, stood to attention, at ease, easy, and finally when Lord Trenchard himself arrived, arranged ourselves in a semi-circle around him and sat on the ground, whilst a rip roaring sandstorm blew up, intermittently blotting out the so-called landscape and reducing visibility to a few yards. By the time we had heard what the RAF was, what it is today, and what it is going to do in the future, we were well and truly full of 'grit' and those of us who had not before had the pleasure of hearing Lord Trenchard, realised something of the driving force behind this great man.

The parade concluded by three rousing cheers for the famous ex-policeman and by 1445 hours we were hurrying away to take cover from the blast. The LG was completely u/s. The wind increased, the dust rose higher, tents flapped, and we waited expectantly for the worst sandstorm many of us ever experienced. Wherever one looked one saw a yellow haze of light, which changed gradually to a most fascinating orange and reddish-orange colour, reminding one vaguely of neon lighting on a foggy day in London. We breathed sand, we ate it, we cursed it, and finally resigned ourselves to it. The rains came, the wind howled, the Mess threatened to take off at full boost. We held a Mess meeting, declared that the messing was of a remarkably high standard, had one for the road, and then perhaps another one, and slunk off through the rain, hoping to find our tents upright, and the Mess still standing in the morning. A most memorable day.

Tedder was quite clear on the requirement for his units in the run-up to the attack. 'What we have got to do is to try and knock the enemy air right out of the ring.' In the few days prior to the launch of the Alamein offensive 213 Squadron ground personnel prepared a forward landing ground and on the evening of 23 October, 'the aircraft arrive, 18 planes and 18 hungry pilots'. Prior to the move, as Peter Olver recalled, 'We were flying every day, keeping the Huns at bay. We were always attacking not letting them settle down.' On the night of 23 October Peter listened to the 'tremendous barrage of shells' as the artillery opened the battle and the next day the opposing armies clashed. Over the next week losses would mount on both sides but Rommel's forces were the first to crack and early in November he ordered a withdrawal.

The air forces were instrumental in the success of the battle, Churchill signalling Tedder, 'Many congratulations on the magnificent way in which you are cutting into the enemy in the air, on the ground, and on the sea.' 213 Squadron's daily presence over the front line kept the skies hostile to the enemy. As Peter, who was usually leading the squadron, recalled, 'We did most of our work flying as a twelve aircraft squadron up and down the line. When the Germans would come in and try and bomb our troops, or strafe our troops, we'd shoot them down.' And certainly 213 Squadron was having by far the better of the intense air battle.

On 2 November 1942, according to his combat report, Peter would make his own addition to the rapidly rising squadron score:

> As Punnet Leader I was airborne from LG172 at 1540 hours, the squadron having been ordered to patrol the area around 856295. Whilst patrolling in the battle area in square 8630, control reported 20+ bandits approaching from the south west at 17,000 feet. They were first reported as the squadron was flying westwards at 8,000 feet, and were travelling eastwards at 13,000 feet, 8 miles away at 12 o'clock and then 9 o'clock. The 20+ Stukas in vics of 3 and in line astern had an escort of 9 Me109s about 3,000 feet above them.
>
> I turned south and then east, climbing to 11,000 feet to engage them calling up combat leader as I did so.
>
> I attacked a Ju87 from astern, firing several short bursts and closing from 100 yards to 50 yards before breaking

away. This aircraft had not time to jettison its bombs. I saw smoke issuing from the Ju87, glycol coming from the port side and pieces falling from the fuselage and tail. I last saw it out of control at 2,000 feet diving vertically. (NB this aircraft was seen to hit the ground by Sergeant Usher.)

I then attacked another Ju87 which jettisoned its bombs. I fired two bursts from fairly close range and saw strikes on the engine and fuselage. Pieces broke away from the aircraft, which I last saw going north eastwards in a steep dive at 1,000 feet. I claim this Ju87 as probably destroyed. Attacking a third Stuka and closing, to a range of 50 yards, I fired two bursts in a stern attack and saw pieces break away from it. I gave it another long burst when my guns ceased to fire. I claim this Ju87 as damaged.

In addition the squadron claimed two further Stukas destroyed, two probably destroyed, one damaged and one Me109 destroyed. The squadron diarist recorded, 'all landed safely at base at 1625 hours amid much excitement as the various attacks and more important still the results were discussed... a highly satisfactory sortie.'

Air engagement was not the only operational activity at this time. 213 Squadron was also called on to harass enemy ground troops. For example at 1335 hours on 3 November, Peter led 213 Squadron with 1 SAAF Squadron detailed to strafe motorised transport and pretty much anything else on or in the vicinity of the road east of Daba. Peter took the pilots out to sea and then across the coast, 'swinging south and then north to the road strafing as they went, and finally flying out to sea before reaching Sidi Abd El Rahman. The enemy was completely taken by surprise. Some small arms fire was experienced.' At the end of the sortie the squadron claimed nine to thirteen tanks, two staff cars, groups of tents, men, twenty-two lorries, an armoured car and two gun pits.

Rommel was now in full retreat and the pursuit was on. The fighter squadrons began their move forward, coming across landing grounds with the odd abandoned German aircraft attracting the attention of souvenir hunters.

Between 13 and 16 November Peter would be leading 213 Squadron on operations, whilst based behind enemy lines. A 243 Wing report sets the scene.

With the intention of establishing a secret base deep into enemy territory from whence the routed Axis forces could be most effectively hammered, 243 Wing, under the command of Wing Commander J Darwen DFC, was ready to move to LG [landing ground] 125 at first light on Friday November 13.

The Wing consisted of 18 aircraft of 238 Squadron, commanded by Squadron Leader Marples and 18 of 213 Squadron, commanded by Squadron Leader Olver, and essential ground personnel from Wing and Squadrons amounting to approximately 105. These and vital equipment were transported by 12 Hudsons. All aircraft arrived safely, with the exception of 2 of 238 Squadron, which force landed en route.

Stores and rations had been dumped by aircraft at the LG the previous day, and on arrival at 1130 all pilots assisted in refuelling their aircraft in readiness for the first operation. This was a combined strafe of the coastal road from Agedabia to Agheila.

Years later, Peter recalls:

We were operating behind the German lines. They tried to attack us but didn't achieve it. We were on an old landing strip that had been used before. Don't think of an aerodrome, a landing strip is merely a couple of drums at the end of it. When the aircraft are gone there is nothing there. We were inland a bit and behind their lines and we strafed them all the way back to Agedabia.

At 1345 hours on 13 November Peter led fifteen 213 Squadron Hurricane IICs, and Marples led twelve 238 Squadron aircraft, all under the command of Wing Commander Darwen, on the successful strafing sortie of the raid from Agheila to Agedabia, again apparently surprising the enemy, finding German and Italian troops. 213 Squadron's contribution was a Fiesler Storch shot from the sky and ten MT claimed destroyed and forty-four damaged. However 213 Squadron did not achieve this without cost, two pilots failing to return.

It would prove to be an extraordinary few days for the Wing. From 156 sorties the return was two aircraft destroyed in the air, twelve on the ground, three damaged on the ground, 138 MT destroyed, 173 MT knocked out.

Peter had been in action again on the morning of 14 November. At 0930 hours he led twelve of 213 Squadron's aircraft on a strafe of the Agedabia landing grounds. On approach to the target a Savoia 79 was dispatched by Flight Lieutenant Cameron. Peter, in his Hurricane IIC, led the attack on the aerodrome and a 244 Wing intelligence summary described his actions.

> Not many aircraft were visible on this drome but 6 CR42s [Italian fighters] were seen on the tarmac and a further 3 in line abreast, one of which was beginning to taxy. Squadron Leader Olver sprayed the three of them scoring a direct hit on one which blew up so violently that his own aircraft was engulfed in the flames that shot up from it.

Peter was to recall later:

> There were two lines, the rear line had got four aircraft. The leader was there and he drove forward just at the wrong moment. I managed to get him just as he was in line with all the others.

> *244 Wing intelligence summary:* The other CR42s already damaged by Squadron Leader Olver's attack were destroyed by the explosion. Flying over the town he shot up troops in the main square and on the LG to the west of the road attacked and damaged a Ju87B.

Whilst conducting the strafing Peter had somewhat of a close call.

> When you are going along on a road you don't notice that the road doesn't ride on top of the sand all the time. Sometimes there's a cutting and the road goes through it and then comes up again. It waves up and down as you are going along. There was a line of telephone poles on the side of the road where it was a cutting. And they had gone to the top and that's when I hit one without seeing it. We were flying as low as you could go.
>
> I hit the pole with my starboard wing, just out of the arc of the airscrew. It nearly had me down and I did a sort of circle, scraping on the ground, just managing to get up and fly back. You couldn't do less than a certain speed because it stalled, but there was such a bloody great gash in the wing.

On 17 November the squadron ground crews and equipment were on the move forward again, this time to El Adem, but having to deal with heavy downpours and the resultant mud, they didn't arrive until 20 November. Meanwhile the squadron pilots had remained operational notably on 18 November.

213 Squadron report: 12 aircraft were airborne from El Adem at 1030 hours and flew on a course on 250 degrees. After 1 hour's flying time what appeared to be a wireless station was observed. The CO Squadron Leader P Olver went down to strafe this, observing on nearer approach that it was a water pump with concrete block house . . . Continuing on course, the road was crossed 10 miles north of Agedabia, between 40 and 50 MT being seen between this point and the town. On first crossing the road Squadron Leader P Olver strafed a 3 ton MT, which blew up. He also knocked out 4 other MT and on flying over the LG at the west of the town, he fired a burst at a Ju87 which he had damaged on a previous strafe. The road was crossed and recrossed and just before reaching the town, a section led by the CO passed it to the west, the two other sections passing it to the east. Intense Breda fire was experienced from the south east and northern corners of the LG and to the east 88mm dual purpose guns, which were being towed along the road north of the town, also opened fire. One of our aircraft was presumed to be hit, as the pilot called up over the R/T saying he was not hurt and was seen to climb out of the cockpit. Squadron Leader Olver went down in an attempt to pick him up, but the nature of the ground prevented his landing. F/O R P Baines, F/O C Luxton, F/Sgt H M Compton and F/Sgt J R Rebstock failed to return to base with the other pilots, but F/Sgt J R Compton subsequently returned on the 24th.

Further moves came, to Martuba, new pilots came in and the squadron operated patrols over Benghazi harbour and to cover the convoys. In December there were further patrols to defend against any enemy aircraft that had the audacity to threaten the Martuba landing grounds, and also to provide convoy cover. But operational activity had lessened, indeed heavy rain would now intervene to make the landing grounds unusable and conditions for the airmen were far from pleasant. Although there were the odd occasions when spirits were raised.

> *21 December 1942, 213 Squadron ORB:* News that Squadron Leader Peter Olver, our CO, had been awarded the DFC reaches us, and in consequence the ban on the sale of beer (which we had been saving for Christmas) was lifted, each member of the Mess being allowed a ration of two cans.

Peter's DFC citation read:

> Squadron Leader Olver has flown with great distinction on recent sorties during which fierce attacks have been made on aircraft and transport well behind the enemy's lines. In November 1942 when his squadron attacked an airfield at Agedabia, 6 enemy aircraft were destroyed; 3 of these were destroyed by Squadron Leader Olver. Although one of the fuel tanks in his aircraft caught fire and exploded, he led his squadron back to a landing ground. In spite of many difficulties and adverse weather he kept his formation together and so enabled further operations to be undertaken on subsequent days.

The 213 Squadron ORB recorded the unit's level of morale on Christmas Day 1942.

> At about 11 o'clock the CO returned as most of us were watching an excellent game of soccer between 'England' and 'The Rest'.
> At 1330 hours the airmen were served in the open air with the Xmas dinner, and there were positively no complaints. There was soup, pork, roast potatoes, peas, cauliflowers, Xmas pudding, oranges, nuts, and beer, and the meal concluded with three cheers for the cooks called for by the CO who spoke briefly.
> In contrast to the very fine soccer match of the morning, in the afternoon two teams, officers and sergeant pilots versus senior NCOs, took the field and played a game which was one glorious rag from start to finish. Rugger and soccer was played, spectators joined in the adlib, goal posts moved to accommodate wild shots, and there was much merriment, players and spectators alike declaring it was the funniest game that had been seen for a long time. Three

cheers were given, three more, then we hurried away, hoping to be in time to hear the King's Christmas broadcast.

The new year would bring fresh responsibilities for Peter, with a change of command, in the form of a posting to 1 SAAF (South African Air Force) Squadron.

> They had been equipped with Spitfires and they had lost three South African majors one after the other. There wasn't a great rush to command the squadron after that. So the AOC said he wanted a British pilot, so he got me and told me to command 1 SAAF squadron and see what the matter with it was. Well there was plenty wrong with it. They weren't particularly good as a squadron to begin with, but they got better. There were perfectly good fellows in the squadron they just needed experience, which they got. We sorted it out and got rid of a lot of surplus people. It was quite a good squadron in the end.

As well as their food rations, the pilots were also making their own arrangements for obtaining food. On the day of Peter's arrival three hunting parties had been sent out, the squadron ORB recording 'the day's bag... was 21 Gazelle'. The next day, 'the venison obtained yesterday has made a very welcome change from the deadly monotony of bully beef.' Peter set about improving the operational effectiveness of the squadron, as recognised in the ORB on 12 January 1943, 'Our new CO Squadron Leader Olver is rapidly getting this somewhat disorganised squadron back to the line once more. The other 3 squadrons in the Wing have all had recent victories, all except 1 SAAF. The pilots are all keen on redeeming our former good name. With the clueful leader we have now we should soon be pulling our weight for the Wing!'

Throughout January Montgomery's forces had been driving on through Libya, and on the morning of 23 January 1943 Tripoli was reached. Beyond lay Tunisia into which the enemy forces were being squeezed. Not only from the east but from the west also, following the Allied landings in November 1942. From February through to the middle of May the noose would tighten eventually ending the Axis presence in North Africa. Air power was still playing its part, which included 244 Wing, and 1 SAAF Squadron was making its presence felt also. On 21 January 1943

244 Wing's diary recorded offensive patrols over Tripoli and Castel Benito, the airmen witnessing the enemy on the ground ensuring that nothing of value was left behind in the town and aerodrome. The diary was also rather derogatory about their opposition in the air, 'Clueless Mc202s' [Macchis] attacked by 1 SAAF Squadron, two claimed destroyed and one probable. Peter Olver was credited with one of the Mc202s destroyed. Peter was leading by example and certainly making a difference. The 1 SAAF ORB entry for 21 January reads, 'There is a noticeable improvement in the spirit of the squadron now. Under Squadron Leader Olver's influence it has pulled itself together remarkably and is rapidly getting on the top line once more.'

Having done his job, at the end of January Peter Olver left to take up responsibilities as Squadron Leader Flying 244 Wing.

> It was a very big wing, not like an English wing with about three squadrons. It had five, six or seven squadrons in it sometimes. All Spitfire mark Vs, with IXs later on. The Spit IX was the best of the lot, much better at altitude. We were operating all the time, attacking the Germans wherever we could find them.

244 Wing's diary opens in February 1943 with, 'The uneventful lull following the fall of Tripoli continues', and it would be so for the first three weeks. But the land battle in the south of Tunisia was about to escalate, in the air similarly, and 244 Wing echelons move up, 'nearer the front line than ever – only 15 miles from the bomb line'. There would be fierce fighting on the land during the next few months in Tunisia. But it was only really a matter of time before the Allied jaws snapped shut. Allied air power made a great contribution by attacking the Axis forces on the front line, behind the front line and on the air, land and sea supply lines as enemy forces were wastefully thrown in to an inevitable defeat. The 244 Wing diary records claims of enemy aircraft, which far exceed the losses reported. The 244 Wing diarist regularly recorded for posterity the successes of his comrades, for example.

> *27 March 1943:* Today joy fell in considerable measure... formations of enemy bombers were successfully intercepted with 50% damage in the case of Ju88s and more with Me210s, with additional relish that both formations jettisoned their bombs on their own formations.

29 March 1943: Simultaneously with the collapse of the Mareth Line a total of 200 enemy aircraft destroyed was reached by the Wing today when 9 enemy aircraft were destroyed and 5 damaged.

6 April 1943: Today the Wing carried out 247 sorties easily breaking all previous records... and though at first the Luftwaffe showed a singular reluctance to appear, later in the day they endeavoured to oblige, adding to the Wing score a total of 3 destroyed, one probable and four damaged.

8 April 1943: This was the third day of continuous high pressure operations. From dawn onwards, offensive patrols were maintained over the bomb line... in the hope that the enemy would sally forth, which he did not. If this was the result of intimidation there was certainly cause for it when the biggest 'strafe' of all was laid on at 1700 hours. At one time there were 221 aircraft over the area of the Axis retreat, but though considerable damage was done on the ground, we had complete supremacy in the air and not a single enemy aircraft dared to put in an appearance.

Peter Olver was, of course, in the midst of all the action, and had some success. On 17 March he and Wing Commander Ian Gleed, whilst returning from a conference at 211 Group HQ, engaged two Me109s a few miles north of the landing ground. The airmen on the ground watched through the fading light as Gleed downed one and Peter damaged another. On 16 April 244 Wing recorded, 'what otherwise would have been an outstanding day in the Wing history was overshadowed by the loss of Wing Commander Gleed', and the diary recorded at length the deep sense of loss. However the 'outstanding day' was because seven enemy transport planes, three Me109s and one FW190 were claimed destroyed.

The 244 Wing diary entry for 17 April 1943 opened, 'After the havoc wrought by the Wing on recent enemy air convoys these became conspicuous by their absence, and after a formation of SM81 [transports] [3] and Me110s [3] escorted by 109s and Macchis had been intercepted in the early morning no further activity of this kind was encountered in spite of continuous armed recces of the area throughout the rest of the day.' The aforementioned forma-tion was intercepted by twelve aircraft of

601 Squadron, top cover from six aircraft of 1 SAAF, led by Peter Olver, and six aircraft of 145 Squadron, which were providing escort to Kittyhawks on an armed recce. One SM81, one Mc205 fighter and an Me110 were claimed as falling to 244 Wing's guns. A further three Me109s and an Mc202 were claimed damaged.

Taking off at 0925 hours, the sortie did not start well, one pilot of 1 SAAF Squadron having to force land and his number two returning to base. Then at 20,000 feet as the allied fighters swept round Cape Bon enemy aircraft were reported.

> *Peter Olver's combat report:* I saw 2 Me109s climbing up in front of us. I dived on one and gave him a short burst from 100 yards. He turned underneath me, and I turned and chased him, firing four short bursts. We had dived from 20,000 to 12,000, and were then amongst a lot of Kitties. I followed him through them and gave him another squirt. I saw him going down with smoke pouring from him, but pulled out then to reform my section, and to cover the Kittyhawks. We had climbed to 15,000 when Gilson reported enemy aircraft below. There were 2 of them, Mc205s, crossing the coast west of Cape Bon. We dived on them and I gave one a squirt from 200 yards from dead astern. He was streaming black smoke, and I followed him down to 3,000 feet. As I was not gaining on him I put the nose down, dived below him and as I pulled up gave him a long burst in the belly, from about 50 yards. Flame and white smoke streamed from him. Then Gilson came in and attacked him. When Gilson pulled out I gave him another squirt. Then Gilson fired at him again.

Lieutenant Gilson had already been involved in combat, and would later claim a Me109 damaged. His combat report records his co-operation with Peter Olver.

> As we crossed the coast at Cape Bon I saw one enemy aircraft. Squadron Leader Olver dived after him, chasing him out to sea. The enemy aircraft began a slight climb. There was smoke coming away from him. I closed to 250 yards and gave him a number of bursts from astern. He then turned to the right. I turned with him, firing all the time. I was then about 100 yards from him. I last saw him diving away with smoke pouring from him (Note by Intelligence Officer: Squadron Leader Olver saw this enemy

aircraft, which he states was a Mc205, go down in flames. He suggests sharing it with Lieutenant Gilson...)

The Wing diary recorded two pilots missing, Flight Sergeant Griffiths of 601 Squadron and Lieutenant Mundell of 1 SAAF Squadron.

The next day Peter Olver took over command of the wing, being made an acting wing commander, and his pilots continued to utilise their air superiority through to the end of April and into May, including, 'brilliant results against shipping'. On 5 May, 'one of the largest formation of fighters yet encountered by the Wing – it consisted of 34 Me109s and Mc202s – was intercepted over Creteville by four Spitfires of 92 Squadron led by Wing Commander Olver. In spite of the advantage of height and number, the majority of the formation showed no inclination to stay and fight it out when our aircraft attacked.' Two enemy aircraft were damaged, one credited to Peter.

On 13 May the Allied Commander-in-Chief General Alexander signalled to Winston Churchill, 'It is my duty to report that the Tunisian campaign is over. All enemy resistance has ceased. We are the masters of the North Africa shores.' Attention now switched to the next operations, the seizure of the island of Pantelleria, and then the assault on Sicily. Whilst the army and navy prepared, the Allied air forces kept up the pressure.

> We didn't pause at all. We attacked all the time, trying to engage the Luftwaffe but they were getting crafty by that time. When they went out of Africa they got the wind up rather and tried not to engage. You'd spot them and then they'd fly for home, although you could still get shot down if you weren't careful. We flew over Pantelleria just to put the wind up the Italians. We really had a tremendous number of aircraft flying then.

In preparation for the forthcoming operations, 244 Wing moved to Malta. As Peter recalled, 'I led them across to begin with. It was quite an interesting place, and had had the worst of it before we got there.'

As the day of the seaborne assault on Sicily neared 244 Wing recorded on 4 July, 'the softening process started'. In the following days the wing escorted bombers attacking targets in Sicily. On 7 July, 'the softening up became pulverisation'. The invasion began on 10 July 1943 and 244 Wing maintained

continuous patrols over the beaches, engaging enemy aircraft.
The next day from first to last light the wing kept up its presence.
One particular patrol brought considerable success but also a
significant loss, as recorded in the diary:

> 4 Ju88s were destroyed, one probably destroyed and a sixth
> damaged, when 12 Ju88s were intercepted by 92 Squadron
> (1500-1635) over Priola. There was an escort of 30 fighters
> but these were ahead and did not engage our general
> formation... Unfortunately Wing Commander Olver, who
> was leading the IX's did not return.'

Peter takes up the story:

> The Germans were going to bomb the American landing. I
> saw them coming down towards it, so we dashed along
> towards them. They suddenly saw the Spitfires
> approaching. The Ju88s, at the same height, were coming
> down from the north. They swung round and struggled to
> get home, dropping their bombs on the ground. They
> weren't very brave at that time the Luftwaffe. They wanted
> to bomb the American shipping but they didn't like
> Spitfires. They did a terrific steep turn, which isolated the
> outside one, and I shot it down. The other pilots got onto
> the remaining bombers. Then I got a bullet in my fuel
> tanks, but it wasn't the Junkers 88 that I had shot down
> that had hit me. They started to bale out in no time at all,
> and the aircraft crashed on the ground. Who put the bullet
> into my fuel tank I couldn't say but I pretty soon found my
> aircraft on fire.
>
> I was not very high but I was going to try and get back
> to the coast, to the sea, because burns don't like salt water.
> I put the nose down, heading for the sea, but I couldn't get
> to it. I was hoping that the aircraft wouldn't blow up and
> fortunately the engine was going perfectly right to the end.
>
> I opened the hood, at the last moment, knowing that
> you have to be very quick when you land on water. But the
> flames, which were licking down the fuselage, came in the
> cockpit and over my face. I had to get out fast. I was in a
> bit of a hurry as I was so low down and once out I hit the
> tail. My legs were burnt, I dislocated my shoulder and I
> broke my arm.
>
> The parachute stopped my forward impetus, not the

usual way when they stop you falling. It opened up as I was dashing along and I hit the ground at the same time. I was right on the deck.

Peter had escaped just in time. He had come down in territory still in the hands of the enemy, who were very soon to make their presence known.

I was aware of something like a bee at my feet and on the second bee I realised that somebody was shooting at me from a distance. I took off as best I could but was picked up by some kitchen boy Germans, a ragged sort of mob, who were rather nasty to me. My legs had been burned quite badly. I was marched across a grain field, which the Sicilians had cut by hand. I didn't want the stubble sticking into my burnt legs but these German kitchen boys kept sticking me up the arse with a bayonet, to make me go to a gate across the field. We heard a motorbike behind us and on it and the attached sidecar were two of the smartest senior NCOs you could imagine – Hermann Goering parachute division. Both could speak English, one very well, and he said to me, 'Have these chaps been molesting you in any way?' I said, 'Well they tried to take my watch and a few other things.' They lined them all up, swore at them, shouted at them and smacked them across the face. I was then put in the side car and they took me off to try and find a doctor. But they were very short of doctors.

I finally came across one who became a firm friend of mine. He was German of course. He couldn't do much, but he saw to my arm, which was hanging down and bound it all up. Some days I was on a lorry, on straw, with a lot of German wounded. We got rather fond of each other actually.

The aim was to get us out of Sicily. At the Messina Straits, I was lying on the ground on a very hot day near a bar and some Germans were getting drinks. After a while I thought I could do with a drink, so I got up and went into the bar. None of the Germans stopped me. I said in English that what I had got was a ten shilling British Military authority note and I handed it to this chap. He nearly had a fit behind the bar. He was terrified. But the Germans said, 'Go on, give him a drink and give him his note back to.' So they paid for my drink. The chap in charge of the landing craft taking all these troops across the Straits could speak very good English. I commended him on it and he said, 'Well I was three years at Rugby, so why shouldn't I?' I said, 'you're on the wrong bloody side then.' He said, 'Well I'm German and that's all there is to it.'

On reaching the toe of Italy Peter was put into a hospital with German wounded.

A lot of these chaps had been on the lorry with me and they had become firm friends of mine. I never found the Germans disliked the British, as long as you got a good one, not a bad one. You got the odd chap whose house had been bombed in Berlin, he wasn't so happy with you. Then I went up to a hospital at Naples, and then out of that to a prison camp. Lot of Americans in that camp and I got treatment of a sort but they had no medicaments. An American Jew, who was very frightened of the Germans, was a doctor and he did what he could for me, which wasn't much as they hadn't got much. But all the American troops had been issued with sulphamilamide and they used that on my wounds, which by now had all gone septic. Having no proper bandages, they had put on paper bandages, which had grown into the leg. So they now had to soak them all off and start again. That was painful. He did the best he could, though the hairs have never come back on my legs properly.

Peter now began the long journey to a prisoner-of-war camp in Germany.

The Germans did have an interrogation centre at Dulag Luft but they never sent me to it. I was never questioned officially. Although I was interrogated by many people it was not by anybody who knew anything. They treated me pretty well. I was lucky to get up through Italy. The train ahead of mine was strafed and the train behind mine was strafed. I was shut in for five days and four nights. That was horrible, we hadn't anything to eat or drink and there wasn't room to lie down properly, but I couldn't stand up so I had to. I did try to escape when travelling in a train. I tried to get out of a window. I had a tap on the shoulder and turned to find a German NCO with a bloody great gun pointing at me, telling me to get back in.

Peter went through a number of camps before finally arriving at East Compound, Stalag Luft III, Sagan. The war still had twenty-two months to run.

It was like going into the wolves den at Whipsnade zoo, seeing all these chaps shouting and talking like mad. I had been wounded a bit and was not feeling particularly proud. You couldn't tell when the war was going to end. The troops were doing well but for us it was not fast enough. There were little problems. I hadn't got enough bedboards. They were being used for shoring up escape tunnels. So I couldn't sleep very well. Food was inadequate, there was a shortage. I passed the time reading, playing games, walking round the circuit, discussing the course of the war with other people. We had a wireless in my room and a chap who could take down the news in shorthand.

In 1945 the situation for the Germans on the eastern front was deteriorating. The Russians were advancing and the POWs at Stalag Luft III began to hear the front-line guns. The decision was made to evacuate the camp and march the prisoners west, an evacuation which was carried out in haste.

I had prepared for it. I could see what was going to happen. I had four pairs of socks which were fresh. I had them round my belt and would change them on the walk. I had made a pack for my back and one for my front to counter balance it. I was in command of a lot of people but what could you do in such conditions, nothing really. It was extremely cold, there was not enough to eat and then there was the problem of finding somewhere to go at night. The first night of the march I kicked the door in of an old chapel and got the chaps in there. Still cold but not as cold as outside. Perishing. And the German guards were as badly off as we were.

East Compound had left the camp at Sagan very early on the morning of 28 January, meeting up with fellow POWs from North and Belaria Compounds on 31 January at Muskau. From here half of East Compound, including Peter Olver, along with North Compound marched to Spremberg railyards, arriving late in the afternoon of 2 February. Here they were entrained and sent to the Bremen area, arriving late afternoon on 4 February. All the time, during the march the POWs, and their guards, had to contend with the extreme cold. The search for food was also an ongoing concern for the marching prisoners and Peter took it upon himself to find something to eat from the local population.

> I used to go into their homes and tell them I wanted some food. They were surprisingly fine with this and once they got used to the look of you they'd give you some food. Although not all of them. Some were bloody awful and I used to say that I would call in a few thousand from outside if they didn't give me any food. They started to give it to me. I would have killed them if they hadn't.
>
> I was a hell of a thief. I would just go into people's houses, take some food and go. There weren't enough guards. You'd always walk behind a guard and his dog and he's not likely to be looking out of his arse.
>
> You could have made a break for it easily, but I didn't see a future in it. I could see we would be better off all keeping together. You were sorely tempted but I didn't trust the Russians, just didn't know what the treatment would be like with them.

The POWs spent the rest of February, March and early April at Marlag und Milag Nord, a few miles outside Bremen. Many had arrived in a state of very poor health, with cases of frostbite and bad stomach complaints from eating frozen bread were common. Conditions at the camp, sanitation, bedding, cooking arrangements, were summed up as 'appalling'.

Germany was now rapidly moving towards defeat. The British, Canadian and American armies had crossed the Rhine. On 10 April Marlag und Milag Nord was evacuated, the POWs heading for the Lübeck area. On arrival, dissatisfied with the camp they had been allocated the POWs took up residence in a large farm. All the POWs now had to do was survive. Sourcing food, of course, still occupied the prisoners' minds, including Peter's.

> I went into a farm building and saw this sausage and thought I could do with some of that. There was quite an attractive girl there. I said I wanted some of the sausage and she said she couldn't give me any of that but she would give

me some other food, adding though that if her father saw me he'd kill me. I said, 'well he'll kill me or I shall kill him', and I asked why he wanted to kill me. She responded that his son had been shot down, whilst serving with the Luftwaffe. After a while I heard him coming and far from wishing to kill me, we became firm friends and he took me up the field to show me where his son was buried.

At a certain stage we disarmed the German guards. We were in a large farm that belonged to a very wealthy German cigar importer, a gigantic dairy farm. I went out, took a lorry that I had discovered, and went for a ride round with all these Poles. They wanted to stop and kill some Germans, but I couldn't see any reason for killing them particularly so I didn't let them.

The British army arrived in the area at the beginning of May. Peter, whilst travelling around in a jeep met up with some of the British troops, and when liberation finally came he ended up at Diepholz, 'where I was put in a DC3 and taken back to England. I had lost a lot of weight, weighing then about seven or eight stone.'

Peter Olver's outstanding career had begun just over four and a half years earlier amidst the hostile skies during the Battle of Britain. All the experience he had gained then and during his subsequent operations from the UK, patrols and offensive sweeps, he had utilised during his time in the deserts of North Africa, applying his leadership qualities, rising to command a wing.

On return to the United Kingdom he joined Technical Training Command, overseeing 3 Wing, Wilmslow. He subsequently spent some time at Chivenor, on Spitfire XIVs, then in 1947 chose to break from the RAF. He then took his family to Kenya to realise the passion for farming that he had developed at an early age. In 1963 he came back to England and carried on farming. He is now retired, living in Wiltshire.

Sixty-six years on Peter reflects on the Battle of Britain.

I don't think I realised at the time how important the Battle of Britain was. It has grown in people's imaginations really but it was just a moment in time. The battle as far as I was concerned didn't finish at the end of a particular period of time. It went on. The Germans were still coming in, over our coast. It's all very well to say that the Battle of Britain is from this date to this date, but they were still killing your pals.

People were overclaiming like hell, so were the Germans tremendously. There's every reason why they should, their government wanted them to do it, their units wanted them to do it and the individuals after a bit wanted to do it. It's very easy to do. If you shoot at something you think you've got it and you don't stop to look around at it because then you'll get shot down. Overclaiming's what lost the Germans the battle, no doubt about that.

And Peter's final thoughts, 'The airmen should be remembered. They were a wonderful lot of people.'

Flight Lieutenant William Terence Montague Clark DFM

Chapter 9

Contact

Tony Cheney was eleven in September 1940, living in a small terrace house, just off the Harrow road in north-west London. Tony would experience, and never forget, the Luftwaffe's attempts to crack London and the morale of its people.

A lot of our time was spent in a brick air-raid shelter in the playground, as the Battle of Britain was just reaching its climax, and we were having air raids every day and night.

But Wednesday, September 18th was a rather special day.....

About 8.30 in the evening the sirens sounded again, a wailing up-and-down note which we were getting familiar with. My Mum called out, 'Tony, put your homework away and go down to the shelter.' The Germans had started to bomb London in a big way, by night as well as by day.

I put my books and things in my satchel, which was hanging up in the hallway, grabbed my little first-aid kit in a tin box, put on a coat, trotted out into the small backyard and down the steps into the Anderson shelter. I could hear my Mum calling to my Dad, 'I've got Derek (my younger brother, who was in bed and asleep) – hurry up, George, and get down to the shelter.' She came bustling out, with Derek in her arms, wrapped up in a blanket. Already the unsteady drone of German bombers could be heard, and the noise of anti-aircraft guns was getting louder as the bombers came nearer. Searchlights were weaving about in the sky, and the night was lit up by the flashes of exploding anti-aircraft shells. 'Don't stand up there watching, George', said my Mum, 'Come on in, it's dangerous out there.' Dad liked to lean against the Anderson shelter, and watch the scene, whilst he finished off his pipe of tobacco. He had been in the trenches in the first world war, and was quite unmoved by the noise and commotion – and the danger – going on around. But tonight, unusually, he hadn't lit up his pipe, and came on in when my Mum called to him. They sat together on the side of one of the lower bunks in the shelter, talking quietly. I sat on the other bunk, and my brother was in the top bunk, still asleep. The noise of the air-raid came nearer, with the whistle, whoosh and bang of the bombs, the fire-engine bells, and the sharp crack of nearby anti-aircraft guns getting louder all the time.

I was sitting on the edge of the bunk, when, without warning, everything went black. I don't know how long it lasted, probably only a few seconds, then the air was full of choking dust, people were shouting and screaming outside. In the light of my torch, through the fog of dust, I could see my Mum looking very white and shaken. My Dad said calmly, 'I expect that's the house gone, a direct hit probably.' The curtain over the entrance to the shelter was pulled aside, a torch shone in, and an air-raid warden shouted, 'Anyone hurt, you alright in here?' 'Yes, alright, but what happened, are we hit?' my Dad replied. 'A mine over Buller Road, everywhere's flattened, a lot killed', the warden said, and disappeared. 'Go and have a look, George', my Mum whispered, 'but do be careful.' My Dad pulled himself up through the entrance to the shelter and surveyed the scene. 'My God', I heard him say, 'what a mess.' He came back in, and spoke to my Mum. 'The house is standing, but the roof's gone, there's timber everywhere, there's lots of buildings down over the back, where Compton Road was.' Just then we heard whistles blowing, people shouting, and the clang of fire-engine bells. A voice shouted, 'Everybody out, get out of here, a gas-mains busted, there's going to be a bloody great bang in a moment.' 'You go with Derek, I'll bring Tony', she said to my Dad. 'Mind how you go, love', the warden said in a friendly voice, 'there's glass everywhere.' The backyard and the shelter were covered, criss-cross, with broken roof timbers, bits of wood, tiles, bricks, bits of furniture. The windows of the house were gone and the back door, ripped open, hung forlornly on one hinge. The tiles were gone from the roof of the house, and a few remaining timbers stuck up blackly against the clouds in the moonlight. The crash of anti-aircraft guns, and the drone of aircraft engines increased again.[12]

Massive explosions, sheets of flame and multiple fire conflagrations lit the night sky. All caused by the high explosive and incendiary bombs that were being dropped that night by the German bombers, which had droned across the city virtually from the onset of darkness to the verge of daybreak. London was suffering its heaviest night bombardment of the war to date. Docks and industry and the surrounding areas beside the river Thames to the east of the Tower of London were burning. Not that the bombing was that concentrated. Hospitals, churches, gas works, residential areas, the railways, the roads were destroyed or damaged. Many many lives were lost. Many people were seriously injured. Many people lost their homes.

It was the night of 16/17 April 1941, and Londoners were into their eighth month of suffering under the German night-bombing offensive. Tens of thousands had been killed. The German daylight air offensive had been seen off by the RAF the summer before. But seeing off the Luftwaffe night-time intruders required new thinking, new technology, new equipment and new tactics. Air defence against the 'Blitz' would test that system.

Fighter Command put up 164 aircraft to counter the stream of German bombers on this night. One was a 219 Squadron twin-engined Bristol Beaufighter flown by Wing Commander Tom Pike accompanied by Sergeant Terry Clark. Pike listened intently, and reacted to, the ground controller's instructions, as they successfully positioned the Beaufighter in close proximity to an enemy raider. Terry Clark stared into the cathode ray tubes in front of him, eager to see the blip indicating their foe had been found. The blip appeared and Terry spoke to his pilot. 'Contact'.

William Terence Montague Clark was born on 11 April 1919 in a nursing home at Broad Green, a suburb of Croydon.

> One thing that does still stand out in my mind is the sight of men, not that old, walking the streets carrying a little wooden tray and selling shoe laces and boxes of matches – proudly wearing their war medals.

Times were hard and Terry left school at fourteen, 'not because I liked work, but to make some money.' He worked for a couple of years at Croydon Gas works, but clearly wasn't satisfied, 'I began to think about joining the forces, RAF perhaps.' He had taken the opportunity to make the odd visit to Croydon airport, 'you might be lucky and see Imperial Airways Hannibal aircraft take off bound for Paris. To me though flying looked dangerous – so I considered the navy.' Terry applied to join the Royal Navy Volunteer Reserve but a certain necessary medical procedure led to a change of mind, 'I learnt that I would be vaccinated. I wasn't going to have needles stuck in my arm. So my plan to join the navy died a very quick death.'

A few months later he came across a notice at the office stating that Auxiliary Air Force Squadron No. 615 was forming at RAF Station Kenley and men were required for training as fitters, armourers and air gunners.

> 'Air Gunners'. That sounded interesting, but would I like flying? The thought of being in the air with my machine gun at the ready, the wind flying past me, my pilot hurtling

through the sky chasing the enemy, seemed exciting at the time.

For an expensive ten shillings Terry was able to take a ten-minute flight on a De Havilland Rapide, 'but it was worth every penny. I enjoyed every moment and I was hooked. My next move was to get to RAF Kenley.' Small in stature but with pride in his heart, Terry arrived in March 1938, was shown around the airfield, coming across some Hawker Hector biplanes, 'The machine had two cockpits, one for the pilot and the other for the air gunner. My interest in this aircraft increased!' Next he had an interview with the CO.

He asked me why I wanted to join the Auxiliary Air Force. My reply was that I had a great interest in flying. When he next asked me if I had flown before I mentioned the flight in the Rapide at Croydon. He seemed impressed and asked me what I wanted to do in the squadron. In a flash I said air gunner. He then looked at the officer to his side, smiled and said, 'Clark, I don't think you would see over the scarf ring.' I replied very quickly that I would, not for one moment knowing what a scarf ring was! He paused looked again at his companion and then told me he would put me down for training as an air gunner. I left the room feeling somewhat pleased with myself.

Terry returned to Kenley the following Saturday, 'All keyed up, I thought I might even have a trip in the Hector.' But there were more mundane matters to deal with first. Drill without rifles, how to salute an officer, drilling with rifles, 'I found this instrument of war difficult to handle, after all it was nearly as tall as me.' Collecting kit, dismantling a machine gun and putting it back together, making your bed in a certain way, 'or you would be told in a certain fashion to do it again.' Then came an opportunity to use the rifles at the rifle range, 'We were going to fire them! One bullet for each man, so we had better make it count. I duly fired at the target. Ouch! I thought the recoil had broken my shoulder. Where my bullet was heaven only knew. I think they are still looking for it.' Training continued.

Although I was an untrained air gunner, it was decided we should have instruction on map reading and after a few lectures I braved the air. I was kitted out with flying helmet, goggles, flying suit, and really super leather flying boots. At last this was the real thing. My pilot was Flying Officer Fieldsend. My first RAF airborne trip from RAF Kenley was on 9 June 1938 and we were airborne for one hour. To say it was terrific is an understatement.

Terry attended lectures in meteorology and was a passenger during formation flying practice, 'It was a grand sight to see three aircraft so close together, but not too close! For all these trips I just sat in my cockpit and enjoyed the views.'

In August 1938 Terry went with the squadron to RAF Thorney Island for two weeks training, sleeping under canvas, attending numerous lectures, and practicing landings and take-offs.

On 27 August three of us air gunners were detailed to be at the hangar ready to take off at 2.00 pm, complete with mae wests, as flying would be over the sea. We went down to the hangar, and the other two lads having found mae wests, went down to the dispersal leaving me still looking (I'm convinced the RAF was being economical with equipment). I was lucky and I rushed off to the aircraft complete with all the necessary bits and pieces. They were waiting for me and I duly climbed into my cockpit. As I settled I was handed a small cardboard box and was told that the pilot would tell me what to do with it. Out to sea we went, and my instructions with regard the box were as follows – my pilot would fly low over the sea whilst the other two aircraft would gain height. Then when nearing sea level I would throw the box out and the pilot would then gain height and join the other two aircraft. I know that the box contained aluminium powder and when it hit the sea it would burst, spread and make a very suitable target for air-to-sea firing. However, after all that the mission was abandoned due to poor visibility and after fifty minutes in the air we returned to base. On stepping out of my cockpit a sergeant approached and said, 'Clark, you are on a charge.' In amazement I said, 'What for? What have I done?' The sergeant replied that I was to report to his office immediately and he would let me know. Off I went and was duly marched in to see the flight commander. 'Do you know', he said , 'if it had been wartime, the delay of a flight could have serious consequences.' My defence was that I had great trouble finding a mae west. I did not think it wise to say that I thought the RAF was penny pinching. I was duly charged, and for my punishment was confined to camp, so no boozy trip out. Armed with scrubbing brush, pail and carbolic soap I set about scrubbing the flight commander's office floor. My earlier visions of flying were somewhat dulled – I did not think that flying entailed this sort of work.

Despite being confined to camp, Terry still managed to find a way out.

I laid on the back floor of a car with a blanket over me and there were three chaps sitting in the back with their feet on me. We passed the guard room OK and we eventually returned. I had had my full share of the necessary liquid.

International events then took over. The Munich crisis enforced a move for the squadron to its wartime station at RAF Old Sarum, but Terry, as an auxiliary remained behind, 'I can only assume that if matters really became serious the air gunners and all other auxiliary personnel would have been called up.' The crisis passed and 615 Squadron returned to Kenley, soon to learn that they would be coming under the direction of Fighter Command with conversion to Gloster Gauntlets and then to Gloster Gladiators. Such a change however made certain airmen rather redundant.

Gladiators were single-seater aircraft. So no room for an air gunner. We AGs [air gunners] now had a problem. What to do? We asked if we could transfer to another squadron. The answer was no. Jobs like aero fitter and engine mechanic were offered but personally I did not want to do either. I was then asked, 'Well what can you do?' Craftily I thought of a nice warm job in the orderly room, so I said I could type. 'Right then orderly room for you.' So from air gunner to orderly room in one sharp stroke.

Terry then moved with the squadron for the annual camp, to HMS Peregrine, which became RAF Ford, 'Being in the OR one began to notice an air of urgency. Signals were flying to and fro. Then in the middle of the second week it all happened.' The squadron was sent back to Kenley, call-up papers were handed out and then a medical check up, involving, 'a jab in the arm, my first. I am sure that by the time the doctor got to me the needle was blunt.' A move to Croydon airport followed. The squadron settled in to newly named RAF Croydon.

As I remember, my main task was typing weekly reports of aircraft status. In those early days at Croydon life seemed to go on quite calmly, but there was excitement in the air. There were rumours of the squadron going overseas.

Which indeed they did, but one member was kept behind to maintain the orderly room. As Terry lived close to the aerodrome he was granted a sleeping out pass, and was able to spend some time at home. Some weeks later he was sent to Kenley, and there, 'took up residence in the armoury'. But he became impatient and requested an interview to try and establish what the future had in store for him. A few weeks later a posting came through to a refresher course at No.5 Bombing and Gunnery School at RAF Jurby, on the Isle of Man.

At the beginning of April 1940, for five consecutive days, I was flying twice a day in Fairey Battle aircraft, firing a machine gun at last, at a drogue towed by another aircraft. On one occasion I hit the cable towing the drogue, which I thought was a good shot. But of course the drogue fell away, which put pay to any shooting training for the second air gunner who was with me in the cockpit. On landing the instructor came up to me and in RAF language stated that he was not amused.

219 Sqn Blenheim

A couple of days later Terry had his first flight in a Bristol Blenheim, 'which had a fitted turret for the air gunner, his own private office.' After three weeks at Jurby he heard that he would be returning to Kenley.

> To the best of my knowledge there was no passing out parade and no brevet to say that I had passed the course OK. All my logbook shows is that I spent 9.25 hours flying in Fairey Battle and Blenheim aircraft. Not much to show.

Back at Kenley Terry again requested an interview, 'with the Adj, subject POSTING!' On 12 July the news Terry was after came through, a posting to 219 Squadron, at Catterick, to fly in Bristol Blenheims. 'At last I was going to get in on the action. It had been a long wait.' Arriving in the evening at Catterick Terry refreshed himself at the airmen's mess and then found a bed for the night.

> The next morning I presented myself at the orderly room. 'Ah Clark', said the corporal, 'we were expecting you but where are your stripes and brevet?' Sergeant stripes! I had heard rumours that aircrew were to be made sergeants. He went on, 'You cannot see the CO as you are. Here is a clothing chit, go down to the clothing store and get your stripes and brevet and come back at 2.00 pm.' I had had breakfast in the airmen's mess. I was now going to have lunch in the sergeants' mess. Life in the RAF was getting better by the minute.

Terry began to settle down, acquainting himself with fellow airmen.

> Life as a sergeant was improving, but I am sorry to say we young sergeants were not exactly welcomed in the sergeants' mess. The old sweats were somewhat peeved that we had received our stripes so soon. I could understand that the older NCOs would be annoyed. After all it had probably taken them many years to attain that rank, and we achieved it in a matter of days. Myself – one day AC2 and sergeant the next. Our argument was that we were risking our necks as well. As time went by there were more aircrew NCOs and so we had to be accepted. In the end all were happy to share a pint.

An Air Historical Branch narrative covering the early stages of night air defence in the Second World War succinctly puts the difficulties associated with air combat in the darkness.

> The problem of air defence is well conceived in three subsidiary but interrelated phases. Simply stated, these are early detection of the enemy, his continuous and accurate location and, finally, engagement and destruction. In broad terms, these are prerequisites of successful interception both by day and by night, with the important difference that by night the limitations of human vision had somehow to be made good.[13]

Indeed day-fighter pilots often relate, that after flying through and engaging an enemy formation, with their squadron, they suddenly found themselves all alone in the sky. At night that sense of isolation is of course even greater.

So one of the main problems at night was that once an enemy aircraft had been found, the key was to remain in contact. Airborne radar could provide the answer, but when the war broke out its development was still in its infancy. In December 1938, 25 Squadron received twin-engined Bristol Blenheim IFs and the squadron would be top of the list for equipping with airborne radar electronics. The tactics and techniques of operational night fighting both in the air and with ground control, would be developed attempting to counter German minelaying aircraft early in the war but as the AHB narrative put it, 'Neither effort nor ardour could overcome the technical weaknesses inherent in the primitive airborne radar equipment of those days, nor the drawbacks in the sets used for ground control.' A Night Interception Committee was formed in March 1940 and it had the foresight to realise that the enemy daylight offensive would soon be forced through losses to resorting to bombing in the dark. These night attacks would begin in England in June 1940, a few months later they would become an onslaught. During the summer improvements were made in airborne interception AI radar and as Dowding would state when the night-bombing campaign escalated:

> An AI sight must eventually be developed, capable of being laid and fixed without seeing the enemy, and every fighter should be capable of leaving and returning to its aerodrome blind. Our task will not be finished until we can locate, pursue and shoot down the enemy in cloud by day and by

night, and the AI must become a gun-sight... nothing less will suffice for the defence of the country.[14]

Of course someone would be required to look down that 'gun sight'. This duty would be taken up by men such as Terry Clark.

219 Squadron crews detailed for night duties in July 1940 would make an evening ten-minute flight to RAF Leeming, from where they would operate, 'Relax in flying control and await our turn to get airborne. Not many chairs and the concrete was hard.' Despite such hardships Terry was enjoying his new experiences.

> Life in the squadron was great. Our aircraft was the short nose Blenheim Mark I. Not the best aircraft for night fighting, but the best at that time. Looking back it seemed clear that we were not at all prepared for war. In some of the aircraft we carried AI mark 3 [which had been installed in some of the squadron aircraft in August 1940]. In those days to operate the AI we carried an LAC who had to lie flat on his stomach and gaze into the magic box. The trouble was that the vibrations of the aircraft, nine times out of ten, made the AI unserviceable.

On 1 August 1940 Terry took off at 2120 hours in a Blenheim piloted by Pilot Officer Lake for the ten-minute flight to Leeming, returning at 0720 the next morning. These trips too and from Leeming would become routine.

> We were operating a bus service, to and from Leeming. Await our turn, be scrambled and roam the sky, ever hopeful that the AI operator would pick up a contact, or the ground controller would put us in the direction of the enemy. AI was very unreliable and to be honest the AI equipment was still in its infancy and very secret. The boffins were working hard to improve the equipment, but like everything else it took time. So we struggled on with the poor old Blenheim and infant AI.

219 Squadron's main responsibilities prior to 15 August 1940 had been to undertake night operations. But on this particular day the squadron's aircrews would take part in a most memorable operation. The Luftwaffe, extending its attack front, went for targets in the north and north-east of England. This proved costly as sixteen bombers and seven fighters would not be

making the return trip across the North Sea. 219 Squadron claimed a share of the success. At 1310 hours four Blenheims took off to intercept one of the raids and the squadron diary recorded 'two aircraft were believed to be destroyed'.

Operations continued, with various pilots, and as Terry recalled, 'What one would have given for a faster aircraft and better AI. We were ever on the look out for any enemy who had the nerve to invade our area. I remember asking myself whenever were we going to get to grips with the opposition?' 219 Squadron ORB records with regularity in this period, 'no results' or 'without result' and sometimes the suggestion of frustration was also apparent in the occasional entries such as, 'AI again employed without result', '...sent off to intercept X raid with customary lack of success', '...as usual plots faded out as soon as the aircraft took off'. It was not just 219 Squadron who were frustrated, the Air Historical Branch narrative records, 'During August Fighter Command saw small return for their attempts against the night raider. 828 sorties were flown on twenty-six nights of the month, an average of about thirty-one sorties a night, and there were claims to the destruction of four enemy aircraft, only three of which were allowed.'

Despite the lack of engagements with the enemy, this is not to say that night flying in itself was not a perilous occupation. The 219 Squadron diary kept a record of such perils. On 6 August, on a searchlight co-op, the two airmen in a Blenheim diving low over a river, which hit a high tension cable and crashed, suffered facial injuries. On 27 August a Blenheim on return from a patrol was on the receiving end of friendly fire from a Lewis gun, the bullet passing through the wing. On 29 August one pilot whilst on operations suddenly found his Blenheim lit by searchlights and he came under 'friendly' AA fire.

Into September 1940 and the great night trial in the air and on the ground was about to begin. The seed of fear had actually already been sown in the minds of the people of England. Certain popular movies had made the population aware of what a bombing attack could do. *Things to Come* released a couple of years prior to the war, dramatised H G Wells' vision of the aerial bombing of a city and the threat of air attack by a mass of bombers and the resultant widespread fear. How could propaganda counter this fear? *The Lion Has Wings* released a few weeks into the war showed Spitfires turning back the bombers. Then there was *London Can Take It*, regarded as one of the greatest war films of all time, which somewhat demonised the actions of the enemy air forces, including the narrator using lines such as 'German bombers are creatures of the night. They melt away before the dawn and scurry back to the safety of their own aerodromes.'

The German night creatures began their attempt to crack their enemy's civilian morale, in earnest, early in September 1940, following up on the mass attack on London, during the previous daylight hours. The Air Historical Branch narrative stated, 'All that had gone before was a prelude to the great night bombardment of London which commenced on 7/8 September.' The night bombing would continue, for days, which became weeks and then months. Pressure grew on the RAF to provide effective opposition. For interception of the enemy aircraft there were eight night squadrons, six Blenheim and two Defiant, available, along with some aircraft from the fighter interception unit. There were also some single-engine squadrons on hand but not all pilots had night-flying experience, the aircraft were not really suitable and day pilots were tired enough as it was.

The 219 Squadron diarist made the following notes on 24 and 25 September respectively, 'The enemy appear to be concentrating on the south with all his aircraft', 'There were no X raid patrols during the night apparently for the same reasons as the previous night'. Indeed to the south was where the night battle was escalating. So unsurprisingly on 12 October there was a move in this direction for Terry's squadron, to RAF Redhill, 11 Group and a new aircraft, the twin-engined Bristol Beaufighter. The first couple of weeks at Redhill proved frustrating, however. Contacts were made occasionally but 'no results' would again feature. The entry on 21 October commenting on operations recorded, 'no results were obtained except that an AI expert who accompanied Flight Lieutenant Goddard succeeded in setting that apparatus on fire.' Nevertheless despite ongoing frustrations the new aircraft were certainly welcomed, as Terry Clark relates:

> At last we had an aircraft built for the job. However, on inspection of the Beau we noticed the absence of a turret! No machine gun! What were they up to? Where were the air gunners going to sit? The answer was simple. There were no air gunners and we were to be retrained as AI

operators. This of course, for most of us, was not on. We had been trained as air gunners and air gunners we wanted to remain. Some of us requested an interview with the CO and we stated that we did not want to gaze into a cathode ray tube and we would like to be transferred to Bomber Command. The CO's response was that he did not think that 11 Group, Fighter Command would approve, but he would try. The answer came back, 'air gunners would re-train as AI operators and like it.' I thought that our offer to go to Bomber Command would have been accepted with open arms, they were having severe losses. I could only think that our slight knowledge of AI was sufficient to keep us in this country. And it would be understandable as AI was still a closely guarded secret.

In addition to a new aircraft Terry had now to familiarise himself with the new Mark IV AI and also to make better acquaintance with a permanent pilot, Pilot Officer Dudley Hobbis. Terry still felt bitter about the change in his responsibilities though, 'but along came a boost'. On the night of 25/26 October 1940 Sergeant Arthur Hodgkinson, with his AI operator Sergeant Benn, intercepted and shot down a Dornier 17. The first confirmed claim in a Beaufighter.

Everybody was absolutely delighted and it helped us air gunners to accept our new role. We now had to get our eyes glued to that tube and make it work not only for us but for the squadron. By now we had a flight of three aircraft at RAF Kenley and three aircraft at RAF Tangmere. We were still using some Blenheims but gradually they were replaced by the Beau. For me, operating from Kenley was somewhat uplifting and made me feel that I had done something for myself. At Kenley in 1938/9 I was an AC2 air gunner untrained with 615 Squadron and now I was a sergeant AI operator flying a fast Bristol Beaufighter and operating against the enemy.

As Terry's operational station was near home he still took the opportunity to make a visit to his mother and father. He would also strike up a relationship with the proprietors of the local pub, of which one member of the family, Margaret, worked at the Air Ministry. Terry would be spending more and more time with Margaret.

At the beginning of November bad weather interfered with, and curtailed flying duties. Mid month however the squadron would suffer a serious set back. Terry recalls the effect on him and mentions putting up the barricade of indifference that airmen would commonly adopt, when trying to deal with the realities of the air war.

> I am sorry to say that during November we had a couple of crashes of which both were fatal. Losing friends after just getting to know them was for me very upsetting. I was not used to the thought of death and having four was a great shock. But it was a case however of getting on with the job. That might sound callous, but it would not help us to dwell on it. Life and our work had to go on. Better comradeship one could not have had. Happy days and sad days, and if we had that bad luck to lose a pilot and navigator, we would down a pint and drink to them for taking their last flight. It may seem unkind but it was the best way of all.

So operational life, of course, had to continue. On 27 November Terry recalled the trip was 'a little more exciting'. Terry was crewed up with a Sergeant Nightingale. Scrambled at 2300 hours they searched the sky for a couple of hours without luck. Nevertheless Terry felt pleased.

> This was my first real operational flight. All the others had been routine night patrols, ever hopeful that we should see something. I began to feel excited. At last I felt I was getting somewhere, and I was even beginning to like the two little AI tubes.

On 8 December 1940 Dudley and Terry flew to RAF Debden to improve their night flying and combat skills.

> Here we joined a school which was designed to give us AI exercises, with another aircraft acting as target. We would make various approaches i.e. head on, 90 degrees, etc., in order that the AI operator could see what it looked like on the tubes, and to be able to take the necessary action to follow. It meant instruction to my pilot and a quick response from him. Practice made perfect – nearly! It was all very exciting and sometimes bewildering, but the only way to learn. It also helped to build up a rapport with the

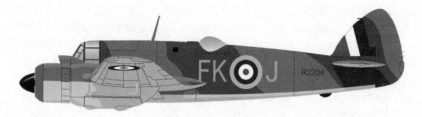

219 Sqn Beaufighter

pilot, and from the changes in my voice he would know exactly what I wanted him to do. It built up perfect teamwork. I had a good pilot and I was determined to be a good operator for him.

On 10 December the squadron made the move to Tangmere, 'and not before time. At last a fully operational station that was equipped for night flying'. Bombing damage to the aerodrome was still evident and, as such accommodation for the squadron's aircrew was found at an old manor house in the nearby village of Oving. The airmen soon established their presence in the Tangmere Arms however, with the odd foray out to try, 'the delights of Chichester – never knew it had so many pubs.' Into the new year and Terry had the opportunity to gain further flying experience.

13 January was my big day. Dudley came to me at dispersal and said that it would be a good idea for me to have some flying practice, believing it might come in useful one day! My thoughts were, 'I hope not'. Anyway off we went in the squadron's Magister. We were barely airborne for ten minutes when Dudley told me to hold the stick and get a feel of the aircraft. Thank God he was in the second seat. I held the stick rather loosely and we started heading downwards rather smartly. Dudley let it continue downwards for a moment. I think he was playing the fool with me, giving me a fright. He was a bit of a prankster, as I would know to my cost at a later date. Unfortunately the weather began to close in so my trip in the Magister was brought swiftly to an end. Dudley merely remarked, 'Never mind we can have another go some other time.'

Operations continued, two days on, two days off. But there was little activity. Poor weather curtailed flying and 'No contact made' is the regular entry in the diary when operations were carried out. Terry along with his New Zealand friend Colin Pyne continued to enjoy the pleasant surroundings of Chichester and the local hostelries. In February 1941 a new CO arrived at the squadron, Wing Commander Tom Pike, 'a severe looking man, but underneath the solemn face I detected fairness and at times a touch of humour.'

> It was the usual events for the month, local flying practice, searchlight co-operation with the army, night patrols, and as a bonus some more flying in the Magister. My logbook now shows that I was having dual flying practice. In that month I had a total of five trips. I was getting the hang of it, well I thought so. On one occasion Dudley suggested that I try a landing. I should have known better. Into the circuit I went, lined up the runway and made my approach. I was as nervous as hell and I was concentrating too much on the instruments. It appears that I was aiming for the flying control instead of the runway. I realised afterwards what had happened, Dudley had let me drift. I imagined the control officer beginning to wet his knickers as a lonely Magister came towards him. Of course Dudley knew exactly what he was doing, took control and made a perfect landing. To this day I am convinced it was another of his pranks. Little did I know what next he had in mind.

From November to February 1941, 219 Squadron claimed four enemy aircraft destroyed.

> Not much you might say, but when you change to a new aircraft such as the Beaufighter it takes a while for the pilot to get used to a much more efficient and faster plane. Also the aircraft being new will result in teething problems. Indeed getting used to the Beau cost the squadron four lives.

In mid-November 1940, a new phase in the night air battle began, which would go on into February 1941. On 14/15 November 1940 the Luftwaffe smashed Coventry. This was the first of thirty-one major attacks during this time, nine on inland industrial cities, fourteen on ports and eight on London.

The operational requirements on Terry and Dudley would steadily rise as 1941 progressed. Two night-flying patrols in

January, two in February and a searchlight co-operation. During March three dusk patrols and five night patrols. In this period three more lives would be lost when another Beaufighter crashed on 8 February 1941. Possibly someone could see that the lack of success and the loss of colleagues could damage squadron morale. Accordingly, on 14 February Marshal of the Royal Air Force Lord Trenchard made a visit.

> *219 Squadron ORB:* ...during the course of his inspection he chatted to the aircrews... General course of the conversation was admitting that night fighting was a difficult proposition, and although we have had several disappointments, which tended to make us downhearted, he urged us to keep going and he was confident that this unit would achieve success in the near future.

Three days later the success came. Squadron Leader Little shooting down a Dornier, with the ORB recording, 'this success coming as it did has a noticeable tonic effect on the squadron throughout, after rather a long period of hard luck.' But the squadron diarist does perhaps start to show his cynicism on 24 February about one method of night fighting, 'At 2300 hours Sergeant Crook carried out a searchlight co-operation only proving the usual magnificent proficiency of this type of defence.'

During March Terry took the opportunity to return home to visit his mother and father and hear news of his brother Stanley, a veteran of Dunkirk, who was now in Egypt. He also took the opportunity to refresh his relationship with Margaret, but his mind was on other things.

> To be honest the love of my life, at the time, was flying. I must confess that I would get up in the air at every possible moment. To me every flight was a thrill. I did not think about being killed, it just did not enter my head. If it happened, well it happened and nothing could be done about it.

By now the night air battle was into what the AHB narrative called the third phase, the 'War on Ports'. Up until 12 May the Luftwaffe mustered for sixty-one raids involving more than fifty aircraft. Approximately 80% of these attacks were against ports, and 60% of all the raids were in the west and south-west, targeting the Atlantic entry ports of food and supplies.

With March 1941 came further success for 219 Squadron. 13 March, 'was a red letter day for the flight [A]. By 2000 hours the station commander made a PA announcement congratulating the squadron on bringing down two hostile aircraft.' Another enemy aircraft was, 'sent down in flames', the next day. But again the dangers of flying were never far away. On 21 March Sergeant Gee crashed on the aerodrome circuit. He was killed, his observer surviving.

April would be the month that Terry would now experience first hand the life and death struggle of the night air battle. He would at last come face to face with the enemy in the sky. But he had an inner foe to deal with first – creeping doubt. Up until the middle of the month he was on four night patrols and one dawn patrol.

I was at last beginning to feel that I had the hang of AI and I must confess enjoying it. On 16 April though I had a shock. It all started in the sergeants' mess. I was called to the phone and told that I would be flying with the CO that night and to report to B Flight dispersal at 1400 hours for a night-flying test with Wing Commander Pike. I had just finished two nights on with my own flight, so why me? I felt a little wobbly at the knees. What if I made a balls of an interception. Supposing of course we got one. I could see myself complete with bowler hat, which did not suit me, being sent away to a training unit. Why me? There must have been other operators on B Flight. Please open up the earth and swallow me. I will fail and that will be that. Nevertheless at 1400 hours I arrived at B Flight dispersal and met the CO. I had seen him before but it never entered my head that I would ever fly with him. 'Good afternoon Clark,' 'Good afternoon sir.' He gave me a smile, which I thought was a good sign, hopefully. 'Rather a change from being an air gunner Clark. Were you disappointed not to be transferred to Bomber Command?' 'Well I was at first sir, but I have grown to like AI and I must admit it is more interesting. I am glad to be staying with the squadron.' 'Good show Clark. We are glad to have you with us. In about ten minutes we'll do a night-flying test and then you can go and get some food. I shall see you later.'

Well so far so good I thought, he didn't seem a bad guy

after all. I did not enjoy my supper however. My thoughts were all about failure and being kicked off the squadron. What would Mum and Dad say? How could I face them as a failure? What I needed was a good stiff drink but of course that was taboo. I felt very miserable and yet at the same time somewhat elated that I was chosen to fly with the CO. I wondered if Dudley had recommended me. Had he said I was quite good? I hoped not. If he said that it would have reflected on Dudley and I would have been responsible. The more I thought about it the worse it got. 'Oh well', I thought, 'Let's get down to dispersal and get the whole thing over and done with. If I am kicked back to training school it will be my own bloody fault.' I prayed for a little help.

The test went smoothly and Terry was impressed with his pilot. Later back at dispersal Wing Commander Pike and Sergeant Clark awaited their call to scramble. Others wore night glasses, accustoming their eyes to the dark. Terry found this a disadvantage in one respect.

How could you play pontoon and have a flutter if you were wearing night glasses? I might have missed a trick and lost money and then the metal stuff was hard to come by. I recall being on the losing side when the telephone rang. We all looked at the telephone orderly. I gave a little prayer as we were next. 'Telephone call for the CO'. My internal response, 'Phew, what a relief'. I went back to the pontoon but the phone rang again. The orderly answered and said, 'CO to scramble sir.' My thoughts, 'Oh God that's me as well.' I grabbed my flying helmet and goggles and followed Wing Commander Pike. The ground crew were there at the ready and I climbed into my little office and pulled the trap door up and shut. I plugged in my oxygen and RT. 'Are you OK Clark?' 'Yes sir.' 'Right off we go.' We taxied out to the end of the runway, opened up and away we went. My thoughts, 'please up there take pity on a small soul down here. I want to stay with the squadron. Can you give just a little help?'

Using Wing Commander Pike's combat report interspersed with Terry's present-day memories, we can track what happened that night.

Wing Commander Pike's combat report – Night 16/17 April 1941
I took off from Tangmere at 0020 hours in Beaufighter R2253 with Sergeant Clark as AI operator. After a short time I was handed to Durrington and chased an enemy aircraft on a northerly vector. No contact or AI or visual was made. I was then returned to the coast and vectored onto another enemy aircraft. This time AI contact was quickly made.

Terry Clark: I immediately saw a blip on my tubes and gave Wing Commander Pike the much wanted word, 'Contact'. The enemy aircraft was about two miles ahead of us at a height of 17,000 feet. I think they must have either seen us or possibly a backward looking radar was on. He took violent action.

Wing Commander Pike's combat report: AI contact was maintained by Sergeant Clark in spite of three 90 degree turns by the enemy.

Terry Clark: 'Hard starboard', I called out, 'and keep turning. Steady the turn now he is ahead of us. Hard starboard again, I think the bugger knows we are after him. Keep turning and maintain height. Ease your turn now, we are getting close. He is off starboard again, hard turn. Now ease up that's it. He is ahead of you now. You should be able to see him.'

Wing Commander Pike's combat report: Finally the enemy was closed to minimum range and was sighted by means of 2 exhaust flames at about 500 yards range and 300 feet above. Range was closed to about 200 yards and a one second burst from four cannon and four MG guns set the enemy on fire.

Terry Clark: The burst made the enemy aircraft cough a bit and indeed set the aircraft on fire. We followed him down for several thousand feet and then he took a vertical dive, struck the ground and exploded with a shower of incendiaries. I felt like a child with a new toy. I had at last proved myself, and with the CO. For some reason I suddenly felt a little sad. How many men had we killed? Back in Germany a wife or mother would be grieving over their loss. Did I come into this world to kill people? Sadness went when I realised that it might have been us in that situation. All is fair in love and war they said (I had yet to learn about love). With both of us feeling quite pleased with ourselves we returned to Tangmere control and whilst we were on a homing vector we noticed a few bombs explode nearby. We turned towards the line of bombs and I 'flashed my weapon', the code for switching on the AI.

Wing Commander Pike's combat report: AI contact was obtained almost immediately at 1,500 yards range. Tangmere were asked if any friendly aircraft were nearby.

Terry Clark: 'One', said Tangmere, 'and we have told him to move away.' I still had contact so the hunt was on again. Once again the enemy started to take evasive action. It seemed to me that it was like a cat chasing a mouse, and I was bloody certain that this mouse was not going to get away. Contact was maintained and we were slowly creeping up on him. He went off again to starboard. Not quick enough. I had my beady eye on him and a quick call to Tom Pike and we were back behind him again. Then a sudden call from Tom, 'I can see him. It is a Heinkel 111.' The moon had risen and there he was about 300 yards away.

Wing Commander Pike's combat report: Two exhaust flames (one under each wing) were then seen and range was closed to 250-300 yards. A four second burst was given at this range and enemy exploded in the air. Burning fragments blew back and hit the Beaufighter.

Terry Clark: A moment later I saw two parachutes in the air. Well at least they were alive and would become POWs. We watched the aircraft until it struck the ground. Enemy number two to our credit and I was beginning to feel a little cocky. Tom Pike decided that we had done our share and set course for Tangmere. However, fog had set in and we were diverted to Middle Wallop, landing at about 0300 hours. We had been in the air for 2 hours 40 minutes. I hoped that I had proved my worth with the CO. I had satisfied myself.

Terry inscribed two swastikas in his logbook. In addition to his

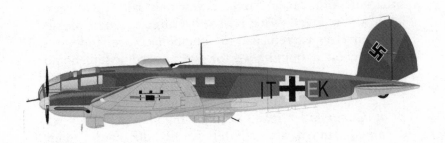

Heinkel 111 H-5

and Tom Pike's claims a further enemy aircraft was destroyed by another of the squadron's pilots.

An intelligence report is available giving further details of one of the aircraft that fell to Terry Clark and Tom Pike's teamwork that night.

> *Place, date and time:* Near Gorse Hill House, Hambledon, Surrey
> *Type and Marks:* Heinkel 111 – 1T+EK
> *Unit:* 2/KG 28
> *Start and Mission:* Started from Nantes at 0030 hrs, together with one other aircraft of the staffel to lay mines in the Thames estuary near Chatham. Two mines carried.
> 12 aircraft of the Gruppe had set off about 30 minutes previously for a different objective. This and one other aircraft were the only 2 of KG 28 going to Chatham. Whilst flying south of London at 16,000 feet on the way to the Thames estuary, this aircraft was hit and the starboard engine set on fire. There was AA fire at the time and no fighter was seen but it is understood that the wreckage showed many MG and cannon strikes. The crew baled out but the W/T operator and B/M were killed. The parachute of one failed to open and in the other case, the harness was apparently faulty. The aircraft crashed in flames and an explosion, probably due to one of the mines, caused a crater 30' wide and about 12/15' deep. The second mine

was found unexploded in the neighbourhood. The pilot of the aircraft, who had the disc of 7/KG 77, left that unit to join KG 28 in Sep 40. His Staffel had been based at Nantes since Nov. Since Nov, owing to sickness and leave, he had done only 10 war flights, all of which were minelaying operations except for the big raid on Coventry on which bombs were carried.

Morale: High

Crew: Pilot – Unteroffizier Thomas Hammerl – wounded.
Observer – Oberfeldwebel Albert Engel – unwounded.
W/T – Gefreiter Wolfgang Schuler – dead
B/M – Gefreiter Richard Mattern – dead.

On the afternoon of 17 April Terry, and a friend Sergeant Dye, celebrated at the Tangmere Arms. Unaccustomed to whisky Terry suffered somewhat.

> I must say that I felt a little woosey. I arrived at the dispersal as usual and saw the CO. Whether or not I looked a little dopey I do not know, but he gave me a rather old fashioned look, but made no comment. Fortunately bad weather closed in and flying for the night was cancelled. I was sorry because I thought we might be able to have a repeat performance. Greedy – well why not?

When Terry next met Dudley Hobbis, his usual pilot, he felt rather ashamed, 'that with him I had not scored but immediately I had gone with the CO we were lucky. I did not want him to think that I had tried harder with the CO and not him.' Terry's opportunity to set matters straight would soon arrive however. On 20 April Dudley and Terry completed a night patrol. On 23 April a dusk patrol and on 27 April a dawn patrol. That night Terry and Dudley's chance would come. On taking off in Beaufighter R2154 from Tangmere at 2034 hours, and after climbing to 14,000 feet, Terry and Dudley were informed that there was a 'bogey' in the area.

> I had my AI switched on and made contact with an aircraft that was over to starboard. We turned about ten degrees to starboard and increased speed. This one was for Dudley and I was not going to let him get away. He had my constant attention. Dudley then spotted the aircraft. It was a Ju88.

His combat report records the following:

> Keeping him in sight [the pilot] lowered flaps to fly slowly about 140 mph and worked himself into position to attack from the darkest part of the horizon, our pilot keeping slightly on the enemy aircraft starboard and closed in to about 100 yards, then went directly behind and slightly underneath him and lifted the nose to get sights on him and gave him a burst of 1 second. It was obvious that a short burst was good enough. Our pilot saw the flames of the shells hitting the fuselage and starboard engine.

Terry continues the story:

> The aircraft was set alight and took a steep dive. It hit the sea and burst into a mass of flames. Dudley had always said during exercise that that was the position he liked to be in before firing. I now had number three to my credit and must confess that I was feeling rather pleased with myself. Dudley had now made his first kill and I sincerely hoped that I would be with him for some more.

The Ju88 fell into the Solent, the crew of four killed. Terry and Dudley landed at 2255 hours. They were airborne again at 0350 hours the next morning on a dawn patrol, as Terry recalled, 'It was quite a busy time.'

News came through that Tom Pike had received the DFC and a few days later he came up to Terry.

> 'Clark', he said, 'I did try to get you the DFM but the powers that be want four kills before it can be awarded. I really did try for two but they would not agree.' I felt somewhat choked that he had taken the trouble to tell me this. I think that he felt I deserved it for the two which had given us such a hectic time. I have never forgotten this act of kindness.

Over the next few weeks operations continued, one further patrol in April, six patrols in May. The rate of success for the squadron had improved, the diary recording on 3 May, 'The total bag for the squadron up to date being 20 destroyed, 4 probables, 5 damaged'. Further enemy aircraft fell to 219 Squadron in the next few days. On 11 May the squadron diarist took the opportunity to once more make comment on other forms of night defence. The aerodrome, 'was blitzed for about three hours', the Magister was burned out and there was surface damage, fortunately with no casualties. 'Owing to the marvellous display of our ground defences again the Huns returned safely to their native land.'

This date saw a turning point in the night air battle. The resources of the Luftwaffe were going to be required elsewhere, to the east and the attack on Russia. The scale of the night offensive was now to dramatically reduce, although the German threat was not completely to disappear from the darkness over Britain. There would still be opportunities, if they can be called such, for the RAF nightfighters to engage their foe.

Chapter 10

The Cat and Mouse Game

On 24 May 1941 Terry Clark was posted to RAF Cranage for an AI navigation course, 'It was naturally very interesting and useful but I missed my friends and having got used to one pilot I was not keen on flying with the unknown.' Terry 'survived' the course and on 11 June returned to Tangmere, 'to be told that in my absence Dudley, now Flying Officer, had taken a spare operator and shot down a Ju88 on 1/2 June. Good for him but I thought, "What bloody cheek – he might have had the decency to wait for me!"'

> I couldn't have Dudley shooting down enemy aircraft every time I was sent away on a course. It really wasn't cricket. I felt therefore that I had to do something about it. On 13 June, whilst at dispersal and awaiting our turn to scramble, and still trying to get to grips with bridge, the telephone rang. All heads turned towards the telephone orderly. 'Flying Officer Hobbis scramble sir.' Off we went again. The ground crew were already out there. There should have been a ground crew medal of some sort for them. 'Beau R2326 Sergeant'. 'Thanks chaps'. Into my little office again and check the escape door is tightly closed. Check oxygen plug in socket. Inter com plugged in. Dudley calls, 'All OK?' 'Yes.' 'Right off we go.'

Flying Officer Dudley Hobbis lifted his Beaufighter and instructions came through to patrol Shoreham-Beachy Head at 15,000 feet. When on patrol the nightfighters were handed over to Durrington GCI, who gave them vectors, 'up and down for about an hour'.

Sitting way down the aircraft and all on my Jack Jones I was in no mood to be going up and down all the time. 'Come on you German aircrew it's about time we were hearing from you.' Durrington must have heard me. 'We have a customer for you.' We were given a vector of 190 and instructed to climb to Angels 20 (20,000 feet). It was bloody cold up there. After a short while Durrington gave us a change of course to 030 and we were told to flash our weapon. 'Flash weapon?' I thought. It had been flashing for some time hoping to get a blip on this customer. Well he had come to the right store, and we would certainly give him all he asked for and more! 'Bandit 3-4 miles ahead of you'. I asked Dudley to increase speed and shortly after I picked up a good strong blip. This one was a bit cheeky and dropped down a couple of thousand feet and at the same time veering off to port. 'Oh', I thought, 'I've got a clever little bugger here.' Down we went after him and I put Dudley once again behind him. 'Keep same speed', I said to Dudley, 'we are gaining.' 'Starboard ten quick!' Our customer obviously didn't want to shop at our store. 'Steady now, hold this course.' If only he knew we had on board the very goods that would make him sit up. He was on the way up again, 'Climb 1,000 feet and level out. Port ten. Steady now and he is ahead and slightly above you. We are nearly at minimum range.' 'I can see him!' said Dudley. 'It's a Heinkel 111. I can see 4 exhaust flames.'

Dudley Hobbis' combat report: I closed in to point blank range in line astern and gave about a two second burst. I saw flashes of explosive shell hitting enemy aircraft and one particularly large and brilliant flash from his port engine. Enemy aircraft dived down belching black smoke and I broke away over him to his right. There was no moon and enemy aircraft disappeared into darkness. Just after this incident I saw a tremendous lamination of incendiary bombs ignite on the ground, and the following day learned from the prisoners that they had jettisoned their incendiaries (a total load) after they had been hit. They said that their port engine packed up immediately and some moments later the starboard engine caught fire. The sky was clear but dark with no moon.

There is an interesting aside to this story of life and death in the air. After the war Terry was put in touch with one of the crew shot down that night, W/T Feldwebel Herbert Schick.

> I was invited to be his guest at one of the 100 Gruppe reunions. The 100 Gruppe was, I am told, a specialist bombing unit. I made excuses not to attend as I felt that it would be somewhat strange to enjoy a weekend with someone I had tried to kill. I have been told many times that I should have gone and that they would have made me most welcome.

Terry corresponded with Herbert on many occasions, Herbert's son providing the translation. Herbert is no longer alive but Terry still exchanges Christmas cards with his son.

Terry's doubts and concerns about this still relatively new form of aerial warfare were fading. The 'kill' on 13/14 June, 'made it three for Dudley and four for me. I was beginning to like this cat and mouse game, so long as I remained the cat! Life in the RAF was really becoming interesting. But then disaster struck.' News came through that Dudley and Terry were to be posted to RAF Hunsdon, to fly on Turbinlite Havocs, 'instead of our beloved Beaufighter'. This did not meet with approval, 'The Havocs of the Turbinlite Flights did not have any guns, not even a pea shooter.'

> Instead it carried a bloody ton of batteries stowed in the bomb bay. The nose section of the aircraft had been modified to include a reflector and carbon arcs, which would become a searchlight. That was not all. Underneath the port wing was a white strip *illuminated at night*! This we were told was for the Hurricane aircraft that would be formating with us at night. I do not know what Dudley thought of the idea, he never said. I was not asked and just as well. My remarks would have certainly been cause for a court martial and that bowler hat might have been mine.

Terry's logbook records 11 hours 30 minutes training at Hunsdon, but nothing about it impressed him.

> We would be flying around at night naked. Not a single gun and illuminated for all to see. What if we had a blip, which turned out to be hostile and we chased it. I would be

giving Dudley various vectors and possible changes of height. Suppose the enemy suddenly swerved off to the right, with the Hurricane on our left. It would be OK for us, I could still follow it. But would the Hurricane? Come back 219 and bring the Beau with you please!

Whilst at Hunsdon Terry heard the news that Dudley had received the DFC and he had received the DFM, with respect to their time at 219 Squadron. The squadron commander had made the following comment, 'Sergeant Clark has been in this squadron since 12 July 1940 during which time he has shown outstanding keenness and considerable ability as a radio operator. In company with his pilot he has now destroyed 4 enemy aircraft at night.' The Tangmere station commander added, 'Sergeant Clark has by his teamwork with his pilot shown an example to the other radio operators in the squadron. I wholeheartedly agree with the recommendation of his squadron commander.'

Terry and Dudley were posted to 1455 Turbinlite Flight in July, coincidentally at Tangmere. Terry felt it some consolation that he had been promoted to Flight Sergeant and Dudley to Flight Lieutenant. 219 Squadron were also still at Tangmere, 'and when the Beaus took off at night I would be thinking lucky sods. In a way it was like rubbing salt into a sore wound.'

I would rather have stayed with 219 Squadron as a sergeant than fly in what I think (for what it's worth) was a bloody silly idea. I recall wondering what the lads would be saying, 'Terry, are you carrying your torch with you tonight.'

Dudley cheered me up one day when he suggested that I had some more time flying – this time in the Tiger Moth. I note in my logbook that we flew twice on 15 and 16 October. In the course of those trips Dudley showed me how he did a loop, and as I understood it, when you did a loop you should have ended up in the same place you started. Dudley's loop was perfect. 'Now you have a try', he said. 'What me!' 'Yes. Come and get on with it.' I thought, 'Well what have I got to lose. Only his life and mine, but if he is willing well here goes.' Down I went then up and over and back to first position. Dudley was laughing. 'What's up?' I said. 'Well I think we are in the next county!' I decided to make no comment. I could imagine a damn great grin on his face. Anybody watching from the ground would probably be saying that pilot needs to go back to training school or better still, join the navy.

Some more leave came Terry's way, giving him an opportunity to further his relationship with Margaret. But Terry would always be yearning to return to his RAF colleagues.

> I was very happy to be back with the lads. I know it was all male company, but it was the comradeship that was formed and I think missed when away. We were all in the same boat and we all shared the love of flying and its risks. We shared a pint or two together and our talk was mostly about what and when, and what silly sod of a pilot did that. Even back with 1455 Flight did not seem so bad, but my view of Turbinlites had not changed, they were no bloody good.

Through the second half of 1941 and into 1942 Terry and Dudley amassed flying hours in the Havoc, but there was nothing to inspire Terry. In February 1942, came something slightly out of the ordinary, an altitude test on the Havoc, to 23,000 feet, 'It was rather chilly up there and my only thoughts were, "Hell". It was a long way to drop.' Further opportunities came Terry's way to fly in the Tiger Moth, 'What a lovely little aircraft. Up there with the wind whistling by you, who could possibly think that there was a war being fought in this clear blue sky?' Terry was also given the chance to try out another type of pilot training.

> Dudley asked me to meet him at the Link Trainer for a little instrument flying. The Link Trainer was a mock-up of an aircraft cockpit complete with hood so that pilots could get experience on instruments at night. The instructor would sit at a desk and give instruction as required to the pilot. I duly arrived at the trainer and Dudley told me to get into the cockpit and close the hood. I was now in complete darkness except for the glow of the instruments on the panel. Dudley called me up via the telephone on his desk. 'Climb to 16,000 feet and maintain course of 260 degrees.' Watching the instruments very carefully I carried out his orders and reported back when I had made the necessary height and course. He then continued to give me various

vectors and changes in height. He thought I should know all about this as it could be useful in an emergency. I was giving these changes all my attention, my eyes were glued to the instrument panel. I really wanted to do well at this, so I was giving it my full and complete concentration. Suddenly Dudley called out, 'Get out! Get out! You are on fire!' At that moment smoke started to drift up by my feet, 'My God I bloody well am on fire.' And with that thought I flung the hood open and prepared to jump. I had no parachute, but I could not stay in a burning aircraft. I made to jump and suddenly realised that I was only about three feet from the ground. I was trying to gather my thoughts when I saw Dudley and another officer laughing their heads off. Dudley had organised for another officer friend to get a mop head, set it alight and then smother the flames so that it only smoked. He then pushed it under the Link Trainer. Just another joke from Dudley, but I must be honest I thought my time had come. In the end of course I had to laugh as well.

There was further training in March, mostly by day, then in April a rumour that Dudley and Terry would be moving. But the months dragged on. Finally a posting came through to RAF Hunsdon. 'Dudley was to become CO of No. 1451 Turbinlite.'

My thoughts at that moment were unprintable. There was only one consolation. Dudley was now a squadron leader and I was a warrant officer. Good news in a way, but I would rather have stayed as a flight sergeant and moved to an operational squadron. Good news for Dudley so I was pleased for him, but flying in bloody torches again. Sheer hell!

Prompted by Dudley, Terry applied for a commission, involving an interview with the station commander and then another interview at 11 Group Headquarters with Air Vice-Marshal Leigh-Mallory.

He looked at me and said, 'I see Clark that you had some success with your pilot Squadron Leader Hobbis.' 'That is correct sir', I replied. He nodded and murmured 'good', and then said, 'thank you'. This was obviously the signal for me to retire and when outside the aide said, 'that's all Mr Clark, you will be notified of the result in due course.' About three weeks went by of nail biting and wondering.

On 18 May 1942 Terry's commission came through, 'in a way I shall remember to my dying day.'

I had just been that morning to collect my new warrant officer uniform. I went to my room and changed. If it had not been for the warrant badges on my sleeves I would have looked just like a pilot officer. I must say that I was extra pleased and wanted to show myself in new uniform to Dudley. Back to the sergeants' mess and I had not been there very long when Dudley phoned. 'It's through', he said, 'Congratulations'. 'How did you know?' I said. 'I only got it this morning.' 'What are you talking about?' said Dudley. I thought Dudley was being a bit strange. 'Warrant Officer uniform', I said. 'Oh never mind that. I am talking about your commission Pilot Officer Clark. Have some lunch in the mess and I will pick you up at 2 o'clock and we'll go and see a film in Hertford and then have tea.' He came promptly at 2 o'clock in his staff car and off we went to Hertford and the cinema. I have no idea what we saw and at the end of it we came out and he said, 'Now we'll have some tea.' I wondered where we would go for tea. We got in the car and I saw that we were leaving Hertford. I thought he was going to find a nice place in the countryside. I was wrong we were making our way back to Hunsdon. 'Bang goes tea then', I thought. We entered the station and went straight to the tailor's shop. Dudley said, 'Take off your coat.' I was beginning to wonder if this was another of Dudley's jokes. He took my coat and gave it to the tailor. 'Take off those warrant badges and put on a thin blue ribbon (pilot officer) on each sleeve.' The tailor did this and Dudley gave me back my coat. I was still in a daze, not certain what was going on. 'Now Pilot Officer Clark', said Dudley, 'we can go back to the officers' mess for tea.' He had not forgotten. In a way another of his jokes, and I am sorry to say the last he would pull on me.

Tea followed. Then a party and as Terry recalled, 'I woke up the next morning to hear a voice saying, "Wake up Mr Clark sir, I have a nice cup of tea for you." I was in my own room with a nice bed equipped with white sheets and white pillow. I thought I must be in heaven.' That afternoon Terry went to the mess and was greeted by his fellow officers and was 'forced' into a few more drinks. 'I will never forget that short moment in time and as I write it I can close my eyes and see it all again.' A few weeks later Terry went to London to collect his new pilot officer uniform and when Dudley took some leave this enabled Terry to also have some leave and return home to surprise his parents, 'I knocked at the door and my mother answered, "Oh – are you alright? Is that a new uniform?" I had to explain and tears came into her eyes. Her baby son had made it!' Celebrations were held at the local pub, Terry met up with Margaret and they arranged to have their photograph taken together.

The week's leave soon passed. On the journey back to Hunsdon I felt really pleased. The surprise about my promotion worked well. Life despite Turbinlites was definitely improving. The month of June and July passed with the usual practices and a little formation flying. August was to be a month or should I say a day in which I shall never forget. Dudley and I took off on 13 August for an aircraft test. At the end of the test we were nearing the station when he decided to beat-up a house. I assumed that it was a friend's and so I just sat back to enjoy the ride. The house was situated near a wood and it was not until he had finished the beat-up that I noticed some small branches of a tree sticking out of the starboard leading wing edge. I spoke to Dudley and told him to look along the starboard wing. 'Why?' he said. 'Just look' I replied. There was a 'bloody hell' and I knew that he had seen the problem. It was obvious on the beat-up we had sunk just a little bit low and hit the top of the trees. We returned to base and on leaving the aircraft at dispersal Dudley was told to report to the station commander. I did not see Dudley again until 11 October and he had been reduced to the rank of a flight lieutenant.

Terry flew with Dudley on 13 October, then Dudley went to an OTU as an instructor and Terry was posted to 62 OTU at RAF Usworth as a radar instructor. Terry spent six months there, 'flying in draughty old Ansons. Three hours a day, half as fighter and half as target. I was not cut out to be a teacher and I have to say it was a bind from beginning to end. I was also missing my pal Dudley even though it was all his fault.' On 26 March 1943 Terry was posted to 51 OTU RAF Cranfield, where he met up with Dudley again, 'and not before time. We also became reacquainted with my old friend the Beaufighter, it was good to see her again.' On 27 April Terry and Dudley were posted to 488 (New Zealand) Squadron at RAF Ayr. 'I had never been so far up country before, but it was worth it. We were operational again and it was so good to be back with Squadron Leader Dudley Hobbis at the helm. We seemed to be very busy with air-to-sea firing and various exercises with Fullerton GCI control. We were not however offered any customers.' Indeed Terry would be missing out on any contact with 'customers' for a further few months.

> I was sitting in the mess one evening with my feet propped up against the bar and having a quiet drink, when a lovely young WAAF officer spoke to me from behind. Being a gentleman I turned or should I say swivelled around to see who it was and promptly over balanced. I fell backwards (so I was told) and struck my head on the brickwork of a fireplace. I remember no more. Apparently I just lay there not moving, and some of the lads thought that I was playing silly buggers. I was still lying there when they saw blood coming from my right ear.

The Medical Officer was called and Terry was taken to hospital and a fractured skull fissure was diagnosed. When Terry came to, 'I found myself in a very nice room, complete en-suite and a very nice nurse standing by me.' Terry spent three weeks, 'under the care of the lovely young nurses and my health improved rapidly.' He received some visitors, 'Dudley gave me some very nice large oranges although when I say gave me, I mean he threw them on the bed aiming at a spot which could have done me serious damage. Trust Dudley.' Eventually Terry was discharged, with a warning to be more careful about 'Scottish water'. He was required to go through some more aircrew medicals to test his fitness, which included a visit to a psychoanalyst at Gleneagles, 'It appeared that in the case of head accidents, one had to be checked, to make certain I had not turned "funny".' Terry passed.

I was told all was well and that I would soon be back on flying. I made my way to the officers common room at Gleneagles to have a cup of tea, only to find about two dozen officers all in various stages of bandaging, being lined up in two rows. Before I could say Jack Robinson I found myself in one of the rows. We had just sorted ourselves out when in through the door came His Majesty King George VI together with Her Majesty Queen Elizabeth. The King walked down one row and the Queen the other and stopped at me. Her Majesty said, 'The gardens here are lovely.' I replied, 'Yes Maam they are.' The Queen walked on. I felt rather embarrassed, I had not seen the gardens.

Terry eventually rejoined his squadron in October 1943, then at Bradwell Bay, Essex.

I was back flying with Dudley again. Regretfully this was not to last. Dudley came into dispersal one afternoon and said, 'I am afraid that you will have to get yourself another pilot. I am leaving the squadron shortly.' He did not say why, but I think he was going to be promoted and would probably have a desk job. He did not seem upset about it. I was shattered. We had been pilot and navigator since December 1940. He had gone from flying officer to squadron leader and I from sergeant to flying officer. We had had our problems and our successes. I would have flown with him anywhere at any time. I just could not believe that I would not enter his name in my logbook again. I was fed up and far from home.

Terry soon teamed up with his new pilot, Pilot Officer Douglas Robinson, known as Robbie, 'It was good to be back on ops and I soon found out that I had another good pilot.' On their first patrol together there was almost success. Terry writing in his logbook, 'chased bogey but no luck'. There were four further operational sorties in November, without contact with the enemy.

On 25 November 1943 Dudley Hobbis came to Terry at dispersal and told him that he was going to be making one last operation trip. He was taking as his radar operator Flight Sergeant Oliver Hills.

I really do not know why Dudley came to tell me. It could have been his way of saying that he would be leaving the squadron very soon and that would be the last I would see him.

I was sitting in the mess that evening playing bridge, when another officer came up to me and said, 'I hear that Dudley has bought it.' I could not believe what I had heard. I hurried down to A Flight dispersal to find out for myself what was going on. The only information they had was that Dudley had reported to the controller that one engine was on fire and that he had ordered his navigator to bale out. Nothing more was ever heard and it was assumed that Dudley had also baled out. I cannot explain my feelings but it would not sink in that Dudley had gone. Both would have gone into the North Sea, which would have been icy cold.

Thirty-three-year-old Dudley Hobbis' body was never found and his loss is recorded on the Runnymede memorial. A loss such as this has no closure, no formal process to mourn the departure of a friend; a burial and a ceremony. Only the disorder of uncertainty which gives no satisfaction. How Dudley Hobbis lost his life remains pure conjecture. The body of thirty-two-year-old Flight Sergeant Oliver Hills (whose commission was confirmed after his loss) was washed ashore a few months after the event. He is buried in Epsom cemetery.

Terry Clark now had to face up to the loss of his former friend and colleague.

Robbie gave me much help in coming to terms with Dudley's death and of course his navigator. Getting back on operations was the best way of dealing with the loss, and life as they say must go on. November came and Robbie and I were coming together as a team. I had every confidence in him, but I still missed Dudley. I still wanted to know what happened. Was it a result of enemy action or was it friendly fire? Sadly I will never know.

The relationship Terry was developing with Doug Robinson now paid off and Terry would soon be inscribing another swastika in his logbook.

Flying Officer Terry Clark DFM and Pilot Officer Douglas Robinson took off from Bradwell Bay in their Mosquito XIII, AI

Mk VIII, at 0005 hours on the morning of 20 December 1943 and began patrolling under the control of Trimley Heath GCI. A warning came through of possible activity. The combat report records the incident.

[They] were ordered to climb to 15,000 feet, being taken over by Sandwich GCI (Controller F/Lt Kirby). Pilot was given several vectors but was unable to make contact with a bandit so was then given vectors on to another enemy aircraft, climbing to 21,000 feet. A contact was obtained at twelve o'clock, range 2 miles, with the enemy aircraft well above so pilot climbed to 25,000 feet and obtained a visual on an Me410, 2,000 feet ahead and slightly below. Speed of enemy aircraft approx 300 mph.

Pilot closed to 250 yards and opened fire with a 2/3 second burst but owing to vapour trails no strikes were seen. The enemy aircraft took violent evasive action, climbing and diving in tight turns but the searchlights illuminated and held the enemy aircraft and our pilot plainly saw the black crosses on the wings. A second attack was made from 150 yards, closing to 100 yards, several short bursts during which strikes were seen on the port engine and fuselage. A red glow appearing from the engine. Inaccurate tracer from the barbettes was passing above our aircraft and pieces flew off the enemy aircraft which then did a steep port turn and dived towards the ground. The visual was temporarily lost but the aircraft was seen to hit the ground and explode shortly afterwards.

Pilot states that prior to first attack he was above and starboard of enemy aircraft and to escape illumination and possible sighting by enemy aircraft he did very steep turn to port, thus bringing himself just above and slightly to port of the Me410, which was well held by searchlights from the port beam and he feels his first attack was made before the enemy aircraft knew our fighter was in the vicinity.

Again an intelligence report is available providing some detail of the consequence of the combat.

Place, date and time: Boonshill Farm, Iden near Rye,
  Sussex. 20 December 1943, 0235 hours.
Type and marks: Me410
Unit: (V/KG 2)

According to local eye witnesses, this aircraft was attacked by nightfighters and seen on fire in the air. It then crashed into the ground and was completely burnt out. There were no bombs on board.

The pilot's body was found in the wreckage and the W/T operator, who had baled out, was located some 20 miles away suffering from severe injuries. He was taken to hospital and as yet his condition has made interrogation impossible.

Amongst the documents recovered was a movement order dated 27 August 1943 for the pilot and a Gefr Gillman of FPN 31730 to travel by rail from Vendeville to Utrecht and then to Soesterberg on 28 August 43 for the purpose of collecting an operational aircraft in accordance with instructions from V/KG 2. This was the only document found which gave any possible indication of the unit.

Crew: Pilot – Leutnant Heinz Baack, 11 September 24, EK I, dead. W/T – Unteroffizier Michael Strasser, 13 December 20, badly wounded and broken leg.

Terry looks back on the event:

Robbie had made his first kill and on the way back to base he did a beat-up of dispersal. I was really pleased for Robbie but it brought back memories of my old pilot Dudley Hobbis. Why couldn't it have been him and I celebrating another victory. I continued flying with Robbie, but for some reason, and one that I cannot explain, I suddenly felt unhappy. I could not get the memory of Dudley out of my mind. Robbie tried hard to help me with this problem, but we both realised that things were not right. I went to the Medical Officer and he said it would be good for me to have a rest. I agreed, and in due course I was posted to RAF North Weald Sector Ops. I would become a u/t controller. Well at least I would still be with aeroplanes.

Before his move Terry would complete six operations with Doug Robinson in January, three operations in February and two in the first week of March. 'No joy' summed up the results of these flights. Terry arrived at North Weald on 15 March 1944 and would spend five months there. On numerous operational flights

Terry had heard the words of controllers as they tried to place him and his pilot close enough to obtain a radar contact. Now Terry would be seeing what the controllers had been working with.

> The operations room was set up in part of a large mansion and it had one of the best ops rooms I had ever seen. Three floors with the senior controller of the day on the top floor, looking down on two very large plotting tables. It was really very impressive. For the first week or two I sat alongside a controller on a lower floor and just watched proceedings. We also had some American controllers who looked after their aircraft when on sweeps. The whole set up was excellent, and I felt that all aircrew should at some time spend a few hours in an ops room to see how the 'voices' one heard on the R/T did their work looking after you.

Terry enjoyed his time at North Weald, making lasting friendships. In particular one friendship was secured for life. On a trip to the theatre in London, Terry proposed to Margaret, 'She was taken aback for a moment, then with a big smile on her face gave her assent.' An engagement party followed and plans for the wedding were made. Meanwhile the course of the war was about to change significantly.

> 5 June 1944 came and we could see that something big was in the wind. All officers were confined to the station and no incoming or outgoing calls were allowed. Margaret tried to call me but the mess steward who answered the phone just said that I was not available. Activity was building up and all controllers were on duty including my good self. I was, for a short time, loaned to the Americans, and I was in constant touch with an American aircraft that conveyed our instructions to other fighters further over enemy territory. The operations room was a scene of tense activity from that day onwards.

Whilst at North Weald Terry took the opportunity of taking two operations room WAAFs to Bradwell Bay to meet the aircrew of 488 (NZ) Squadron. 'The lads were always keen to meet a couple of very good looking females, and it certainly did liven up the atmosphere when I took them down to dispersal that evening.'

Terry and Margaret's wedding date was set for 16 July and just prior to that he was promoted to flight lieutenant. He managed to survive the stag party two days prior to the big day. However, the war would not let things go as smoothly as he'd intended.

Before setting off for church I received a telegram marked priority. It was from Wing Commander Raymond, who had agreed to be my best man, and said that together with other officers from ops they had been called to 11 Group for a conference and very much regretted that they wouldn't be with us. I pounced on my good friend Ray Vernon, and he took his place. The sun was shining as Ray and I made our way to Beddington Church, on the edge of Beddington Park. A lovely old church that had suffered some bomb damage. We arrived at the church and Ray went off to park his car. I walked down the aisle and took my place. I felt nervous as a kitten. Time was now getting close to Margaret's arrival and Ray had not returned. Had I lost another best man? I turned to Ken Simms, another officer friend, and asked him to take over. So it was that Margaret and I had a 'different' best man. At last we managed to sign the registry in the church and so everything was at least legal! Cars then took us to the Grange, a lovely old house set in the middle of Beddington Park. No-one could want a better setting, except that it also had suffered some bomb damage. As some of our RAF friends would not now be at the reception, we moved some of the chairs closer to the top table. Just as well. During my short speech of thanks to all, we had an air raid warning. Some bombs dropped a distance away and where the ops friends would have been sitting, the ceiling collapsed.

The rest of the day went without further intrusion from the enemy, and the newlyweds went off on their honeymoon, to the village of Cove. Expecting to be there for a week, a 'priority' telegram arrived after four days, recalling Terry to North Weald. 'What could go wrong next? I said sorry to Margaret, but I knew she would understand the situation. Margaret had not worked at the Air Ministry without knowing that problems could arise at any time.' The couple returned home and Terry made his way to North Weald.

The next morning on duty in the ops room and suddenly

there was call from Group. 'Diver Diver Diver' came over the telephone. This was the code word for the rocket propelled bombs known to all as Buzzbombs. Looking at the plotting board one could see the plot arriving all over London and some were coming our way. Tin hats were the order of the day, and whilst one or two were near, the ops room was not hit. Now I know why I was recalled. But after a few days the excitement calmed down and everything was as before, calm, cool and collected.

Terry at times now began to feel, 'like a spare part – they certainly did not need me.' So he requested to spend a few days with 488 (NZ) Squadron, then at Colerne. Wing Commander Raymond gave permission, 'I think he realised that I was aching to get back to squadron life.'

I travelled down to Colerne, just itching to see the lads again. That evening down at dispersal fate, I think, stepped in. Whilst I was there, Doug Robinson's navigator had felt sick. Robbie was left without a navigator. I jokingly said I would be happy to take his place, and to my surprise the CO said OK. Robbie and I, it was like old times, were to carry out a beach head patrol.

Doug and Terry took off from Colerne at 2325 hours on the night of 28 July 1944 and were directed to the beachhead area, where they were taken over by 'Yardley' ground control, to patrol south of Caen. They were then asked to investigate a 'bogey' as outlined by Doug Robinson's combat report.

After various vectors my observer reported he had contact 2½ miles range 2 o'clock height, 10,000 feet. We took over from Yardley and I obtained a visual on a Ju188 at a range of 600 feet, 10 degrees above 12 o'clock. He was flying in a layer of haze proceeding north. I realised that my overtaking speed was too great and to avoid overshooting I throttled right back. Enemy aircraft was doing 220 mph. He must have seen my exhaust flames at this moment and opened fire. Ventral guns which fired tracer and which disappeared below. There were no strikes. Enemy aircraft immediately peeled off to port and I followed and closed in to 150 yards range. We were both going down. I opened fire and gave him a short burst, but there were no strikes,

owing to the fact that I had too much deflection. I closed in
again to 100 yards still going down. I opened fire and gave
a short burst and enemy aircraft blew up. He was still going
down when he blew up. I levelled out and did a steep turn
to port continuing an orbit and watching enemy aircraft go
down in flames hitting ground with a terrific explosion,
lighting up area. The kill took place at 0118 hours, 10/15
miles north of Mayenne. Claim – one Ju188 destroyed.

After being airborne for about two hours Doug Robinson
decided it was time to return to base, but the excitement of the
night was not over. Terry takes up the tale:

On the way back I noticed white puffs of smoke coming up
around us and suddenly realised that we were being fired
upon, what a bloody cheek. Not knowing whether we were
over enemy or friendly areas I suggested to Robbie that we
fire off colours of the day. He agreed, I pulled on the cord
and nothing happened. The damn thing had jammed. So
Robbie put the nose down and removed us from the area
pretty damn quick. I must admit that when we were being
fired upon my thoughts were, 'My God. I have just got
married. What will Margaret say?' We duly arrived back at
base and the following morning I was flown back to North
Weald. I did not say a word to anyone but next day the
teleprinter in ops room gave all the details. The ops room
personnel were quite pleased to hear of my little adventure
and I tried very hard not to let my head get any bigger.

On 20 August, quite possibly as a result of his 'little adventure'
Terry was sent back to 488 (NZ) squadron to fly with Flight
Lieutenant Bill Cook. However the partnership wasn't to last
long. In September Terry was summoned to 11 Group
headquarters and was told that he would be going on a course at
RAF Detling, but before which he could take a week's leave, 'I
said no more and immediately carried out 11 Group's orders.
Home to Margaret for a whole week. What more could one ask?'

That week went far too quickly and I duly reported to
Detling. The adjutant was just as confused as I was. He
wanted to know what I was doing at Detling. For want of
something else I became assistant to the adjutant. I seem to
remember I did a good job signing leave passes.

A few weeks passed and Terry received further instructions, to go to RAF Honiley, to attend a course at the Ground Control Approach School.

> Back at school! I was not very happy at the idea, but the 'school' turned out to be quite interesting. GCA was a system where if an aircraft was in distress due to weather or any other problem, you could identify him by means of radar, bring him over base and then talk him down to land – giving him instructions when to lower flaps, undercarriage, and land. It was a good idea but pilots were not very happy about trying it. It was rather like a car driver being blindfolded and you as passenger tell him how to drive. I must agree not a pleasant thought. In fairness it would be better than stooging about in bad weather and then spreading yourself all over the countryside. Any port in a storm.

Terry followed this up spending time with a unit in France and then with No.1 GCA unit at RAF Prestwick as second in command, 'I regret to say that whilst at Prestwick we did little work. We had to beg, borrow or steal (yes steal) an aircraft so that we could get in some practice.'

In November 1945 Terry was released from service and told he could go home. He recorded his thoughts at the time.

> I left the Croydon Gas Company in August 1939 to attend the Annual Summer Camp of No. 615 Squadron AAF. I returned to dear old Croydon Gas in January 1946 a somewhat toughened young man, full of confidence, and ready to meet the world. I now have a dear wife, and a very young son. Dear God, may we have a calm wind and a steady course to steer into the future.

Terry now describes his life postwar.

> After some three years being assistant to the store's manager, I decided that it was time to look elsewhere. Still having a yearning to get back into uniform, I applied, with my wife's happy consent, for a permanent commission in the RAF. I failed the medical due to deafness in the right ear (I wonder if that fall at RAF Ayr was the cause?) Not to be outdone, I applied for a commission in the RAFVR and

was accepted. My base would be RAF Kenley, dear old Kenley, and for two weeks a year I would receive training as a fighter control officer at various stations in England.

At the same time I decided that I needed something better than my job at the gas company, and along came the chance. I took over the clerical duties of a small engineering company. The firm prospered and grew and after a couple of years I was appointed company secretary. A year later I was appointed a director. I then formed, at the request of the directors, another company and became its secretary and director. Life with my wife and two young sons was now on a secure base.

At the end of five years in the RAFVR I obtained my release and I must say that I was not sorry. The comradeship was not as it had been before.

And finally Terry sums up his feelings about his involvement in the events of 1940 and 1941.

Straight after the war I wasn't really aware of what we had been involved in. I wasn't aware that it was going to turn round as it has. It was just another part of the war. Whenever I attend a signing session and people thank me for what I have done, I just say, 'Well we were just doing our job.' It is very nice for people to appreciate what we had done. I always feel sorry for the bomber boys though. They suffered terrific hardships.

I was pleased I was part of it, absolutely. I feel that what I have done was worthwhile. I would not have missed it for the world. It was a wonderful experience the whole time in the RAF. It's not pride, it's satisfaction. Every sailor, soldier, airmen did their bit. They should all be thanked.

Winston Churchill, House of Commons, 20 August 1940:
The gratitude of every home in our Island, in our Empire, and
indeed throughout the world, except in the abodes of the guilty,
goes out to the British airmen, who, undaunted by odds,
unwearied in their constant challenge and mortal danger,
are turning the tide of the world by their prowess and
by their devotion. Never in the field of human
conflict was so much owed by so many to so few. All hearts
go out to the fighter pilots whose brilliant actions we see with
our own eyes day after day...

Appendix

Example Variants of Principal Aircraft Featured in the Book[15]

Royal Air Force

Hawker Hurricane Mk I

Type: Fighter
Crew: 1
Dimensions: length: 31ft 5in; height: 13ft 1½in; wingspan: 40ft 0in; wing area: 257½ sq. ft.
Weights: Empty: 4,670lbs; Loaded: 6,660lbs
Performance: Ceiling: 34,000ft; Maximum Speed: 325mph at 18,000ft; Range: 600 miles at 175mph
Armament: Eight .303 Browning machine guns
Engines: Rolls-Royce Merlin II or III 1,030 hp

Supermarine Spitfire Mk IA

Type: Fighter
Crew: 1
Dimensions: length: 29ft 11in; height: 11ft 5in; wingspan: 36ft 10in; wing area: 242 sq. ft.
Weights: Empty: 5,067lbs; Loaded: 6,409lbs
Performance: Ceiling: 34,000ft; Maximum Speed: 355mph at 19,000 feet; Maximum Range: 575 miles
Armament: Eight .303 Browning machine-guns
Engines: Rolls-Royce Merlin II or III 1,030 hp

Bristol Blenheim IF

Type: Fighter/fighter bomber/nightfighter
Crew: 2/3
Dimensions: length: 39ft 9in; height: 9ft 10in; wingspan:
56ft 4in; wing area: 469 sq. ft.
Weights: Empty: 8,840lbs; Loaded: 12,200lbs
Performance: Ceiling: 24,600ft; Maximum Speed:
(sea level) 237mph, (10,000ft) 263 mph, (15,000ft) 278mph;
Cruising Speed: 215 mph at 15,000ft; Maximum Range:
1,050 miles
Armament: (Port wing) one .303 Browning machine gun
(c, fairing) four Browning machine guns, (turret) one Vickers
K303 machine gun
Engines: Two Bristol Mercury VIII 840 hp radial engines

Boulton Paul Defiant Mk I

Type: Fighter
Crew: 2
Dimensions: length: 35ft 4in; height: 12ft 2in; wingspan:
39ft 4in; wing area: 250 sq. ft.
Weights: Empty: 6,282lbs; Loaded: 7,110lbs
Performance: Ceiling: 30,200ft; Maximum Speed: 304mph
at 16,500ft; Range: 600 miles
Armament: Four .303 Browning machine guns in the dorsal
turret
Engines: Rolls-Royce Merlin III 1,030 hp

Bristol Beaufighter IF

Type: Nightfighter
Crew: 2
Dimensions: length: 41ft 4in; height: 15ft 10in; wingspan:
57ft 10in; wing area: 503 sq. ft.
Weights: Empty: 14,069lb; Loaded: 21,100lb
Performance: Ceiling: 28,900ft; Maximum Speed: (sea level)
306mph; Range: 1,500 miles
Armament: Four 20mm Hispano cannon in fuselage nose, six
wing mounted .303in Browning machine guns (two to port and
four to starboard)
Engines: Two 1,590 hp Bristol Hercules VI

Luftwaffe

Junkers Ju87B Stuka
Type: Anti-tank/anti-shipping strike aircraft
Crew: 2
Dimension: length: 36ft 5in; height: 12ft 9in; wingspan: 45ft 4in;
   wing area: 344 sq. ft.
Weights: Empty: 6,085lbs; Loaded: 9,370lbs
Performance: Ceiling: 24,500ft; Maximum Speed: 232mph at
   13,500ft; Cruising Speed: 175mph at 15,000ft; Range: (with
   1,100lb of bombs) 370 miles
Armament: Two fixed MG81 machine guns and one removable
   MG81
Engines: One 1,150hp Junkers Jumo 211Da

Dornier 17Z
Type: Medium bomber
Crew: 4
Dimensions: length: 53ft 5½ in; height: 15ft 9in; wingspan: 59ft;
   wing area: 592 sq. ft.
Weights: Empty: 11,484lbs; Normal loaded: 18,913lbs;
   Overloaded: 19,481lbs
Performance: Ceiling: 26,740ft; Maximum Speed: 265mph at
   16,400ft; Cruising Speed: 236mph at 14,200ft; Maximum
   Range: (normal load) 745 miles
Armament: One 20mm MG FF cannon (on some versions), one
   13mm MG131 machine gun (on some versions), six 7.9mm
   MG 15 and/or MG81 machine guns, 2,200lb bombload
   (carried internally) or 1,100lb bombload plus max fuel (all
   carried internally)
Engines: Two Bramo 323P 1,000 hp radial engines

Heinkel 111H-3
Type: Long-range medium bomber
Crew: 5
Dimensions: length: 54ft 6in; height: 13ft 9in; wingspan: 74ft
   3in; wing area: 942 sq. ft.
Weights: Empty: 14,355lbs; Normal loaded: 25,520lbs;
   Maximum overload: 27,400lbs
Performance: Ceiling: 25,500; Maximum Speed: 255 mph at
   16,000ft; Cruising Speed: 225mph at 16,000ft; Range:
   (normal) 1,540 miles; with overload tanks, 2,640 miles; with
   4,400lbs of bombs range was reduced to 760 miles
Armament: One 20mm MG FF cannon, one 13mm MG 131
   machine gun, seven 7.92mm MG 15 and/or MG81 machine
   guns, one 4,409lb bomb (carried externally) and one 1,102lb
   bomb (carried internally) or eight 551lb bombs (all carried
   internally)
Engines: Two 1,200 hp Junkers Jumo 221D-I

Junkers Ju88A-I
Type: Medium-range bomber
Crew: 4
Dimensions; length: 47ft 1in; height: 15ft 5in; wingspan: 59ft
   $10^3/4$ in; wing area: 540 sq. ft.
Weights: Maximum loaded: 27,500lbs
Performance: Ceiling: 26,500ft; Maximum Speed: approx
   286mph at 16,000ft; Range: 1,553 miles
Armament: Three or five 7.9mm MG15 machine guns; normal
   bombload: 3,968lbs; maximum bombload: 5,510lbs
Engines: Two Junkers Jumo 211B 1,200hp

Messerschmitt Bf110C-4
Type: Fighter escort/fighter bomber
Crew: 2
Dimensions: length: 40ft 4in; height: 11ft 6in; wingspan: 53ft
   5in; wing area: 413 sq. ft.
Weights: Loaded: 15,290lbs
Performance: Ceiling: 32,000ft; Maximum Speed: 340mph at
   22,000ft; Cruising Speed: 285mph at 16,500ft; economic
   cruising range: 680 miles; highspeed cruise range: 565 miles at

301 mph at 23,000ft
Armament: Two MG FF cannon in nose of aircraft, four 7.9mm
  machine guns of 1,000 rpg, one 7.9mm machine gun of
  750 rpg
Engines: Two 1,100hp Daimler-Benz DB601A.

Messerschmitt Bf109E-3

Type: Fighter
Crew: 1
Dimensions: length: 26ft 8in; height: 7ft 5½in; wingspan: 32ft
  4in; wing area: 174 sq. ft.
Weights: Empty 4,421lbs; Loaded: 5,520lbs
Performance: Ceiling: 36,500ft; Maximum Speed: 354mph at
  12,300ft; Cruising Speed: 298mph; Range: 412 miles at
  cruising speed
Armament: Two MG FF cannon, two 7.9mm MG 17 machine
  guns
Engines: One 1,150 hp Daimler-Benz DB601 Aa inline

The Western Desert

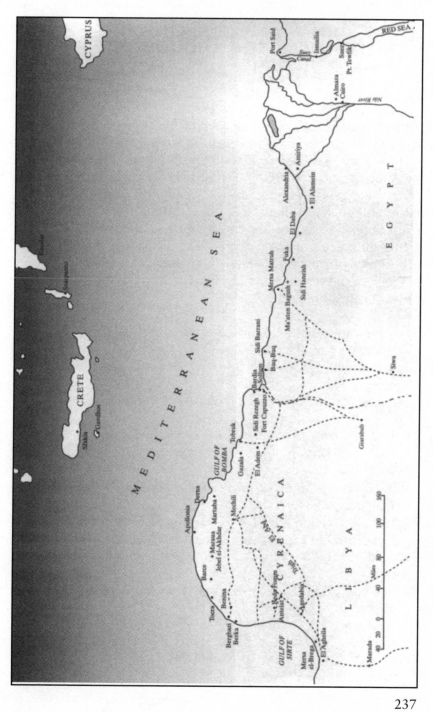

Sources and Bibliography

To put together the context of each of the airmen's stories I have sourced a lot of primary information from squadron and group records at the national archives, Kew, London. This is supported by information from the Air Historical Branch narratives. Of course there is also available a wealth of general published information, concerning the Battle of Britain. I have used as my main published source, for the conduct of the battle, Wood & Dempster's *The Narrow Margin*. The airmen's personal stories are drawn from interviews, wartime correspondence and logbooks and every attempt has been made to tie the information up with official records.

The publication dates are the editions consulted, rather than the first year of publication.

Clutton-Brock, O. *Footprints in the Sands of Time* (Grub Street, 2003)

Churchill, W. *The Speeches of Winston Churchill* (Penguin, 1990)

Darlow, S. *Victory Fighters* (Grub Street, 2005)

Darlow, S. *D-Day Bombers – The Veterans' Story* (Grub Street, 2004)

Gelb, N. *Scramble: A Narrative History of the Battle of Britain* (Harcourt, 1985)

Holmes, R. *Acts of War, The Behaviour of Men in Battle* (Cassell, 2004)

Liddell Hart, B.H. *The Other Side of the Hill* (Pan Books, 1999)

Liddell Hart, B.H. *History of the Second World War* (Papermac, 1992)

Oliver, D. *Fighter Command 1939-45* (HarperCollins, 2000)

Price, Dr A. *The Luftwaffe Data Book* (Greenhill Books, 1997)

Ramsey, W.G. *The Battle of Britain Then and Now* (After the Battle, 2000)

Ramsey, W.G. *The Blitz Then and Now Volume 2* (After the Battle, 1988)

Rawnsley, C.F. & Wright, R. *Night Fighter* (Crécy, 1998)

Ross D., Blanche B. and Simpson W. *The Greatest Squadron of Them All Vol. 1* (Grub Street, 2003)

Shores, C. & Williams, C. *Aces High* (Grub Street, 1994)

Shores, C. *Aces High Volume 2* (Grub Street, 1999)

Shores, C. *Those Other Eagles* (Grub Street, 2004)

Tedder, *Without Prejudice* (Cassell, 1966)

Terraine, J. *The Right of the Line* (Hodder and Stoughton, 1985)

Various authors, *The Battle of Britain* (Salamander Books, 1997)

Watkins, D. *Fear Nothing. The History of No. 501 (County of Gloucester) Fighter Squadron, Royal Auxiliary Air Force* (Newton Publishers, 1990)

Wood, D. & Dempster, D. *The Narrow Margin* (Pen & Sword, 2003)

Wilmot, C. *The Struggle for Europe* (Collins, 1952)

Endnotes

1 Doug Bukin, WW2 People's War website.
2 Wilmot, C. *The Struggle for Europe* (Collins, 1952)
3 Holmes, R. *Acts of War, The Behaviour of Men in Battle* (Cassell, 2004).
4 Douglas Cooper, WW2 People's War website.
5 Gelb, N. *Scramble: A Narrative History of the Battle of Britain* (Harcourt, 1985).
6 Shores, C. & Williams, C. *Aces High* (Grub Street, 1994).
7 Hazel Roberts, WW2 People's War website.
8 Audrey Middlemas, WW2 People's War website.
9 Ross D., Blanche B. and Simpson W. *The Greatest Squadron of Them All Vol. 1* (Grub Street, 2003) p180.
10 Ross D., Blanche B. and Simpson W. *The Greatest Squadron of Them All Vol. 1* (Grub Street, 2003) p289.
11 Tedder, *Without Prejudice* (Cassell, 1966) p309.
12 Tony Cheney, WW2 People's War website.
13 Public Record Office AIR 41/17.
14 Ibid.
15 Primarily based upon specifications detailed in Wood and Dempster's *The Narrow Margin* (Pen & Sword, 2003).

Index